News and Society in the Greek Polis

News and Society
in the
Greek Polis

Sian Lewis

The University of North Carolina Press
Chapel Hill

First published in the
United States in 1996
by the University of
North Carolina Press

First published in 1996 by
Gerald Duckworth & Co. Ltd.
The Old Piano Factory
48 Hoxton Square, London N1 6PB
Tel: 0171 729 5986
Fax: 0171 729 0015

Library of Congress Cataloging–in–Publication Data

Lewis, Sian.
News and society in the Greek polis / Sian Lewis.
    p.   cm. — (Studies in the history of Greece and Rome)
Includes bibliographical references and index.
    ISBN 0–8078–2309–0 (cloth : alk. paper). — ISBN 0–8078–4621–X
(pbk. : alk. paper)
    1. Communication—Greece—History.   2. Greece—Politics and
government—To 146 B.C.   3. Greece—Social conditions—To 146 B.C.
I. Title. II. Series.
P92.G75L48   1996
302.2′09495—dc20   96–7496
                                                              CIP

Typeset by Ray Davies
Printed in Great Britain by
Redwood Books Ltd, Trowbridge

Contents

Preface

We live in a society in which more and better communication is seen as the key to the future. Information, we are told, is vital, the lifeblood of civilisation. All individuals are offered ever greater access to information, our sources vying to tell us not only what has happened, but also how we should understand and react to it. A topic of such significance in our own time surely deserves investigation in the ancient world.

A book which would do full justice to all aspects of news and communication in the ancient Greek world would need to be far longer than this one. When the project was still in its early stages as a D. Phil. thesis, my supervisor Robin Osborne warned me against using the term 'communication' in any description of the project, because, as he said, 'Communication is about everything'. This was sound advice for the limitation of an enormous subject, but it also became a theme. I believe that there was no area of life in the ancient polis which was not influenced by the constant reception and dissemination of information. Accordingly I have not attempted to be exhaustive, and those searching for, as an example, a discussion of military communications and signalling will seek in vain. Instead I have tried to isolate those elements of information exchange which were important within the polis, and to analyse them in the light of modern theories about communication and its effect on society. This area of the experience of the Greek citizen has received scant attention, and my aim is first to present the evidence for topics hitherto undiscussed, and secondly to demonstrate how the means and methods of communication shaped Greek polis society. I hope that this book may be of interest not only to classical historians, but to anyone concerned with news and its social context, and to this end all Greek has been transliterated or translated.

As the project took shape, some ideas appeared in earlier forms elsewhere: certain sections of Chapter 1 are reproduced from an article 'Barbers' shops and perfume shops: "symposia without wine" ', in A. Powell (ed.), *The Greek World* (Routledge 1995), by permission of Routledge; my thanks are also due to the editor of *Hermathena*, for permission to reprint part of Chapter 6 (from *Hermathena* 152 (1992)), and to the British Museum for the jacket illustration.

The final form of the study was influenced by the contribution of three people in particular: Robin Osborne, whose unfailing enthusiasm and wide-ranging knowledge improved the work beyond measure; and Christiane Sourvinou-Inwood and Nicholas Purcell, both of whom offered advice and encouragement at exactly the right time. I am also grateful for the acute and helpful observations of my examiners, Robin Lane-Fox and Michel Austin, of Peter Rhodes, and of the anonymous reader for Duckworth. Needless to say, they bear no responsibility for any errors that remain. Finally I am happy to record my gratitude to the friends who helped in different ways: Nick Groom, Anton Powell, Paul Snow and Heidi Kaye, Katherine Turner, and (last but by no means least) Robin MacKenzie.

This book is dedicated to my parents, Diana and Colin Lewis, because it represents the fruition of all those Sunday afternoons.

S.L.

We are all tainted with the Athenian Itch
News and *New Things* do the whole World bewitch.

Robert Wild, *In Nova Fert Animus* (1679)

Introduction

Information =
$$\log \frac{\text{odds that addressee will know content of message after receiving it}}{\text{odds that addressee will know content of message before receiving it}}$$

The quantity of information conveyed by a given message is equal to the binary logarithm of the number of possibilities necessary to define the message without ambiguity.

Umberto Eco, *The Open Work*

In 396 news came to the Spartans that the Persian King was preparing a fleet of warships for use in the campaign against the Spartan allies in Asia Minor. Xenophon gives an account of the means by which the news reached Sparta: a Syracusan called Herodas had been in Phoenicia 'with a shipowner', and when he saw the preparations, he sailed on the first boat for Greece to warn the Spartans. Acting on his information, they began to mobilise their allies and make plans.[1] This story is typical of Xenophon; he is obviously using his specialised knowledge of Sparta to add colour to a minor event, and he shows us only half the picture. Despite Xenophon's indefinite description ('a Syracusan'), Herodas appears to have a recognised role, like 'the man with the tattooed head' carrying a secret message in Herodotos, and the implication is that he was no insignificant stranger at Sparta.[2]

It is also a paradigmatic story about news in Greece. The coming of the news is haphazard; it is only chance that brings it to the attention of the Spartans. The messenger is not official, but there appears to be more to the story than meets the eye, since he was accepted without question by the Spartans. The news was brought as quickly as possible within normal means – Herodas found the first ship that he could going to Sparta. It illustrates some of the problems experienced by the Greeks in the field of news. This kind of information, about the military plans of the Persians, was clearly of great importance to the Spartans – they immediately set defensive plans in motion. Yet they had made no effort to obtain such information first: that is, they had no permanent system of intelligence gathering, and nor did any other polis, relying instead on the action of chance partisans like Herodas to bring them the informa-

tion that they needed. The contradiction between the perceived importance of news, and the lack of institutions to gather it, is one of the roots
of this survey.

Modern historians have tended to treat the episode with scepticism.
Starr refers to 'the Syracusan Herodas, who "happened" to be in Phoenicia with a shipowner'.[3] The reasoning behind this appears to be that
the receipt of so important a piece of news could not have been left to
chance, and that Herodas was in the Hellespont not solely for reasons
of trade, but with some idea of discovering the Persian plans. This view
may or may not be right (we have no means of telling), but it is
symptomatic of modern assumptions about news. Contemporary perceptions of the importance of information to military security and
planning make it hard for the historian not to impute the same concern
to the Greeks. There is certainly more to Xenophon's story than meets
the eye, but one cannot conclude from it that Herodas played a defined
role in a Spartan information network.

1. News in society

News enjoys 'a privileged and prestigious position in our culture's
hierarchy of values'.[4] It constitutes the most regular and frequent type
of broadcast and publication, and attention to it is considered a marker
of intelligence and awareness. In a culture such as ours, the existence
of news is never questioned; newsworthy events are assumed to happen
all the time, of necessity. Indeed, the word 'news' itself is considered by
some to be culture-specific, denoting written, or printed, information
only.[5] Is it possible to free ourselves from this association and consider
news and its dissemination as a process fundamental to all societies? It
is certainly easier to do so when considering primarily oral cultures: the
transmission of news is at once more basic and more clearly discernible.
The desire to hear news is documented in all societies ancient and
modern, from the Athenian in the Agora asking *'Legetai ti kainon?'*,
(What's new?) to islanders in the west of Ireland in the 1960s awaiting
the boat bringing news from the mainland.[6]

But what is the purpose of news in society? Why is the desire to hear
it so fundamental? On the individual level, it is relatively easy to see
the benefits derived by both teller and listener in the exchange of news.
The hearer gains knowledge of public affairs, information potentially of
practical or economic value, diversion, and news which he or she can in
turn pass on. The teller gains prestige in appearing well-informed, the
chance to capture attention, and the opportunity to tell the news in the
way that best suits his or her own purposes. These benefits, and some
others, are examined in detail in Chapters 1 and 2.

Within society as a whole, however, news has a further set of
functions. Beyond the practical advantages to be secured for the com-

munity from the gathering of information, news and the telling of news serves to strengthen the cohesion of a community. According to Mitchell Stephens:

> Societies depend on news of violations of the law to reinforce under-standing of their laws and fear of their punishments; they depend on accounts of the out of the ordinary to strengthen the consensus on what qualifies as ordinary.[7]

News supplies and reinforces a shared set of cultural values within a community, and by acknowledging the authority of leadership and political systems, reinforces the support for those authorities. With reference to classical Athens, Stephens brackets news with history, art and religion as a means of constantly legitimating and maintaining systems of authority.[8] The function of news in the Greek polis system provides the theme of Chapters 4 and 5.

The aim of this book, then, is to indicate the ways in which the ancient Greek concept and exploitation of news differed from twentieth-century conceptions. Examining how and why news and information were disseminated in the Greek world offers a new perspective on the polis, and fresh interpretations of Greek society. Looking beyond purely historical sources, I will expose the ways in which Greek ideas about information structured social and political life.

2. Defining news

What is news? News is defined by the *Oxford English Dictionary* as 'new information of recent events'; Stephens defines it more usefully as 'new information about a subject of some public interest that is shared with some portion of the public'.[9] Clearly the size of the public concerned will influence the nature of events considered newsworthy; what is merely gossip in a large community takes on a greater importance as news in a smaller group.[10] News can, in turn, be interpreted only against a background of information, the dissemination of which is equally im-portant. Information can be said to comprise knowledge about persons, events, ideas or objects at any time. It is not necessarily new, or relevant to the public: the fact that Sophokles composed the *Philoktetes* is information; the fact that Sophokles' *Philoktetes* has won the first prize at the Dionysia is news. News can then be defined as a specific type of information. It is not practically possible to separate out news proper, and the processes by which it was disseminated, from that of other types of information which are not news in the strictest sense. For instance, a discussion of how a new medical theory might be dissemi-nated necessarily involves discussion of how medical knowledge in general was spread, and the question of how an Athenian citizen heard news through the assembly is not separable from the role of the assembly in spreading information of any other kind, such as of historical events.

Some further related categories of information require definition, because the term news alone will not cover every pattern of exchange, especially when motivation is in question. Should the public announcement (to Athenians assembled in the theatre) of honours paid to a foreign king be considered as news, according to the above definition? Since the matter will already have been debated in the assembly by the citizens, and since the relevance of foreign kings to the individual is small, it falls rather into the class of affirmation. Affirmation occurs when the information reported through news channels is not new, and is deliberately told to an audience who substantially possess the information already. This may appear remote from the idea of news in twentieth-century culture, with its emphasis on constantly updated new information, but it can be seen, for instance, in reports of confirmation of details of arrests by the police, even though the arrest has previously been reported in full. The concept of affirmation is important in mapping the role of ancient news within the community.

Propaganda is a wider category which intersects with that of news; not all news is propaganda, and not all propaganda is news. Visual and literary propaganda, as well as oral, also played a large part in ancient society, for instance, architectural display or encomiastic poetry.[11] Certainly information travels by all means of display, but for the purpose of this study I am confining myself to spoken and written information. Some news, nevertheless, is disseminated with a primary motive not to inform or entertain, but to shape the opinion of its hearers, and this is propaganda. The relation of news to these categories – affirmation and propaganda – determines its operation in society.

We are accustomed to think of news as something that happens all the time, and which needs constant monitoring, but news is in fact what happens when an event is reported, not the event itself. Greek vocabulary for news is closely attuned to this idea. There is no Greek word for news as such, or a newsworthy event; instead, words focus on process. *Ta kaina*, new things, or *kainoi logoi*, new stories, are reported, but the primary word is *aggellô*, I report, and its cognates. To bring news is to bring a message or report, and the advent of news is described impersonally: *êggeilen*, it was reported. An *aggelma* is both news and a message – clearly the act of reporting is what creates news.

It is worth noting that Greek vocabulary for news does not distinguish between truth and falsity – *phêmê*, common report, is not intrinsically less trustworthy than *logos* (story) or *epistolê* (message); the distinction is one of source. A newsmonger, someone who makes up news, is in Greek a *logopoios*, a fabricator of stories. This word also denotes a poet, but this is less surprising when placed in a Greek context. There was no correlation made between history and truth as opposed to poetry and fiction; on the contrary the Homeric poems, for instance, were treated by historical writers as legitimate history.[12] The tales of poets and dramatists, equally, were drawn from myth, and hence true, as opposed to invented stories. A *logopoios*, then, is not necessarily a liar; as Demosthenes makes clear in his condemnation of newsmongers, it is because they are able to be plausible and authoritative that they are so dangerous.[13]

3. The significance of news in Greek society

The Greeks themselves saw news as one of the factors that could define their communities. Aristotle defined the ideal polis as one which is neither too small to be self-sufficient, nor too large to have effective political institutions; he asks of the oversize polis, 'Who could be the general to so great a mass of people? Who could be their herald unless he were Stentor?'[14] Thus in the ideal polis, the populace can be addressed by one speaker, and that this should be so demonstrates that the dissemination of news was one of the key roles of a polis. To belong to a community was to share in the spread of information in that community: misanthropy, in the Greek tradition, took the form of cutting oneself off from all forms of contact, and living outside the polis in the uncivilised wild, as did Timon or Meleager.[15] Refusal to communicate removed one from society. Similarly, in a system in which each polis was in competition with others, for territory, resources or prestige, the communication of news from state to state was obviously vital to determine their interactions.

The very ordinariness of news means that its transmission is often present in our sources in inexplicit form, because it required no explanation. In many cases, where it is clear that the transmission of news was a significant event, historians give no indication of how the news was brought. For example, after the Spartan surrender at Pylos in 425, Thucydides passes directly from an account of the aftermath of the siege to the surprise caused in the rest of Greece by the news of the capture of the Spartans.[16] He gives no explanation of how quickly, or by what means, the news became known. In other cases, however, specific accounts are given of how news was brought – partisans from Mytilene, for instance, informed the Athenians of impending revolt in 428, while the battle of Aigospotamoi was reported by 'Theopompos the Milesian pirate'.[17] Are such cases documented because they were unusual, or are they simply vignettes of normal practice?

Implicit assumptions are no less a problem for modern historians. Because Western beliefs about news are so firmly rooted in the print culture that has grown up since the eighteenth century, many previous treatments of news in the ancient Greek world have undervalued the transmission of news in what were mainly oral societies. Historians regularly comment on the lack of organised media for the transmission of news in the ancient Greek world, but such comment rarely goes beyond noting the importance of some presumed substitute for the mass media, such as the statue of the Eponymous Heroes at Athens.[18] The most common form of misconception can be conveniently called the 'progressive model'; it assumes that human society necessarily progresses from oral communication, which is poor, through written, to printed, telegraphic and electronic methods, with an improvement in the volume and quality of communication consequent on each step. Modern communication technology is implicitly seen as the goal towards which all ancient societies develop.[19] This alone is problematic enough, assuming that more and better communication is always perceived as desirable. But this model also sees ancient societies as limited by a failure to develop appropriate technology, always striving to achieve the next step. In Greece, especially in the case of oral and written communication, this view is highly misleading, as is discussed in detail in Chapter 6. Ideological reasons, either for the failure to invent a technique, or for the lack of interest in exploiting such an invention, are of paramount importance, as we shall see, and it is precisely here that the role of information in shaping society is most clearly exposed.

A second feature of modern writing on ancient news is the preoccupation with the military, and the consequent overvaluing of certain visible institutions. Riepl (*Das Nachrichtenwesen des Altertums*) is led astray by the invention of forms of telegraphic signalling in ancient warfare: since these were, in informational terms, uncomplicated, used in specific circumstances and for a limited purpose, questions of reception and interpretation simply do not apply, and they can have little relevance to an understanding of the dissemination of news in society at large.[20] Starr, similarly, produced a book of small scope, because he deliberately set out to consider news only in military-political terms.[21] Most of our historical sources deal with warfare, and a study of news must consider this aspect alongside all others. But to assume that the only field in which the dissemination of information is important is the military would be entirely wrong.

The historian, then, should attempt to identify peculiarly twentieth-century perspectives. In particular, one should beware of using contemporary rules of what is newsworthy to analyse events in the ancient world. For instance, when Dionysius of Syracuse was victorious in the Lenaia at Athens with his play *The Ransom of Hector* in 368, one of the chorus made special efforts to be first to bring news of his victory to the tyrant, and was duly rewarded when he did.[22] The concept of news as a saleable commodity is one to which I will return. But this event should not be taken to indicate that victory in the Lenaia was newsworthy *per se*. The news was of far more relevance to Dionysius than to anyone else, and the message here is direct and personal in form. This is reflected in what we know of victors in ancient athletic contests: efforts were made to send the news of a victory home, to family and fellow-citizens, but we do not see interest in the results of the Games simply as results – they were not generally newsworthy. Stephens falls into this trap when he includes sport in his category of events that are always generally newsworthy; it may be more pertinent to ask why Olympic gold medals for any country are considered generally newsworthy now.[23] We see instead in Greece the news going from the Games to the individual concerned, and then via other media motivated by the victor, such as the victory ode, to the world at large. It is through commemoration in poetry that the victor will have his fame spread, not simply by virtue of being a victor.

4. Approaches

The temporal parameters of this book are dictated at one extreme by the nature of the sources. There is no narrative history before Herodotos, and his references to events before the Persian Invasion rarely provide detailed social information. Herodotos' characters furnish a few, brilliant examples of the transmission of news, such as Harpagos' letter sewn into the belly of a hare, but he offers a much less consistent background.[24] Before the sixth century, it is inevitable to be drawn to the unusual, and hard to find the norm against which such examples are to be set. For this period, we are far more dependent on texts which reflect the preoccupations of the small ruling class of the society for and about whom they are written.

The decision not to extend the discussion beyond 300 BC was influenced by the change during the fourth century in the way that news was communicated. From 350 onward, the Greek states began to come into contact with Macedonia, and were ultimately incorporated into Alexander's empire. With the expanding scale imposed on Greece by contact with a larger single nation, the nature of contact between Greece and external nations changes, and so news and information begin to be transmitted by more formal methods. As I intend to document the processes of information in the city-states, 300 marks a rough boundary in terms of news. Thus the period I have chosen charts the interactions of the Greek poleis until the nature of that interaction has changed.

The chapters that follow paint a cumulative picture of news as one of the factors that structured social and political life. The first two chapters consider the role of news within and between polis communities, independent of political control, including the function of information as a determinant of status, and the ways in which information dictated relations between inhabitants of different states. This raises questions

about the way this kind of information interacted with official information, which are brought out more fully in the next chapters.

The theme of control by the polis underlies the following two chapters, which are concerned with dissemination by the spoken word. This
is where the official and unofficial meet, the envoy or herald and the
passing trader. Announcements both within the polis and at places
outside are the aspect most readily seized on for ancient news, but the
motives behind announcement require investigation. These chapters
demonstrate the methods by which poleis authorities exerted control
over information, and imposed their own structures onto uncontrolled
news.

My last two chapters reinterpret the polis institutions in the light of
the conclusions reached above; I look at both the political assembly, and
the creation of public inscriptions. I argue that these did not constitute
the primary source of news for citizens, as has previously been assumed, but that the polis had an agenda for all the information with
which it presented its citizens.

The discussion thus moves from the importance to the individual
citizen of receiving and exchanging news, to the more complex communication organised by the polis. News and the exchange of news were
vital in delineating relations of status and power in the Greek polis, and
understanding this will allow us a better idea of how ancient poleis
worked.

News Within the Community

For most of us, if we do not talk of ourselves, or at any rate of the individual circles of which we are the centres, we can talk of nothing. I cannot hold with those who wish to put down the insignificant chatter of the world.

Anthony Trollope, *Framley Parsonage*

News about events and individuals, public and private, flowed ceaselessly in the ancient polis. People talked in their own houses, with their neighbours, on street-corners, in the shops and markets, and in the public spaces, about themselves, their fellow-citizens and their affairs. A polis was, naturally, made up of smaller communities, the village, deme or neighbourhood, and news flowed in these too. Villages, in turn, were composed of individual households, families and groups of friends, and among these circulated the news of the locality. Within all of these groupings, the exchange of news was not merely a diversion. This chapter will examine how the telling and hearing of news helped to strengthen the bonds between members of a community, impose common moral standards, and define the social strata within the community.

Any distinction between news and gossip depends solely on the size of public among whom an item of news circulates. News in communities as small (by modern standards) as the polis did not concern solely events of international importance or serious topics – the chatter of the Agora could be described by Aristophanes as 'rude jokes about other people's sex lives'.[1] Indeed, to distinguish between news as public and gossip as private at all is inappropriate to the ancient polis, since private matters were clearly understood to be relevant to public life. Tales of private affairs between neighbours, though no doubt interesting, had a relevance beyond casual interest. For example, the circulation of news about individuals and their families in their locality was what allowed a person to establish his or her identity.

In a society where personal documentation was absent, only the word of others could attest to identity, legitimacy or right to citizenship. In the case brought by Mantitheos against his half-brother Boiotos, both parties called witnesses to attest to to events, such as the dekate (tenth-day naming ceremony of a child), the giving of a dowry, and the enrolment of a son in a deme.[2] The word of a witness was the only proof one could bring that such an event had taken place. A legal marriage was proved not by the existence of a written document, but by the production of witnesses to its ceremonies; to establish citizenship, one needed witnesses not only to one's descent, but also to ceremonies of legitimation.[3] Without a network of contact between friends, neighbours, fellow-demesmen and fellow-citizens at local level, circulating information about local people and their affairs, such cases could not be substantiated. Speakers in legal cases also call on witnesses, neighbours or friends, for knowledge of character, such as profligacy, propensity for violence or generosity, and for knowledge of relationships within families, for instance between husband and wife.[4] Recent studies on political oratory have demonstrated how wide a range of affairs neighbours could be expected to know about, and that the dissemination of this knowledge among the community was seen as natural and necessary.[5]

Information determined interaction in three key areas: reputation, public life and defining status. Reputation decides how you are seen in public life; participation in public life in turn reflects on your status as a citizen, and becomes a definition applied within the polis, to distinguish the citizen from the non-citizen by their participation in the public exchange of information.

1. Reputation

Success in public life depended on perceptions of an individual's character, as well as of his actions. Hunter has described how the *dokimasia* (scrutiny of a magistrate for fitness) drew evidence about an individual's own and family's private deeds as part of the procedure of scrutiny.[6] The institution of political comedy, which ridicules political figures on non-political grounds, also illustrates the popular judgement of character as a factor which should affect public standing. Hyperbolos, in the *Knights*, is lampooned for a proposal to lead an Athenian expedition against Carthage, and described at the same time as '*andra mochthêron politên oxinên*' – a sour and knavish fellow.[7] Summary of character in comedy tends to be unsubtle, for instance of Theramenes, as the 'boot that fits either foot', but the distinction between analysis of character and political action is not easily made.[8]

The private and personal information circulated about citizens and their private behaviour had a direct relevance to legal and political affairs, because gossip played a major part in conditioning popular opinion. Of course the courts transmitted gossip at the same time as they used it; reputation was on constant display. Hunter emphasises that gossip was essentially information of a private nature, but needed to be brought into a public setting in order to be effective.[9] In this way the gossip spread among one's neighbours could have great significance: an individual who mistreated his mother, or caused a scandal within his family, could find this being brought into the public arena and used against him. We can see a tension between the desire to protect the reputation and keep harmful information secret, and a complementary desire to discover information about others.

This illuminates an interesting connection between women and gossip. The image of women as over-talkative, and as gossips in a harmful sense, is present in Greek literature from the poetry of the seventh century to the rhetoric of the fourth. Semonides of Amorgos, for instance, defines the good woman as one who does not spend time sitting and telling bawdy stories, and the bad woman as one who talks all the time. One of his negative female stereotypes, the Dog woman, is a creature who both talks too much, and is curious to find things out about her neighbours:

> who hears everything and wants to know everything, and runs round yapping.[10]

Aristotle states that women habitually talk more than men, while both tragic and comic poets play on the image of women as gossips:

> Praxagora: Hurry up and tie on your beard, and any other woman with experience of speaking do the same.
> First woman: My dear, which of us women doesn't know how to talk?[11]

On the face of it, gossiping women would seem to be a bad thing. The talkativeness of women, however, played a significant part in the transmission of gossip in the polis. Andokides records a story told against Hipponikos, father of his prosecutor Kallias, that Kallias had an evil spirit in his house, in the shape of his son. Andokides dismisses this story as foolish, but nevertheless artlessly uses it to undermine Kallias.[12] The story, claims Andokides, is the kind told by 'silly women and children', yet in his speech the story is intended to influence the decision of the jury in an Athenian court. In Demosthenes' speech *Against Aristogeiton* we hear that Aristogeiton escaped from prison and fled Attika with the help of a woman called Zobia, but when he was not appropriately grateful, she acted in a typically feminine way (*gunaiou pragm' epoiei*), and spread the tale of his shabby behaviour around her acquaintances.[13]

Clearly women's gossip could be used to good effect in exposing areas of private behaviour to public view. Although women's gossip could be criticised as petty and harmful, contacts between friends and neighbours for passing on information were vital. Although respectable women were usually supposed to remain inside the house, in this connection women, especially the old, clearly had considerable freedom of movement.[14] In Lysias' speech *Against Eratosthenes*, the news of his wife's infidelity is brought to Euphiletos by an old woman, who has in turn been sent by Eratosthenes' former mistress.[15]

The function of gossip in imposing a common moral standard on the community is well-documented, and it seems that women may have had a particular role to play in policing the morality of others. A society which seeks both to keep women in a separate sphere from men, and to police their activities, must, as Cohen has shown, rely on other women to observe and regulate the behaviour of friends or neighbours who do not conform.[16] Plato, foreshadowing modern China, suggested among his prescriptions for the ideal polis a board of women to regulate family and sexual matters, while Aristotle records that the tyrant Hieron of Syracuse kept power through a ring of informers called the *ôtakoustai* (eavesdropper women).[17] Sources show that women cared a great deal about their reputation as perceived by other women – forensic speeches place much significance on women being allowed by their peers to participate in all-female festivals such as the Thesmophoria, as an indication of respectability.[18] Women as neighbours and gossips, passing on information from the oikos, could and needed to share in this aspect of public life, if it was to fulfil its proper function. The female role was thus a dual one: as wives and daughters they had a duty to prevent potentially harmful information leaving the oikos; as neighbours and fellow-citizens they needed to circulate information about others in order to impose collective moral standards.

The tension between these opposing demands for secrecy and information was obscured to some extent by divorcing rumour from human activity. In situations where we might think of gossip, the Greeks applied the concept of *phêmê*, common report, and the distinction bears examination. *Phêmê* represented more than simply rumour for the Greeks: it was a personification which had been current since the time of Hesiod, and, according to Aischines, the personification of Rumour had an altar at Athens.[19] It is interesting that the Greeks chose to see Rumour as something divine, rather than mundane, information which is passed on by quasi-supernatural means, rather than from person to person. *Phêmê*, in the time of Homer, meant a divine or ominous utterance, and developed from this to mean 'reputation' or 'report'. Hesiod characterises *phêmê* as divine because it cannot be stopped by human means once sent abroad, emphasising its self-generating nature.[20]

One can detect in this a wish to divorce the idea of rumour from that of gossip. Many authors insist on the spontaneous nature of rumour, which springs up and spreads of its own accord, as opposed to slander, which is deliberately passed from one person to another.[21] This attitude towards rumour allowed it to be presented as a neutral force within the

polis. Aischines, in his accusation of Timarchos, argues for the importance of *phêmê* in determining a man's reputation:

> But concerning the life and deeds of men, an incontrovertible rumour
> spreads of its own accord throughout the city, and brings private deeds to
> the attention of all, and often even prophesies what is going to happen.[22]

This is of course a useful claim to make in court; the orators' distinction
between rumour and slander is designed to allow them to gossip about
their opponents while defending themselves: I appeal to common report, you spread slander. But it uses an idea which is current in all
forms of literature, of rumour as an independent entity. The divine
attribution meant that rumour was seen to be generally true, and also
accounts for the thin boundary between news brought by rumour and
that spread by supernatural means.

The best example of supernormal news is the spontaneous rumour
that was supposed to have sprung up among the Greeks at the battle of
Mykale in 479, that the Persian army had been defeated at Plataia.

> As they were advancing, a herald's staff appeared lying in the surf on the
> shore, and at the same time a rumour flew around the whole army, that
> the Greeks had defeated the Persian army under Mardonius in Boiotia.[23]

The rumour was, naturally, true, and Herodotus, through the detail of
the herald's staff found on the beach, implies a completely divine origin
for the information. Rumours were seen to spring up under circumstances in which news could not possibly have been passed by normal
means, and to travel unnaturally fast. The scholion to Aischines associates the establishment of the altar at Athens with another story of this
kind: on the same day that Kimon won his victory over the Persians by
land and sea at Eurymedon, the news was known at Athens before any
messenger could arrive.[24]

Rumour, in the sense of information about individuals in the community, could be presented as divinely rather than humanly circulated,
because news within the community had an ambiguous status, as both
good and bad. It was good to find out about others, but bad to reveal
about yourself and your family. The role of women in this as disseminators of news and gossip is thus also either valuable or harmful, depending on one's standpoint. But without gossip it would have been
impossible to establish reputations.

2. Information and the citizen

Reputation, as we have seen, affected a man's place in public life.
Participation in public life, in turn, can be seen to be the sharpest
indicator of citizen status. Demosthenes, in his speech *Against Aristo-*

geiton, attempts to show that Aristogeiton should be considered suspect by the jurors because he is not seen in public, either in the Agora or in a shop, as Demosthenes claims is normal for any Athenian man.

> Every one of you frequents the Agora, on public or private business. But not Aristogeiton ... he never frequents any barbershop or perfume-seller or workshop in the city.[25]

The implication is not only that Aristogeiton is an unfit member of the citizen body because he does not participate in the public life of the citizen, but also that he must have some shameful secret to hide if he is unwilling to appear in public. Conversely it is the honest man's boast that he lives his life in public and leaves every area of his existence open to the scrutiny of others.[26] Orators state as axiomatic to their audiences not only that a man's private life should be blameless to qualify him for public office, but also that only those committing shameful acts would wish to seek privacy. Aischines emphasises that unlawful love affairs take place in 'private houses and lonely places', and Xenophon offers as evidence for Agesilaos' self-control in sexual matters the fact that he lived all his life in public.[27] Secrecy, and lack of communication, is unnatural – the citizen, by definition, should have nothing to hide. A man should appear in public because by doing so he communicates, by words, action and even appearance, information about his character to his fellow-citizens.

The public appearance par excellence is in the Agora. This is the centre of the polis, and is the place where information was most visibly circulated. It was a place where actions would be observed by others; in Demosthenes' speech *Against Phainippos* the plaintiff asserts that Phainippos, who was supposed to provide him with an inventory of goods, made a point of meeting him in the Agora to hand over a piece of paper, to suggest by public show that he had in fact given the inventory. Accusations in lawsuits of attempts made to spread rumours around the Agora are common.[28] It is thus a place especially associated with the exchange of news between individuals: the 'thronged and fragrant centre', according to Pindar.[29]

Much talk did go on in the Agora – it was the place in which news was most easily made public. The news of the Sicilian Disaster spread among the citizens there; Theophrastos, writing in the 320s, depicts the newsmongering man as accosting his friends in the Agora with all his latest stories; the news of the loss of Elateia in 339 was told there, so that all the citizens knew about it by the following day.[30] But political life did not begin and end with news coming from outside the polis to the citizens: it was an experience shared by all male citizens. Since the radical democracy placed unusual emphasis on the views of the individual male citizen, issues of political significance needed to be discussed in the private as well as the public forum in order for opinion to be formed. That is, discussion in the assembly was only a small part of the whole; one needed to discuss ideas and proposals with one's peers all the time. Finley refers to a 'continuous process of political education' necessary to the democracy – all citizens could participate by engaging in discussion and debate.[31] On the occasion of the launching of the Sicilian Expedition in 415, for instance, Plutarch depicts groups of all ages sitting in public places discussing the proposal for the Expedition:

> ... the young men in the palaistras, and the old sitting together in the workshops and meeting-places would draw maps of Sicily, and of the sea around the coast, and of the harbours and places on the island which look towards Libya.[32]

This demonstrates the sharing of personal knowledge, for example in the drawing of maps, and one of the routes for the dissemination of information between individuals, from those with experience of Sicily to those without. This kind of discussion was a necessary part of the democracy, and to participate in it is a clear marker of citizen status.

The places where the discussions of Alkibiades' proposal were held are interesting. The palaistra was the province of the ephebe, the young citizen, and a space from which other groups, metics and slaves, were barred.[33] Clearly debates here would be the concern of the young and aristocratic. But what should we make of the *ergastêrion*, the workshop, and of the shops to which Demosthenes, in the denunciation of Aristogeiton quoted above, refers?

The shop, whether a barber's, perfume-shop, or cobbler's, served primarily as a meeting place outside the house where friends could gather in an informal setting. This contrast between Agora and shop is part of a distinction which was central to Greek society. Greek life was demarcated into the public domain (the Agora and palaistra) and the private (the house), and the division between these was conceptually sharp.[34] Jameson has demonstrated the difference between the architecture of the house and the shop: a house was inward-looking, planned around a central court with only one entrance, whereas the shop, when it formed part of a private house, had no communication with other rooms, and opened only onto the street.[35] Cohen elaborates further on this theme, emphasising that the distinction between public and private was comparative rather than completely oppositional; what was considered private (or public) could vary depending on circumstances:

> ... in Athens, a symposium taking place within the house is seen as private in relation to conversation in the agora or baths, for example, but public in relation to the free women in the house.[36]

Public life embraced a variety of events ranging from the totally public (such as attending the assembly with six thousand others) to the virtually private (such as two citizens arranging a marriage in a private house). The shop, whatever its nature, was a halfway house. A small group of friends could meet here regularly, to discuss business either public or private, more openly than in a house, but in a semi-private setting.

Lysias suggests that all Athenians were in the habit of visiting some shop and passing their time there, and mainly in those shops closest to the Agora, implying that it was a normative part of Athenian life:

> For every one of you is in the habit of spending time in a shop, one in the perfume-seller's, another at the barber's, a third at the shoemakers, or wherever, and mostly in those shops which are closest to the Agora.[37]

Our evidence supports the idea that one would use a shop as a place outside one's own house to make oneself accessible to anyone else – the speaker of Demosthenes *Against Phormion*, for instance, was trying to serve a summons on one Phormion, and made inquiries as to where he could be found; he was informed that Phormion was at the perfume-market, and accordingly found him there. Similarly Sokrates in the *Memorabilia* goes looking for the youth Euthydemos, and finds him in his usual haunt of a saddler's shop close to the Agora, where he waited to conduct business because he was too young to enter the Agora proper.[38] This last provides a good illustration of the role of the shop between public and private – one can transact public business there without entering the public spaces – and also of access to information increasing in proportion to one's status within the polis.

The shop was, in contrast to the Agora, home to information of a more particular nature, about neighbours, local events, or public figures. Aristophanes' *Wealth*, for instance, depicts the friends and neighbours of Chremes learning from rumours circulating in the barbers' shops that he has become rich overnight, while Peisthetairos, in the *Birds*, describes a scene of older men sitting in the barber's and complaining about their sons' latest enthusiasms; this is the idea of the shop as local centre.[39] Even if ancient Athens was small enough for many people to be known by all, those who met in shops naturally formed smaller communities.[40] We know from our sources that each shop would be host to a regular group of individuals, meeting at a particular place and time.

One of the functions of such centres is well illustrated by Lysias' speech *Against Pankleon* – the speaker was trying to establish the identity of one Pankleon, who claimed to belong to the deme Dekeleia, and to be a citizen of Plataia. Wishing to find out about Pankleon from his fellow demesmen, the speaker went to the barber's shop in the street of the Hermai, where the Dekeleians gathered.[41] It was a recognised place to find the Dekeleians, though one should not accord it an official status – Dekeleia had its own deme assembly to discuss matters of deme administration and religion. It was rather an informal gathering, designed to facilitate business contacts. Similarly the speaker wished to discover whether Pankleon was a Plataian, and after making inquiries of all the other Plataians whom he knew, he was directed to the fresh cheese market on the last day of the month, on which day there was a gathering of the Plataians.[42]

All shops, however, were not the same: there is a detectable difference in class between a cobbler's and a perfume seller's. This depends partly on the nature of the goods for sale. The barber's shop best fills the function of a centre for the casual dissemination of rumour because it is a place where one has to spend time in order to obtain a particular service. It is also a socially fluid place, where numerous people would drop in and out, and it is in the barber's shop (*koureion*) that the idea of unverifiable rumour is strongest – the 'common rumour of the barber's shop' became a pejorative expression.[43] A perfumer's or cobbler's will certainly be a more appealing proposition as a place to spend time than, say, a butcher's or tanner's, and the nature of the clientèle will vary accordingly.[44] Perfume is characterised as the mark of the rich man, and Aristophanes parodies those who sit in the perfume market for their trendy literary chatter, depicting them as leisured, upper-class young men.[45] Conversely in Demosthenes' speech against Konon, Konon claimed to have been dining with friends, in a formal sense, but the speaker depicts him gathering with his friends at the house of Pamphilos the fuller for a drinking session, after which the group went out to ambush the speaker. Naming Pamphilos' profession makes the gathering resemble less a respectable symposion, and more a meeting in low circumstances for criminal purposes.[46]

To some extent the relevance of the distinction depends on the purpose of the speaker – even being barbered regularly could under some circumstances be taken as a sign of aristocratic ambition. Theophrastos' portrait of Petty Pride (*Mikrophilotimia*) is of a man who is barbered many times in the month, as well as keeping his teeth white.[47] This may, however, have more to do with the contrast between city and country than with class. The distance between city- and country-dwellers is satirised by both Theophrastos and Aristophanes, and in this context even visiting a barber's shop becomes a luxury, something one might do on a rare visit to town.[48]

In Lysias' *On the Invalid*, one of the accusations which the complainant attempts to counter is that a group of robbers met in his shop to plot crimes.[49] The motif of the shop as a centre for conspiracy recurs in the common metaphor of an *ergastêrion* (workshop) used to describe a group: Demosthenes refers to *ergastêria* of crooks, conspirators and blackmailers.[50] The *ergastêrion* was a place where slaves and metics would be particularly likely to be found, and a gathering here, where citizen and non-citizen met, would be more suspect than one of citizens alone. Isokrates says of the Athenians 'they sit round in the workshops criticising the constitution', implying that *ergastêria* might be seen as particular centres of disaffection.[51] Obviously the metaphor is not entirely abstract – if these people formed permanent associations, then their meeting-place might well be in a workshop.

We have seen in connection with lower-class shops how a gathering of friends could be cast either as a respectable meeting in public, or a secret conspiracy. This reveals the previously-noted halfway status of the shop – private in one context, public in another. And we have also seen how privacy could be suspect. The fear of private meetings arises from the idea of conspiracy – men getting together to exchange information only among themselves. This was a particular fear of democracies, and a comparison of other states' attitudes illustrates this.

Information was as much a marker of the citizen in societies less concerned with openness than Athens. In Sparta and Crete each citizen belonged to a *sussition* (common mess), membership of which was a prerequisite of citizenship.[52] The *sussition* provided the opportunity not only to share meals, but also to hear conversation intended to reinforce the polis ethic. Sources on Sparta and Crete agree that young men were permitted to attend the *sussitia* in order to learn how to act as citizens. They would hear discussion of political matters, and tales of military prowess, designed to inculcate the morals and standards expected of Spartiates.[53] Further, Plutarch repeats the idea that the talk in the sussition was intended to be exclusive to that particular group – both the young, and foreign visitors, were warned that no talk should go beyond the door.[54] Just as membership of a *sussition* defined a Spartan as a citizen, so the exchange of information within these groups was one of the elements characterising the group, and one of the purposes in its meeting.

The institution of the *symposion*, the private drinking-party, in Athens clearly has some features in common with the *sussition*. In terms of public and private the *symposion* and the meeting in a shop occupy complementary positions within the spectrum: the *symposion* is a public occasion within the private sphere, while the shop is a private meeting in the public sphere. The *symposion* evolved as an aristocratic pursuit, and shared the same purpose of teaching a set of values among a certain class. Bremmer has emphasised the parallels between education through the common meal in Dorian societies, and at the archaic *symposion*: there was in the *symposion* too a tradition of didactic poetry addressed to the young, such as the works of Theognis, and of young men singing songs on topics depicting military valour.[55] Bremmer argues that this aspect of the *symposion* had begun to decline in importance by the end of the fifth century, as the aristocrats abandoned their traditional concern with warfare and individual valour, and the practice of holding *symposia* spread to other classes. In Aristophanes' *Clouds*, one of the ways in which the young Phidippides demonstrates his modernity is by a rejection of the tradition of singing at the *symposion*, and of the traditional kind of song:

> But he immediately said that playing the lyre and singing while people were drinking was old-fashioned, like women do when they're grinding barley ... and he said that Simonides was a rotten poet.[56]

If the *symposion* originally inculcated the ideals of the aristocratic class, it is not surprising if it was seen under the radical democracy as protecting the interests of that class with suspicious exclusivity. The *symposion* became problematic for the Greeks at the point where it became a private, or secret, meeting, and moved towards the idea of the *hetaireia*. The *hetaireia* was a private club which was used for political influence, although it was not a purely political grouping, but a social one as well.[57] However, the *hetaireia* easily attracted suspicion, as a group that could be accused of plotting in private to overthrow the constitution. One of the informers in the Mysteries case made a connection between the *hetaireiai* and the mutilation of the Hermai, and Thucydides saw them as instrumental in the success of the oligarchic revolution in 411.[58] When the *symposion* moves from inculcating the virtues of a class, to passing on exclusive ideals and information, it becomes private, and hence anti-democratic.

The most extreme expression of privacy in this context is the *pistis*, or pledge, by which members of a *hetaireia* guaranteed their loyalty to the group by a certain act. Andokides presents the mutilation of the Hermai as a *pistis*, one which would guarantee secrecy through common guilt, and similarly Thucydides records that the Samian oligarchs in 411 carried out the murder of Hyperbolos as a *pistis*, proving their loyalty to the Athenian oligarchs.[59] Andokides emphasises how seriously he takes the charge of betraying his *hetairoi* by informing on them, by contrasting that betrayal on the one hand with the threat to his own family, and to the polis as a whole, on the other.[60] The symposion, then, could be seem as anti-democratic in the same way as the *hetaireia*, but this depiction has as much to do with the inappropriacy of the private group meeting within the polis, as with its association with the aristocratic class.

3. Status within the polis

Access to information, then, and the groups within one finds it, serve to define the status of citizen. If one considers other groups within the polis, a hierarchy can be seen to affect access to information. Metics could not participate in political life, but formed part of the community of shopkeepers and craftsmen among whom public discussion took place.[61] Women were not supposed to participate in public life at all, but, as we have seen, had an important part to play in the dissemination of local news. They had access to the second tier of information, but not the first. Slaves, as the lowest rank, were not expected to take part in any exchange of information at all. They were both disenfranchised within the polis, and, uniquely, subject to the systematic witholding of information.

Information was systematically kept from slaves, and a strict control exercised over them, in a way different from other classes. They were not automatically excluded from all public places, but we have seen that their presence in an *ergastêrion* could make it an inappropriate place to meet. Concern was manifested over the dangers that would arise from slaves betraying information to outsiders. In the historical sources the desertion of slaves in wartime is emphasised as a major threat, because they will betray information to an enemy, a fear predicated on the belief that slaves have no loyalty to the polis. Chios was put at particular risk in 411, when the city was under siege by the Athenians, because the Chian slaves deserted in large numbers. According to Thucydides, this did the most harm to the Chians, because the slaves passed on their knowledge of the country to the Athenians. In a later treatise Onasander warns against revealing plans to the army too early, and slaves are one of the groups which he singles out as a threat.[62] Any kind of public information was not for slaves' ears: Theophrastos' *Agroikos*, for instance, demonstrates his boorish behaviour by discussing the news from the assembly with his slaves instead of his family, in a way clearly shown to be inappropriate.[63]

The control exercised over slaves is even clearer at Sparta, where secrecy and oppression were specifically aimed at the helot population. Every effort was made to keep the helots in ignorance, both of their own treatment, and of public affairs. Thucydides records the incident of the killing of two thousand of the best helots in 424, when the murders were contrived so that no one knew exactly how each of them was killed. According to Plutarch, the *krypteia* was used as a permanent secret force against them, killing those found out after nightfall. It is suggested that Spartan armies always left Lakonia by night, in order to conceal from the helots the force that had left, and the concern that information should remain within the *sussition* was connected to unwillingness to spread it among disenfranchised groups.[64] Obviously the control of information in this way was intended to prevent the helots turning on Sparta in a time of vulnerability, but it was also a part of a deeper distinction between slave and free in terms of access to information.

Keeping personal information from slaves within the household was clearly more difficult, but the gossip of slaves was nevertheless seen as harmful, with their owners open to betrayal in precisely the same way as the polis. It was especially subversive, because slaves could pass on knowledge to which they had no right, usually to their masters' detriment. In Aristophanes' *Frogs* two slaves find a common bond in resistance to their masters, and one of the forms which this resistance takes is the spreading of gossip about the master's affairs to the neighbours.[65] This concern can be paralleled from more recent history: at the end of the nineteenth century in Northamptonshire, servants recruited locally were not popular because:

> it was felt that gossip carried back into the servants' families and streets might destroy the aura of mystery essential to the maintenance of prestige and social position.[66]

The very existence of slaves creates a potential leakage of information, which citizens must constantly try to plug. In a speech of Demosthenes, slaves are shown passing on information which their master was attempting to keep secret.[67] Hunter suggests that news and gossip spread around local communities may have derived from slaves, but this is difficult to establish.[68] Although gossip specifically said to derive from slaves does not feature in the lawcourts, this is hardly surprising given Athenian attitudes to slave testimony in general; whether or not slaves ultimately were the source for gossip about an individual, the attribution of the information to a slave would tend to undermine it. Only in extreme cases, such as the Mysteries scandal, was slave information used.[69]

It is surprising in the light of the above that Greek authors are much more concerned to show how completely women were excluded from access to political knowledge, than to make the same point about slaves. We find very few direct references to the inaccessibility of information to slaves, and there is in Athenian sources little concern manifested as to what might happen if slaves did gain access to political information and hence power.[70] In contrast, comedy and oratory frequently comment on women's ignorance about the running of the polis. Both *Lysistrata* and *Ekklesiazousai* derive their plots from the idea that women might one day have access to information and power, even though they would be without the requisite knowledge of the democratic process. In Aristophanes' *Lysistrata*, the plot depends on the idea that men usually prevent women from finding out news about political affairs (Lysistrata's husband refuses to answer her questions about affairs in the assembly), while in the *Ekklesiazusai* the women tend to understand political events as far as is necessary for the plot, but do not know how

to make speeches or vote. The humour of the first scene derives entirely
from their attempts to learn the right techniques:

> First woman: But how will we remember to raise our hands when it's time
> to vote? We're more used to raising our legs.[71]

Women, according to Perikles and Ischomachos, should see and hear as
little as possible; politics should be the domain of men.[72] This sits
uneasily with the evidence discussed above for women's participation
in some other areas of public life, disseminating news about private
lives. Why do we see such a concern about women and information?

I stated above that public life for the citizen male did not begin and
end at the assembly. In fact, information about political affairs can be
said to have dominated Athens – notices of forthcoming assemblies and
proposed new laws had to diplayed, with reliance on word-of-mouth to
spread the news to all areas of Attika, orators depict crowds listening
to court cases, heralds made public announcements of both polis and
deme matters, and foreigners and traders were freely permitted in the
city. To borrow an image from Keuls, who describes Athens as a city
dominated by phallic images, it is possible to see Athens also as a city
dominated by information.[73] It was impossible for a person moving in
this milieu to avoid finding things out.

Emphasis on women's exclusion from this domain is based on ideas
of female seclusion in general. The initial reliance on evidence suggesting that most women were kept in seclusion has been superseded in
recent years, by a recognition that not only did many women leave their
houses to play public roles, but that for some it was a necessity.[74] Even
the officially-sanctioned reasons for women to leave the house, attendance at religious festivals and funerals, allowed them the opportunity
to exchange information; more so in the less visible world of women's
work. Women who traded in the markets, supporting themselves and
their families, or worked as nurses, midwives, bakers or sellers, or
shopped if they had no slave to do it for them, entered the areas which
were by definition men's places. The wreath-market, for instance, is a
place where we see women at work, but also a place where men gather
to talk. One of the women in Aristophanes' *Thesmophoriazusai* says
that she earns a living for herself and five children by making wreaths
and selling them; in the *Ekklesiazusai* the Chorus say of the Athenians,
'they sat in the wreath-market and gossiped all day'.[75] The coexistence
of sources insisting on the seclusion of women with those indicating
precisely the opposite, reveal the influence of a normative ideal on
Greek writers.[76] In the same way, much of the insistence in the sources
that women had information kept from them reflects an ideal rather
than reality: the insistence comes precisely because women did have
access to information, because they had an ambiguous status as non-

citizens, but with a prescribed role in the polis. The hierarchy was reinforced by a denial that women had access to any information outside their prescribed sphere.

Slaves, on the other hand, were simply less problematic. The chattel slave faced the very real barrier of language and lack of understanding of how the city worked: slaves truly constituted a group disenfranchised from information. It was not important to insist that a slave had no knowledge of the running of the polis, since there was no question that he or she ever would (hence too the suspicion centring on the *ergastêrion*). Vidal-Naquet explains the lack of fantasies in the Athenian tradition about the rule of slaves by the fact that myth and tradition generally reflected the complete dissociation of the chattel slave from participation in the polis.[77] There was no ambiguity in the relationship of slaves to information, because they held a completely unambiguous social status.

*

When Lysias claimed that all Athenians spent some time in a shop, as well as defending his client, he was saying something about the behaviour to which all free citizens aspired. Only those with sufficient income to be leisured could spend an appreciable amount of time in public talk or discussion, but it was part of the image of the citizen that he did not need to spend all of his time working for a living. As an intermediate stage in public space between the house and the Agora or gymnasium, the shop allowed the citizens to form and maintain relationships larger than kinship groups, but smaller than city-wide structures, providing a milieu in which information could easily circulate. Even at this level, information was controlled by common consensus: there were some things suitable to be discussed before outsiders, and some not, an idea which perhaps underlies Aristophanes' prosecution for criticising the polis at the Dionysia.[78]

Conversely, secrecy in the life of a citizen was hard to achieve, because it contradicted the idea of living one's life in public, and facts about individuals needed to be disseminated as a part of the working of the polis. In some senses information of this kind was more important than external news, or at least more immediate, because it was relevant to the experience of every citizen. On this reading, nothing that was heard in the Agora, even if only 'rude jokes about other people's sex lives', was 'insignificant chatter'.

News Independent of the Polis

For all the Athenians and strangers which were there spent their time in
nothing else, but either to tell, or to hear some new thing.

Acts 17.21

The introduction to Plato's *Phaedo* depicts Echekrates of Phlious, a
philosopher visiting Athens, asking Phaedo to tell him the details of
Sokrates' death. Echekrates has not heard, he says, because no citizen
of Phlious has travelled to Athens recently, nor has any foreigner who
could give an account come to Phlious.[1] The situation is no doubt a
literary convenience, but it illustrates the extent to which the hearing
of news in ancient Greece was dependent on individual travel. An
outline of events had reached Echekrates, namely that Sokrates had
been condemned to death and had drunk hemlock, but to find out more
than this one needed a personal informant. An account of the death of
Sokrates was obviously of importance to those in the small group of his
admirers, yet the information could be spread only by individuals
travelling and carrying the news themselves.

Communication between citizens within the Greek world was governed by a particular set of beliefs and expectations. All Greek poleis
received information and disseminated it to their citizens, but this
alone will not account for all the news which circulated in Greece. News
entering the polis could be analysed by its citizens only against a
background of knowledge, and the orators demonstrate by their appeals
to this knowledge that citizens could be expected to have other sources
of information. Demosthenes, for instance, appeals to the geographical
knowledge of his audience: those of you who have visited Kardia, he
says, will know its situation, and the rest of you will have heard about
it from them.[2] This is an area which has hitherto been little discussed,
yet it is of primary importance for news. Questions of where and how
people heard news, what contact existed between poleis on the individual level, and the nature of the information and news that was circulated, must be answered if a true picture of the dissemination of news
is to be built up.

If many citizens travelled between poleis and had the opportunity to
exchange news and information, this meant that any official version of
events offered by a polis could be enlarged on, or bypassed, by an

alternative source. The opening of Plato's *Charmides* demonstrates the difference between the official report of an event, and the receipt of news from an individual. Sokrates has just returned from camp at Potidaia, and encounters his friends as he comes back to Athens. They have heard that there has been a battle, and that many have died, but want Sokrates to tell them all the details of what has happened.[3]

We should ask what kind of information was passed between citizens of different poleis. The more movement between poleis and contact between citizens there was, the more could be known about other states. This is important for our view of Athenian political life. On the outbreak of hostilities in 431, the Athenians seized and expelled all Boiotians in Attika in response to the aggression of Thebes, indicating that previously there were Boiotians in Attika, who could be perceived as a threat.[4] The reason behind the expulsion and exclusion of foreigners in wartime was surely the perceived danger in the information to be gathered through normal travel. The situation whereby citizens were not informed even adequately of affairs in other states, but relied instead on a few well-informed leaders, who debated the issues and allowed decisions to be made on a factional basis, was most likely to have arisen in wartime, when contact with enemy states was cut; the expulsion of disloyal foreigners would control the passage of information in both directions.

Although the official dissemination of information tended to involve only matters which the polis felt it advantageous to report, this does not mean that states could succeed in suppressing information for long – in fact the opposite was true. It was through individual contacts that information which was neutral or harmful to the polis would be spread. For instance, while Athens was under the rule of the Thirty, they tried to conduct state business as usual, but large numbers of exiles went to Thebes and Megara, where much sympathy was evoked for the exiled democrats.[5] One of the primary areas in which this is important is in the image a polis was able to project. Some information, such as that on manpower, was suppressed, and contact of this kind offered the chance to discover what was not being said on an official level.[6] For instance, the Megarian in Aristophanes' *Acharnians* tells Dikaiopolis that despite the protestations of the government that all is well, things are going from bad to worse in Megara.[7]

Our sources for this chapter are mainly Athenian ones, and as the epigraph indicates, these may be unrepresentative. In the time of St Paul the Athenians had a reputation as being keen to hear news, and, as we have seen, this is a characteristic emphasised by Demosthenes and Theophrastos as well.[8] There is, however, no indication that other poleis necessarily manifested the same concern. Athens was a centre for trade, and a place which set out to attract foreigners in large numbers, with the sanction of the state, so an open attitude towards news is hardly surprising. Xenophon comments in the *Poroi* that all travellers crossing Greece, whether by road or sea, pass through Athens.[9] Similarly the merchants of Rhodes are mentioned by Lykourgos as having a large role in spreading news, and Tenedos is said by Aristotle to be a centre for passenger traffic; distinctions should obviously be made between large cosmopolitan communities and small isolated ones.[10] Athenian evidence may dominate, but does not necessarily represent the norm. In Athenian sources the Spartans are characterised as slow to react, needing to be spurred into action by delegations, but this could simply be in contrast to Athens and Corinth, where news was more readily heard, and reaction could be swifter.[11] So it is necessary to establish what contacts existed, and where they were important.

1. Travel and news

The significance of travel in spreading news is demonstrated by those sources which caution against it. In cities where state control is to be exercised, travellers are seen as a particular problem: Plato dwells on the harmful influence that can come from strangers visiting a city – 'mixing between cities causes the morals of the city to be altogether corrupted, as strangers introduce new ideas; this brings the most harm of all to those states which are well-governed with just laws' – while Aineias Tacticus recommends controls on individual travel to and from the beseiged city.[12] The Spartan effort to prevent foreign influence entering their polis hinged on the control of travel, both to and from Sparta: outsiders could be expelled, because they might spread subversive ideas among the citizens, and Spartiates were not permitted to travel outside the polis unless on official business, in case they learnt foreign customs.[13] It is interesting that the main type of secrecy being practised here is to prevent information reaching the citizens from outside, not to keep internal matters hidden from outsiders.

Two of Plutarch's anecdotes illustrate the expectation behind contact with travellers: in the *Life of Solon*, when Solon is abroad, he hears that a traveller has arrived from Athens, and makes a point of going to ask him what has been happening recently in the city. The news he hears, that his own son has died, is not accurate, but the idea that one would question a new arrival is clear. In the *Apophthegmata Lakonika* a Spartan who has been in Athens is asked by his fellow Spartans how things are there; his reply, 'everything is fine and good', is one to which I will return later on.[14]

Attitudes thus imply that travel was normal and frequent. But frequent among which classes? Should it be seen as the prerogative of the rich? The ability of the rich to travel at all periods cannot be doubted. They had both money and leisure, and, more importantly,

contacts. In the archaic period aristocratic networks grew up, based on
ties of marriage, inherited relationships and visits of friendship, unit-
ing families across polis boundaries. At the betrothal of his daughter
Agariste, for example, Kleisthenes of Sicyon entertained eligible bache-
lors from all over the Greek world, as far as Italy, and including
Diaktorides, from one of the Thessalian ruling families, and Leokedes,
son of Pheidon of Argos.[15] In parallel with such contacts arose the
custom of *xenia*. This kind of relationship existed in the classical period
too, and we see inherited friendships among the leading men of each
polis, as for instance between Perikles and Archidamos, or Alkibiades
and Endios.[16] From the end of the seventh century we see the emergence of a different type of relationship, the *proxenia* whereby an
individual was chosen by a polis to act as its representative in his home
state. According to Herman's study of *xenia* and *proxenia* at Athens, the
development of the institution of *proxenia* was an attempt to exploit the
existing ties of *xenia* between individuals for the benefit of the state.[17]

The development of a public aspect to a private relationship diverted
attention from, but did not supersede, the personal relationship between *xenoi*. Through the fifth and fourth centuries one can still find
some insistence that relations of *xenia* were not in the spirit of polis
loyalty, despite the public use that was made of such contacts. Andokides had connections with various rich men, and offered these
contacts as a potential benefit to the city should he be reinstated, at his
trial in 399. We also see Mantitheos, who claims to be a private enemy
of the tyrant of Mytilene, the Athenian general Timotheos playing host
to Alketas and Jason of Pherai, and the man from Corcyra who was
entertained at Timokrates' house when he came on embassies.[18] There
remained doubts as to the proper relation between public and private
entertainment; Aischines suggests that it was suspiciously oligarchic
for people to meet privately at their houses:

> Doesn't it seem dreadful to you, if the council-chamber and the people are
> being ignored, while letters and embassies are received in private house-
> holds, communications not just from ordinary people, but from the most
> important individuals in Asia and Europe?

Yet the state relied on this system for the conduct of diplomacy.[19] An
embassy still came to the city as a collection of private individuals, and
private influence could be brought to bear. The mutual accusations of
Demosthenes and Aischines over the 'spy' Anaxinos of Oreos illustrate
the tension: Demosthénes accuses Aischines of plotting with Anaxinos,
and it is interesting that Aischines has information about Oreos, and
one of their decrees awarding money to Demosthenes, to read out in his
speech.[20] Aischines' relationship with Anaxinos gives him access to
information from Oreos, but also lays him open to suspicion.

So relations between members of the elite and wealthy could be close. Yet such contacts are still very much at the top of the social scale. Partly this may be because high-level *xeniai* were more likely to attract blame or cause boasting, but nevertheless the men we see are at least middle class, not aristocrats but trierarchs or similar. Even though the institution of *proxenia* had brought these relationships within the democratic ambit of the polis, the poorer citizens do not figure in our sources. Is this simply because they were debarred from travelling?

Greek writers tend to dwell on the dangers inherent in travel: Andokides asks his audience when a man is in greater danger than on a winter sea-voyage. At sea there was the risk of shipwreck or piracy, and on land of attack by bandits, or accidents, but this implies that travel was more common rather than less.[21] The idea of travel as difficult and arduous, and the province only of the rich, has fed the image of a mobile upper class and parochial lower class.[22] Some historians have questioned this image of parochialism in both the archaic and the later classical periods, notably Purcell in 'Mobility and the Polis', and McKechnie in *Outsiders in the Greek Cities*.[23] Purcell argues that the archaic period was a time of great mobility, both for individuals and for whole societies, facilitated by trade and commercial relationships, and that this mobility influenced the form of Greek social institutions. Only in the late sixth and fifth centuries did Greek society become static and insular. Similarly McKechnie argues for the fourth century that the tie binding a citizen to his polis grew weaker, with far greater numbers choosing to live outside the polis in pursuit of a livelihood.

In the light of such conclusions, it is necessary to reappraise the image of the parochial lower class for the classical period too. In an article on communication in the ancient Mediterranean, Casson outlines only the problems of land travel, devoting the major part of his article to sea travel on the assumption that this was always the preferred method of communication.[24] Yet not all journeys were made by sea. During the winter (between November and March), for instance, the seas were closed and travel, limited though it may have been, had to be by land. We have references to mundane journeys undertaken by land – two anecdotes in Xenophon's *Memorabilia* concern Sokrates' words of wisdom to those embarking on long journeys, which are simply assumed to be by land and on foot – and to journeys of considerable importance, such as the embassy of 346 from Athens to Philip of Macedon, which travelled slowly by land.[25]

Casson also comments that there were few real roads between Greek poleis, and that those there were often became impassable in the winter. The road between Athens and Megara, he says, was not made until the time of Hadrian.[26] In fact, Hadrian was responsible for the widening of the existing Skironian road between Megara and Corinth so that two chariots could pass each other, but Casson's preconceptions are significant. He commends Roman roads in contrast to Greek, because they were 'all-weather paved surfaces on key highways', and sees the Greek failure to create such roads as indicative of poor communication. This is misleading for two reasons. First, the built road is something of a red herring, since travellers on foot needed only a recognised route, not an 'all-weather paved surface'. A necessary route would carry traffic whether developed as a road or not.[27] Secondly, Roman roads were built not only to facilitate communication for the army, but also to keep units of soldiers busy, and as an expression of Roman power.[28]

To understand Greek attitudes to roads, we should look to the contexts in which they do occur. Road building in Greece in the fifth and fourth centuries was technologically primitive, and a road made with a standard gauge of incised ruts for wheeled vehicles to use was the most sophisticated way of coping with large volumes of traffic.[29] Most construction of roads involved the creation of 'rut roads' linking important religious sites to large poleis or to the coast, allowing travel to and from festivals. These rut roads were in all cases sacred roads (often named the Sacred Way), linking Athens to Eleusis and Delphi, Sparta to Amyklai (the Hyakinthian Way), and Elis, on the coast, to Olympia. Plutarch relates that a Spartan *theôria* to Delphi, travelling by cart, was attacked by bandits in Megara, indicating that at least one road made Delphi accessible by wheeled traffic from the Peloponnese.[30] The connection between roadbuilding and religion is further demonstrated by a surviving law of the Delphic Amphiktyony from 380/79, referring to the role of this authority in roadbuilding.[31] That a concern to create roads was felt in this area but not elsewhere attests to the position of the religious festival as one of the principal theatres for officially-sanctioned contact between poleis.[32]

The Greek neglect of roadbuilding outside the religious context was connected with the ideological separateness of each polis and its territory – where improvements were made in communications, it tended to be in areas where the autonomy of the state was not affected, by building ports at a distance from the polis, or the diolkos at Corinth. When poleis concerned themselves with roadbuilding, it was only to facilitate movement within their own territory: consider the actions of the Pisistratids at Athens in adding marker-stones and the Altar of the Twelve Gods to the Athenian road system, or the traditional responsibility of the Spartan kings, recorded by Herodotos, for overseeing the roads of Lakonia.[33] But although poleis were keen to facilitate travel within their own territories, they did not extend the same organisation beyond their borders. There was even a distinction in language between the usual word for a road (*hodos*), and that for a road that went abroad, beyond the polis territory (*xenis*). A passage in Plato *Laws* makes the reasons behind the distinction explicit. In Plato's city the *agronomoi* are to dig moats and build fortifications to prevent invasion of the country from outside, and then to look after the roads, to make communication within the land as easy as possible.[34] To facilitate communication between poleis is to create a threat; the opposition between roads and defence becomes clear. A road leading into the heart of a polis from another state could easily be an open invitation to invaders. The building of roads between poleis had to be controlled by apolitical religious bodies, not individual poleis, because the autonomy of a state could be seen to be threatened by the construction of roads.

This has two consequences: first, lack of roads need not be taken to indicate lack of travel, and secondly, attitudes to citizens who travel were likely to be complex. Although in the early period we see only the rich making long journeys for business or pleasure, there is plenty of evidence to demonstrate that the lower classes travelled too. We shall examine the reasons why an individual might travel, and the opportunities for the exchange of news they afforded.

(i) Trade

The relationship between traders and news is obvious; because of this it seems to invite unsubtle treatment by modern historians. The paradigmatic Herodas is often included in the category of merchants carrying information, but his story raises some questions.[35] He was in Phoenicia 'with a shipowner', but his own occupation and motives remain obscure. If he were on a trading voyage as a merchant working with a *nauklêros*, would he necessarily have had to find another ship on which to travel to Sparta?[36]

It is, paradoxically, important to emphasise that traders were not the primary spreaders of all news. The role of the merchant in news-carrying is in fact more complex than some historians have perceived. Starr gives prominence to the role of merchants in spreading news, both of 'ideas and techniques' on a large scale, and of individual items of news. He presents the merchants as one of the primary groups responsible for the unofficial dissemination of news, and offers many examples.[37] His conclusion is that they were 'an important, if unreliable, source of information'. This view is based on some mistaken assumptions. Starr's claim is that in the early period, as well as exporting physical artefacts, 'merchants brought back ideas and techniques, such as the alphabet and the use of molds to make clay figurines'. The role of trade in the dissemination of this kind of knowledge is hardly questioned, but it is often expressed in imprecise terms.[38] In fact, technical information was unlikely to be of much value to a merchant; it would not help him in his trade, and unless he were an expert in some other craft, he would not be able to learn or disseminate a new technique. Bringing a new type of artefact to an area is by no means the same as bringing the knowledge of how to create it. For the spread of this kind of information one must look instead to the craftsmen themselves, travelling in search of work or moving from state to state and taking their knowledge with them. Even an invention like the alphabet was not in any true sense 'spread by traders' – again, the traders were the facilitators, but not the actual disseminators.

The definition of what constitutes news depends to a large extent on the interests of the hearer. Starr comments, 'Undoubtedly they [the merchants] brought back bits of news to their home agoras, which were fed into public knowledge', but merchants in general had a different agenda for news from that of the citizen.[39] What might be news to a merchant, such as crop failure, high prices in Byzantion, or newly-discovered anchorages, did not have the same meaning for the citizen in the Agora. There is no doubt that political news was carried on occasion, where relevant to trading concerns, but it is wrong to see the merchants as primarily responsible for providing political and military news.

The idea of the merchant moving from one small community to another and retailing news in the Agora of each is based on the idea of a fairly primitive social structure. There was in Greece more than one kind of merchant: the *kapêlos*, or small-scale trader, who went from one small community to another, often by land and within a state, and the *emporos*, long-distance trader, travelling and gaining information on a much wider scale.[40] Whereas one trader might be sailing regularly between different countries or different poleis, further along the route followed by commodities, another trader would cover only a limited local area. The large ports, such as Athens, Byzantion and Rhodes, were generally acknowledged to be the centres of trade for *emporoi*, but this does not mean that trade was carried on indiscriminately around the Aegean and Mediterranean from these centres.[41] Much trade at Athens came and went along specific routes, to the grain-producing areas of the Hellespont, to Egypt and to Sicily. Athens (and also Rhodes) acted as entrepôts for many of the smaller states in Greece and Asia Minor, and thus a trader from, say, Naxos, would have to follow only one route, to Athens, in order to find all the goods he wanted. There is thus no compelling evidence to see the traders acting as a large-scale network for the spread of news; the few examples we do have tend to reflect the spread of information at a more local level.

Trade by land in particular was significant in this respect, and the scale of this in Attika was considerable. Demosthenes refers to a law of Drakon banning exiles from the 'border-markets', where, he says, citizens of neighbouring states used to meet in former times. Xenophon suggests in the *Poroi* that much of Attika's trade came by land, and the traders depicted by Aristophanes in the *Acharnians* are part of a local land-based trading system.[42] This implies that the role of long-distance traders in this area was actually quite small, because of the limits on the places they visited, and their need to make a profit rather than provide an information service. Smaller traders, however, played a greater part in bringing information to smaller communities, if not in providing poleis with intelligence.

The distinction that is made in polis life, between the professional merchant and the citizen, is largely one of urban custom, where those engaged in trade inhabit a different milieu, and in which the ideal of the citizen as a leisured stay-at-home who participates in political life could not be reconciled with the occupation of long-distance trader.[43] But this distinction will not hold good for communities outside the urban centre, where we encounter the farmer who may travel short distances to sell surplus produce without becoming a professional trader, and who is not prevented by this from exercising political rights. Through trade with neighbouring communities these people would have access to information from others of their class, about events in the city, public figures, weather or agriculture.[44]

This kind of contact was most affected by war, which could limit both the availability of goods to trade, and the contact permitted between poleis. The best example of this is the Athenians' decree against Megara, the economic nature of which is shown to have affected local trade as well as shipping, and the seizure of Megarian goods as contraband adds to the picture.[45] It has been argued that poleis could not attempt to control trading contacts with enemy states, on the grounds that it would be both economically damaging and difficult to achieve.[46] The only area in which direct control is attested is the supply of commodities specifically for the war effort, namely grain and shipbuilding materials. This does not, however, satisfactorily explain the significance of Athenian comedy on this topic. Aristophanes' plays not only depict Megarian and Boiotian goods being seized as *polemia*, enemy goods, but, more importantly, contain asides on the unavailability of some goods because of the war.[47] Similarly the economic rigours of war, and potential dangers of sailing or travelling to some areas, will have limited trade in other ways. Demosthenes says in the Second Olynthiac that the markets in Macedonia have been closed as a result of the war, and Neaira's trade in Megara was directly affected by the war in 372/1, as fewer foreigners came there.[48] Generally close contacts could be temporarily interrupted by war.

It is of course true that traders appear in our sources in other guises: Apollodoros, for instance, in *Against Polykles*, has friends in Lampsakos and Tenedos from whom to borrow money, and he is explicit about the reason for this:

> Because I was the son of Pasion, and he had ties of friendship with many people abroad, and was trusted throughout Greece, I had no difficulty in borrowing money wherever I needed it.[49]

Thus although the circumstances of his speech relate to a trierarchy, this illustrates the phenomenon of the community of the *emporion*, which covered all major ports, and within which it was possible to be widely known. As a banker and a merchant, Pasion had many opportunities to meet foreign traders or lenders, and these links extended to his son. Equally an itinerant trade may be hidden behind the temporary occupation of an individual, as in the speeches of Demosthenes and Aischines concerning negotiations with Philip; many of the envoys sent by Philip to initiate negotiation of the Peace were in Macedonia as a result of their trade.[50]

But one needs to draw a distinction between traders who lived as part of a distinct community and circulated information only among themselves, as did merchants with centres at the ports of Rhodes and Athens, and those who moved from one polis to another as individual travellers and took up residence there, however briefly.[51] McKechnie argues for an increase in the numbers of those following itinerant professions during the fourth century, ultimately creating the milieu in which the Hellenistic courts could appear. But the experience of wandering traders was not always the same. The sophists, for instance, tended to move to the accepted centres for philosophy, and to attract pupils to these centres, rather than travelling widely from one polis to another.[52] Those who came to hear the sophists comprised a limited audience, and a leisured one too, and the information they shared reached only a narrow circle. Doctors, on the other hand, tended to adopt a more fully itinerant way of life, entering into employment where they could, and interacting with a wider group.[53] *Hetairai* also moved from one city to another relatively freely, and mixed with a varied clientèle.[54] It was not that such professionals disseminated information about their own trade – this was little use to an outsider and usually spread only by apprenticeship – but that they could offer more news as a result of their mobility.

In addition, merchants were important not only as carriers of information themselves, but also as the facilitators of travel for other messengers. Traders carried passengers, as well as travelling themselves, and some of the instances interpreted as merchants carrying information in fact involve the passengers they carried. Some of Starr's examples tend to blur this distinction: the *xenos* of Plutarch's *Nikias* may have been being barbered in the Piraeus, but he is not explicitly stated to have been a merchant, as opposed to a foreigner, and Plutarch elsewhere states that he was a slave.[55]

But did trade actually break down barriers between communities? In one way it simply emphasised the polarity between the citizen and the wanderer: mobility was one of the factors that could in theory isolate the outsider from the citizen. But the concept of the outsider is a complex one, and mobility was not necessarily a determining factor.

Exiles, for instance, could settle within a community, but still be outside the polis proper.[56] The very fact that individuals could move between poleis suggests that the barriers perceived against outsiders were more ideological than actual.

(ii) Military travel

The motive for travel most often advanced to counter assertions about the limited opportunities afforded to the poor is military service.[57] The episode most often cited in this context is the dispatch of the Athenian Expedition to Sicily: Thucydides blames the Athenians' ignorance of the size and population of the island for the failure of the venture, but Plutarch asserts that before the assembly in which the plan was discussed, groups of old and young men sat debating the topic and drawing plans of Sicily and its environs.[58] Such a story argues a knowledge gained from previous campaigns. The experience of those on military service merits investigation. It is a mark of the importance of the military role to the citizen that in forensic speeches an orator will refer to recent campaigns as something in which all or most of the jury have played a part.[59] While this may represent exaggeration in the cause of flattery rather than a reflection of the truth, it does show that participation in foreign expeditions was the norm. Demosthenes suggests that it may have broadened the horizons of the soldier: 'at the inn before the temple of the Dioscuri – if any of you has been to Pherai, he will know the place I mean'.[60] But a closer examination of those speeches which concern military affairs indicates social divisions in the experience of soldiers.

The men who figure in forensic speeches are invariably of the trierarchic or similar class, as Apollodoros in *Against Polykles*, Mantitheos in *Against Boiotos* or Astyphilos in *On the Estate of Astyphilos*. These are all high-ranking men in the military context – Apollodoros is trierarch, Mantitheos taxiarch and Astyphilos lochagos.[61] First, then, these men did have an opportunity to travel, and certainly Mantitheos had used this to form ties of *xenia* – he was on an expedition to collect money from the allies, and evidently became involved in factional strife at Mytilene. He claimed that Kammys, tyrant of Mytilene, was a personal enemy of his and of his father.[62] Apollodoros, on the other hand, accounted for his ties with foreigners by his father's business; the account we have of his trierarchy is interesting precisely because it demonstrates how contained an Athenian expedition in peace-time could be. He was concerned with internal matters such as the return of exiles and the trouble among the trierarchs, and his duties of convoying ships or ferrying messages between posts did not create opportunities for him or his crew to investigate the area where they were stationed. When the Athenians were in Thasos, Apollodoros expressly says that the general Timomachos lodged 'outside the walls', and Apollodoros' only contacts outside the army were either in the market or among his own business acquaintances.[63]

We rarely see, however, the experience of the ordinary soldier or rower, unless through the remarks of speakers addressed to the jury. If the speech of Apollodoros reflects accurately the conditions of service in peacetime, the conditions of war can hardly have offered more scope; the account in Thucydides of the Athenian campaign at Samos depicts a separate camp, where contact between the city of Samos and the camp was initially very small. This contact grew greater only under stress of the soldiers' estrangement from Athens, and issues of contact between individual Athenians and Samians are further obscured by the fact that citizenship was subsequently granted to all Samians in 405.[64]

The need to maintain discipline in a camp was an important factor, and so there was always a concern to exclude foreigners and keep soldiers together. Plutarch relates a story about Epaminondas which illustrates this well: when the Thebans were camped near Arkadia, the Arcadians invited them, because the weather was so cold, to come into the city and be quartered in their houses. Epaminondas refused, saying that if the Arcadians saw the Theban soldiers at close quarters, doing everyday things, they would lose their respect for them.[65] At Syracuse in 415, the Athenian generals were able to draw the Syracusans into attacking the Athenian camp by passing on the information that the Athenians usually spent the night inside the city of Katana, away from their arms.[66] That this constituted an effective lure for an attack suggests that it was unusual for soldiers to spend the night in a friendly city.[67] If one adds to this the fact that much military service was done in Attika itself, in the border forts, it begins to seem that for the rank and file, military service was not such a great opportunity for the extension of knowledge about foreign places.

Thucydides collected his accounts of events during the Peloponnesian War from generals and soldiers who had participated in events, and plainly those interested in the course of the war would find this important. But all an informant could know is what had happened to them, preserved and told as a personal story.[68] Knowledge of people or places would tend to reflect the abnormal circumstances of war, not the normal situation. Geographical knowledge was probably the only type of information that was easily accessible, and this is precisely what we see. It is one of the motives given by Thucydides for the eagerness of the young to sail to Sicily – they had a longing to see different places and for foreign travel – and also the knowledge to which the orators appeal.[69]

Of course to serve as a soldier it was necessary to meet the hoplite qualification; the very poorest served as rowers, and their experience appears to have been even more limited. Pritchett, writing on the experience of the citizen rower, claims that Athenian rowers were expert through continual practice and must have been out on service in most years, but this changed as the fourth century progressed.[70] In Demosthenes' speeches we see trierarchs unable or unwilling to fill their ships with citizen rowers, replacing them with professionals drawn from the Piraeus. The contrast between these two groups is brought out in *Against Polykles*; the professional rowers deserted in the Hellespont, looking for better-paid work in the armies on the mainland, or in the fleets of the Thasians and Maronites, while the Athenian rowers remained with the ships, which were their only means of returning home.[71] The professional rowers evidently formed part of the same international community as mercenaries, whereas the citizens, in contrast, occupied a small and closed world. Through the fourth century, citizens became less and less willing to serve on the rowing benches, replacing their own labour with that of hired rowers, and thus the opportunities for travel connected with the military diminished.

A further dimension is added to this kind of experience by the example of Euxitheos' father, Thoukritos, who was captured during the Dekeleian War, sold as a slave and taken to Akarnania. He was eventually ransomed and returned to Athens, after a period long enough for him to have developed a foreign accent.[72] There are similar stories that some who were captured after the Sicilian disaster and enslaved ultimately found their way back to Athens, with or without the aid of Euripides; Thucydides' account of the hardships they suffered in the quarries certainly appears to be drawn from a first-hand source.[73] We also encounter Nikostratos, who was captured by privateers while pursuing some runaway slaves, and was sold as a slave himself in Aigina. Even Philip II of Macedon spent three years in his youth as a hostage at Thebes, and is believed to have profited from the experience by observing Theban innovations in warfare, gaining knowledge which he later exploited to great effect in the Macedonian army.[74]

Most of the Greeks captured by other Greeks were ultimately ransomed, as were many of the prisoners captured by Philip, and throughout the fourth century we have decrees of thanks to foreigners for ransoming or freeing Athenian citizens.[75] The lack of much explicit testimony to the experiences of ransomed prisoners may perhaps be the result of shame attaching to the situation; Nikostratos, we are told by his opponent, will not want to demonstrate the proof of his experiences.[76] Tales such as that told by Demosthenes about Atrestidas the mercenary returning from Pella to Athens with Olynthian captives are not so useful, since captivity or exile without hope of return could play little part in the dissemination of knowledge.[77] The number of Scythian and other barbarian slaves in Athens did little to diffuse knowledge of their native places – slaves were of such low status as to be untrustworthy as informants, and Greek slaves from cities still in existence were rare.[78]

Thus under force of circumstances ordinary citizens could find themselves abroad for an extended period, with the opportunity (if they were in the frame of mind to appreciate it) to learn about new places and events. Such experience was doubtless different in quality from that of travellers visiting friends abroad, or engaging in tourism, but it was nevertheless a chance to broaden one's horizons.

We also have references to those who undertook foreign military service or activities of their own accord – to the brothers in *On the Estate of Menekles* who earned a living as mercenaries, and to Makartartos, who sold his land and went on a privateering expedition to Crete.[79] This does not by itself argue great mobility, but it does suggest that foreign travel could be seen as a viable option, particularly as one of the brothers in Isaios, Philonides, continued in a travelling life. Even though some of these individuals were absent from Athens for years at a time, this does not mean that they severed their ties with the polis. For example, Nikostratos was absent for eleven years on mercenary service, but his will was contested among his relatives and he clearly remained an Athenian citizen.[80]

Service as a mercenary did not necessarily make the soldier more open-minded than service for the polis. Mercenary armies like the Ten Thousand saw themselves as a self-contained and definitely Greek group, recognising a Lydian among their number by his pierced ears, and promptly expelling him. They remained in distinct units, reflecting polis loyalties, and when the unpopular idea of settling in Asia was raised, its root was the foundation of a new polis on the Greek model, rather than integration with the existing population.[81] Their main aim was to return to Greece, not to gain experience of foreign lands.

Military service, then, was a way of seeing the world, but it had its limits, and declined among citizens as the fourth century went on. In a situation of open hostility soldiers were confined to their camp, and even on peacetime service, the opportunities for meeting citizens of other poleis were small. If the desire to travel did figure in decisions to go to war, as Thucydides suggests, it can only ever have been a minor consideration. War was not a good way of finding out about other poleis, but equally it was not the only way in which poleis interacted.

(iii) Religious travel

Riepl, in *Das Nachrichtenwesen des Altertums*, emphasises the importance of central meeting places for the dissemination of news, and he characterises the four largest panhellenic festivals as the central points of the classical Greek world.[82] These were the Olympia, Pythia, Isthmia and Nemea, which together formed the *periodos*. The Olympic festival took place in midsummer, the Pythian in spring and the Isthmian in spring or summer, which suggests that attendance was meant to be widespread – no Panhellenic festival was held in the months important for agriculture, autumn and early spring, and most took place when a citizen was in any case most likely to leave his land, during the summer campaigning season. Because they were attended by so many, Riepl concludes that they could be considered as the gathering of the whole Greek world. His view is that through the gatherings at these festivals, news could be spread to all parts of the Greek world. I will later examine the extent to which poleis used these for the spread of official news.[83] But how were these festivals important to ordinary people?

In all accounts of ancient travel religion is accorded the largest role as a motive for travel, even among the poor. Finley comments that there were never so many people on the road at once as in the period before the Olympia, while Starr allows that 'seekers of religious shrines were also on the roads'.[84] But is it right to depict these festivals as universal meeting-places independent of the polis? Women were excluded from the Olympic Games, as spectators and competitors, taking part only in a separate festival in honour of Hera held at a different time of year.[85] There was thus a social restriction on those who could attend the Olympia, and one should probably ask whether other restrictions affected those attending.

In Athens social distinctions were clearly a part of religious celebrations in the city. For instance, the female chorus in *Lysistrata* describe the religious offices they have held, in order to demonstrate their importance and position in the polis.[86] While there were no actual legal restrictions on the social status of participants, the evidence does indicate that major roles in festivals were generally seen as the prerogative of the upper classes, even when the festival was theoretically open to all. Isaios uses a woman's election as *archousa* in the Thesmophoria as evidence for her legitimacy and her status:

> But do you think, if our mother were such as these men say, that the wives of the other demesmen would have chosen her to lead the festival along with the wife of Diokles, and would have entrusted her with the sacred objects?[87]

The rich and noble were certainly far more visible in religious matters, holding religious offices and contributing money. Honorific decrees of the Attic demes refer most often to financial benefaction in the cause of deme religion, ensuring that the names recorded in connection with religion are mainly those of the wealthy.[88]

The same is true of religion on a panhellenic scale, at the oracles and festivals of all the Greeks. The epinikian odes of Pindar celebrate not only the victors of the panhellenic games, but also the ideal of the aristocratic victors as descendants of mythological heroes, and leaders of Greece, and this remained true of the Olympic and other festivals for a long time – the nobles went to compete, and the commoners to watch. Those recorded as attending the Olympic festival are either competitors like Alkibiades with his seven chariots, prominent exponents of certain professions, such as Hippias the sophist, or members of *theôroi*, sacred embassies, who were sent from the various poleis at public expense.[89] The *theôroi* tended to be wealthy and important men, another example of the urban élite filling the religious offices. The ambassadors went to the festival either in theoric ships provided by the state, or overland at public expense, while competitors and trainers gathered at Elis to train a month before the date, and then went in procession to the stadium, where they were housed in an official building. Wealthy foreigners, equally, could travel and house themselves luxuriously, as did Thearides, the brother of Dionysios of Syracuse, whose opulence became one of the targets of Lysias' attack in 388.[90]

Does this then mean that the peasant farmer's horizon was narrow, and that the poor worshipped only at local shrines and festivals? There is much evidence to suggest that even the very poor participated fully in other areas of Greek religious life. The Mysteries at Eleusis, for example, were a part of Athenian polis religion, and were quite ostentatiously open to all; the shrines of Asklepios were visited for healing by rich and poor alike.[91] Later authors advance the view that it is better to visit the nearest Asklepieion rather than to travel to the cult centres, but in early times it was only in centres such as Epidauros and Pergamon that Asklepios' healing took place. Even when the cult did spread at a local level, these remained the most famous temples. The inscriptions at Epidauros demonstrate that the temple served as the healing centre of a region, attracting both men and women from Attika, the Peloponnese and Central Greece.[92] That it was not only the rich who benefited from Asklepios is explicitly attested in the sources: he is known as the most philanthropic of gods, and one who treated rich and poor alike.[93]

People also travelled to consult oracles, and these were important in a different way. The stories concerning oracles that have survived in the literary sources are all of consultations by poleis, famous Greeks or foreign kings. The pervasiveness of this idea, that only the important could consult an oracle like that at Delphi, is illustrated by Plutarch; one of his speakers observes that the oracle now exists in times 'when there is nothing complex, or secret, or terrible, but the questions concern petty and mundane matters', in contrast to earlier Greek times.[94] This attitude has led to the assumption by some modern writers that there was an explicit division between the major oracles, patronised by poleis and generals, and those of lesser standing patronised by the lower classes.

It has been suggested that ordinary people simply went to the nearest oracle, regardless of size or reputation, when they wished to make an inquiry, but the fact that travel to distant healing shrines was common makes the contention less likely.[95] The passage of Plutarch quoted above is evidence that in the first century AD, oracles like Delphi did receive mundane enquiries in considerable number, an idea which is supported by the remains discovered at the oracle of Zeus at Dodona. The finds include about 150 lead tablets, on which the enquiries to the oracle were written.[96] Many of these concern mundane or trivial matters, and are obviously not from well-educated or important figures. Obviously some trivial questions would naturally occur, because those living near the oracle, within a few miles of Dodona, would be able to come with a minor request. But the nature of the surviving inquiries from Dodona shows that this was not so. Dodona was an oracle with an international reputation, and three of the eight enquiries preserved from poleis are from outside Epiros, two from Corcyra and one from Tarentum. Of the private queries, some show by a distinctive alphabet or spelling that the enquirer originated from Corinth, Thessaly or Ionia, and there is no difference in subject between these questions and those that apparently originated locally. A few tablets are badly spelt and constructed, suggesting that the writer was not fully literate, and the occupations about which the enquirers ask are as ordinary as fishing and sheep-husbandry.[97]

Xenophon tells us himself that before he embarked on mercenary service in the Ten Thousand, he consulted the oracle at Delphi on Sokrates' advice, asking to which gods he should sacrifice in order to achieve success. Sokrates criticised him for casting his enquiry in this way, instead of first asking whether he should go at all.[98] This provides a clear example of the way questions were posed by individuals at oracular shrines – they tend to be on mundane matters, and often to indicate the desired answer.[99]

There is a surprising gap in our evidence for the attendance and composition of the audience at the Olympic festival during the classical period; only in Hellenistic and later times do we find descriptions of the festivals in literary sources. One reason for this is doubtless the change in perspective: when Greece came under Roman rule, Olympia became the capital of the Greek world, and was thus frequently visited by Roman authors, and a subject of curiosity in Italy. The descriptions of the great crowds attending the Olympia, and of the spectacle of the games themselves, were all written in the first century AD, and so cannot be taken in isolation.[100] Nevertheless, there are some references to participation in the festivals by individuals other than the great and good during the classical period: in Aristophanes' *Peace* there is an obscene reference to staking space for a tent at the Isthmia by a slave, while a scholion to Pindar indicates that temporary shelters were provided at Pisa, close to Olympia, for those who had no accommodation of their own.[101] An anecdote in Aelian claims that Plato shared a tent at Olympia with some strangers who failed to recognise him, while in other anecdotes concerning the reception of speeches by orators or authors at a festival, there is an assumption that a large crowd of listeners was present, such as the audience of Lysias noted above.[102]

It thus seems likely that the later evidence for large crowds and uncomfortable conditions at Olympia is applicable to classical Greece as well; while the attendance from the far corners of the Greek world may have been limited to the *theôroi* sent as an official deputation, men of all classes from mainland Greece had much opportunity to make the journey.

There was more to a *panegyris* than simple religious feeling, particularly in the case of a major gathering like the Olympia: there was the entertainment, of athletic and other kinds, the opportunities for workmen and artists of seeking employment, economic possibilies for sellers of food, shelter, votive offerings and other commodities, and the feeling of participating in a great event – anyone who attended a large festival would enjoy the benefit of local prominence when he returned.[103] The most important news to be gathered was that generated by the games themselves – the names of the victors, the contests that had taken place, the people to be seen or heard there. The significance of this should not be underplayed: Aelian reports that Taurosthenes the Aiginetan brought a wild pigeon with him from Aigina when he came to compete at the Olympic Games, and used it to send a message to his father when he won the pankration.[104]

A spectator returning to his local community would be the means of spreading such news, since there was no official announcement of victory beyond Olympia itself, apart from honours paid to athletes in their individual cities. Compare Plato's *Ion* in which Sokrates, encountering the rhapsode Ion, asks whether he has come from his native Ephesos, and receives an account of Ion's recent victory at the Pythian Games.[105] There is no presumption that Sokrates will have heard any of this already. There was also the element of propaganda; this relates to the building of ornate temples, treasuries and statues at Panhellenic centres. Such constructions were not for the year-round benefit of the Eleians, but for the spectators, and this is how we should imagine descriptions of art or buildings being spread.[106]

Such possibilities for disseminating news raise the question of whether information learned through religious travel could ever pose a threat. Many states held festivals to which they invited outsiders, using it as a state occasion to impress their allies – the Gymnopaidia at Sparta, the Panathenaia at Athens. But the festivals at Athens, the Dionysia in particular, went further than this in drawing large numbers of foreigners to watch the dramatic contests. Of course it was used as a state occasion, with representatives of the allies attending and bringing the annual tribute in the fifth century, but even when the city's role as hegemon of an empire failed in the fourth century, there is still plenty of evidence for unofficial visitors.[107] Isokrates refers in a speech of 380 to the openness of Athenian festivals and the number of outsiders that they attract:

> And the number of those who come here is so great that if there is any benefit to be gained from associating together, this advantage too is embraced by our city

while Theophrastos, writing at the end of the century, refers to an ordinary citizen buying tickets at the theatre for his visiting friends.[108]

The question of how much outsiders could learn has been addressed elsewhere, both in terms of the propaganda of tragedy and the indiscretion of comedy.[109] That comedy might give away secrets seems obvious: comedians used topical material about political matters and public figures, and passages referring to supposed plots between Athenian generals and Spartans or Boiotians, or planned expeditions, might seem unwise.[110] In fact, on the occasions when we know that concern was shown, this was about the slander of an individual citizen, not about the revelation of state secrets in front of *xenoi*.[111] It is true that Aristophanes was not making startling revelations but repeating facts and rumours which an outsider, once in the city, could pick up from general gossip in any case. Comedy was not the main attraction at the Dionysia, tragedy being both more prestigious, and more intelligible to a wider audience, and this suggests that many foreigners may not have been familiar enough with Athenian politics and public figures to get very much out of the political element of comedy. But equally the treatment of Greek affairs in comedy is from an entirely Athenian viewpoint, and it may be that comic playwrights were simply able to ignore outsiders by convention, on the assumption that anything they learned from a comedy would be too little and too late.

(iv) Tourism and personal travel

Having covered the reasons which might compel or encourage a man to travel, we come now to the more problematic area of travel which was neither on behalf of the polis nor for the sake of religion. Was this, travel for pleasure, the province solely of the rich? Some instances in which the ability to travel reflects the old aristocratic ideal are clear: Demosthenes' *Against Neaira* is a case in point. Demosthenes' account of Neaira's life relates how she spent time in various cities, Corinth, Megara and Athens, consorting with different men. Phrynion visited her in Corinth from Athens, and Stephanos visited her in Megara.[112]

Demosthenes is eager to set Neaira firmly in the wealthy demi-monde, and this extends to the men who are described as her companions. There is much circumstantial detail devoted to depicting their lifestyle, and travel forms a part of this:

> He took her to parties at many other men's houses, and also to the house of Chabrias of Aixone, when he won ... a victory in the four-horse chariot race at the Pythian Games, with the team which he bought from the sons of Mityos the Argive ...[113]

A similar depiction of upper-class mores can be found in Antiphon's *Abuse of Alkibiades*, where it is said that Alkibiades went to Abydos to consort with the *hetairai* there. In the same tradition is the young man of Isokrates' *Trapezitikos*; he was the son of a governor of Satyros, king of Bosporos. Because he wished to see Greece, having heard various stories, his father Sopaios provided him with grain to export and money, so that he could travel *kat' emporian kai kata theôrian*, 'to trade and to see the world'.[114] These individuals are rich, they travel by sea, and form the same kind of 'international class' as in the age of the tyrants.

If, however, we turn to the speeches of Antiphon, they illustrate a different type of traveller; in the speech on the poisoning, the prosecutor's father was intending to make a trip to Naxos, while the murder of Herodes took place on a ship full of passengers, going from Mytilene to Ainos. Euxitheos was travelling to Ainos to visit his father, while Herodes was taking some slaves to be ransomed by some Thracians, who were also passengers. In Lysias' speech Against Simon, the defendant is said to have gone abroad for a while because he thought it expedient.[115] These kinds of traveller are not necessarily very rich, nor represented as part of an aristocratic circle, yet they had the motivation to travel quite widely within Greece.

The scale of this kind of travel is striking, as is the apparent ease with which it could be undertaken. Many of the people to be encountered in the orators have friends or relatives abroad; a consideration of some of the recorded contacts between Athens and Megara is illuminating. When the profanation of the Mysteries was discovered, an alien named Teukros withdrew to Megara before making his offer to inform from a place of safety. Apollodoros of Megara was rewarded for involvement in the assassination of Phrynichos, receiving the right of *enktesis* and a plot of Athenian land, while Thucydides says that the accomplice to the assassination was an Argive. In Demosthenes' speech *Against Aphobos*, the defendant is said to have dispersed his property and 'made off' to Megara, where he settled as a metic, and Aristogeiton is said to have escaped from prison and run off to Megara with the help of a woman named Zobia. The speech of Dinarchos against Demosthenes, delivered in 323, refers to a group of Athenian exiles resident in Megara. These men are said to be plotting the overthrow of the Athenian government, and contact with them was a cause for suspicion. Kallimedon was impeached for consorting with them, and Polyeuktos had to clear himself of suspicion by proving that he was visiting his exiled stepfather. For Lykourgos, leaving Athens and settling in Megara are virtually synonymous.[116] All this is very interesting in view of Casson's contention concerning the poor state of the road between Athens and Megara.

In a similar way, the defendant in the case *Against Simon* left the city for a while with his young lover because he felt it expedient to do so, and Leokrates is said to have left Athens, in fear of its capture, for Rhodes in his boat with his mistress.[117] Lykourgos' denunciation of Leokrates' actions turns on the lack of patriotism that such a deed demonstrates; it is not condemned because it is the act of a rich man, nor an act available only to a few, but because only Leokrates would have been so craven as to desert the city. Andokides mentions that certain types of disenfranchisement involved the loss of the right to sail to the Hellespont, or Ionia, and it is clear to see that the first of these provisions was aimed at traders, but as a general principle the curtailment of sailing rights as a form of disenfranchisement is indicative of their importance to the citizen.[118]

One factor limiting mobility among the very poor was the receipt of state handouts. The very poor were naturally tied more closely to the polis: the speaker of Lysias *On the Invalid* would have forfeited his pension by leaving Athens, and if one possessed little else besides citizenship, one had more to lose from moving around. For those dependent on distributions of grain, to which only citizens were entitled, leaving the polis would obviously be uneconomic. Certainly some of the avenues open to the moderately wealthy were closed to the poor; despite the warnings of Isokrates, mercenary service was not the last resort of the destitute. A moderate amount of wealth allowed one to transcend polis boundaries more easily.[119]

We also have evidence of other Greeks visiting Athens. Pyrilampes' peacocks may have enticed visitors from Sparta and Thessaly, but the breeding of exotic birds cannot have motivated large numbers of travellers.[120] Nevertheless, tourism as an explicit motive does appear in ancient writers: Xenophon in the *Poroi* lists among the reasons for people to visit Athens whatever 'sacred and secular' things are worth seeing or hearing, while a fragment of Lysippos refers to Athens as a tourist attraction. Hyperides refers to an episode involving the deaths of some Aeolian tourists at Rheneia, wealthy men who were again travelling *kata theôreian*, and records the Rheneian defence against accusations of murder, that the travellers would not have come to Rheneia of their own accord, 'because they had neither harbours nor markets nor anything else worth visiting'.[121] Further down the scale, the man in jail with Aristogeiton who had his nose swallowed was *tis Tanagraios*, 'some Tanagran', and as we have seen, a Megarian and a Theban were involved in the assassination of Phrynichos.[122]

2. Perceptions of other poleis

It is often asserted by the Athenian orators in forensic speeches that foreigners have come to Athens to hear the verdict in a case, or that the jurors will face the judgement of the Greek world as a whole. Taken at face value, this would imply quite a high level of engagement by outsiders in Athenian affairs. However, rhetorical assertions need to be examined here. The motif that the whole world sees what goes on in the courts at Athens, and that the jurors should make their judgements with this in mind is sometimes asserted as no more than a generalisation: Dinarchos tells his jurors to 'show the world that you have not been corrupted'.[123] In other cases the assertion is far more detailed: Aischines claims that more foreigners than have ever before attended a public trial are present at that of Ktesiphon.[124] There is certainly an element of exaggeration designed to make the crimes of the accused appear worse than they are, but nevertheless these speeches indicate that it was not thought abnormal for outsiders to spectate at trials.

The trials for which the strongest claims are made are political, especially those against Demosthenes, and those conducted by Lysias against representatives of the Thirty, whereas speakers in parochial cases are more likely to assume an all-Athenian audience.[125] Lysias at one point seems to suggest that these foreigners are envoys of a type, sent to report the decision of the jury back to their own polis, and this accords with what has already been shown about the involvement of neighbouring poleis during the rule of the Thirty.[126] Poleis like Thebes and Megara took a large part in sheltering and helping the democratic exiles, and it is not surprising if such interest continued through the early days of the restored democracy. One can certainly conclude from the speeches that the presence of foreigners at Athens was an accepted fact, which might be questioned in wartime for reasons of security, but which normally presented no problem and circulated information.

An extension of this is the idea of notoriety: the claims made by the prosecution of an Alkibiades or an Andokides that all Greece knows of, and is appalled by, the crimes of these men.[127] There can be no doubt that this is true to an extent – Alkibiades was famous for his display at the Olympic Games and for his wealth and charm, while Lysias describes exactly how Andokides became well-known, because of his impiety (obviously) and also because he has travelled widely and flattered many kings, a claim made in slightly different terms by Andokides himself.[128] The speakers assume a popular interest in the trials of such figures which is not confined to their own polis. Again, we may have Athenians attempting to suggest that they have nothing to hide, but trials are certainly represented as part of the wider public domain.

Considerations like these are particularly valuable in understanding how much citizens of one polis could know about another, that is, what background of information did they have, against which to set the news they were offered by the polis? Recreation of the viewpoint of the ancient citizen is difficult, but some indications can be found in comedy and oratory. Comedy is a useful starting-point, because the depiction of foreigners here can indicate what Athenians knew, or felt to be important, about other groups. The foreigners in Attic comedy are all of a stereotypical kind, which is hardly surprising, but the ways in which they are stereotyped are interesting. Those who appear in Aristophanes are drawn from a limited area, from the immediate environs of Attika, and from the larger cities of the Peloponnese: there are Megarian and Boiotian traders, women from Sparta, Corinth and Boiotia, Spartan envoys, and a chorus of Peloponnesians and Athenians.[129] There are no speaking Naxians or Aitolians, and this perhaps indicates a common denominator of familiarity. Apart from these, there is only the Persian envoy of the *Acharnians* (who turns out to be a disguised Athenian) and a few references to other poleis. The first point to be made is that in extant comedy foreigners appear only in the war plays, *Acharnians*, *Lysistrata* and *Peace*. Concern with states outside Attika takes its impetus from external events; other plays with internal themes have only Athenian characters. The foreigners we see are not all hostile – those of the *Acharnians* are traders, the Boiotian professionally – but war is the context in which they generally appear. This is most obvious in *Peace*, where the chorus of Greek farmers is brought on to uncover Peace, but is subsequently forgotten in favour of internal Athenian affairs.[130] Of course in the world of comedy even the Spartans will ultimately turn out to be desirable party guests, but one of the main reasons perceived for interaction between poleis is war.

These characters are foremost Athenian creations; the Megarian is an Athenian's idea of a Megarian, not his own – he makes a joke against himself: 'I've got a typical Megarian trick to play on him.' In the same way untrustworthiness is attributed to the Spartans.[131] The proverbial nature of such statements indicates a conventional Athenian stereotype, in which undesirable characteristics are attributed to any non-Athenian group. Clearly this is common to Greek poleis as a whole (and indeed to most communities, ancient and modern) – inhabitants of other communities are regularly identified as 'other', in terms of morals, social customs, sexual habits, or any other characteristic. Greek terms for different sexual practices, for instance, were often coined from names of cities or countries where the practice was supposedly common.[132]

The characteristics that identify Aristophanes' foreigners are three – dress, language and association with commercial products. One could argue that a delineation of foreign identity by a few obvious references to local products, dress or linguistic mannerisms need imply no great knowledge on the part of the audience, but equally the way that some practices or products are identified with other poleis implies a kind of shorthand based on regular practice. The concentration on food is marked in the war plays, perhaps reflecting a diminution of normal trade during the Archidamian War, and each city has products which are so distinctive as to represent it: in *Peace* leeks represent Prasiai, garlic Megara, cheese Sicily, and honey Attika. Elsewhere Athens is identified with pottery and whitebait, Thebes with eels, Sparta with shoes and Megara with woollen cloaks.[133]

Spartans have the strongest distinction in terms of costume: they are mocked for their long hair, squalid appearance, coarse clothes and sticks.[134] Both Spartans' and other Greeks' language is distinctively dialectal, the most obvious feature being the use of oaths. Foreign religion is presented in a very stylised way, with foreign characters swearing oaths to what were felt to be representative gods – the Spartan envoy in *Lysistrata* swears by the Dioscuri and by Kastor, while the Boiotian of the *Acharnians* swears by Iolaos.[135] Again, this is obvious, but there are enough oblique references to suggest that the audience was alive to differences in religion, for example the invocation of Athena Chalkioikos by the Spartan at the end of *Lysistrata*.[136]

The most significant aspect of the presentation of non-Athenians in comedy is the fact that they are so distanced. While contact between Athenians and outsiders was so common, and foreigners were actually present at the Dionysia, the comedy concentrates on the idea of Athens as the centre of the Greek world, with other poleis deliberately distanced by a stereotypical presentation. They do not enter the world of the Athenian citizen, unless through the regulated contact of warfare. Some lost comedies appear to have been based on Sparta (the *Lakonians* of Kratinos, Eupolis, Plato and Nikochares, and the *Helots* of Eupolis), while the Athenians' nearest neighbours, the Boiotians, who in peacetime were in Attika in numbers, figure only in connection with proverbial stupidity and eels.[137]

This contrast between appearance and reality is demonstrated even more sharply in the speeches of the Athenian orators. On the one hand there are many indications that contact with foreigners was hardly unusual, as all the above examples attest, but on the other the way other poleis are discussed has a deliberate air of unfamiliarity. Demosthenes' appeal to the law of Lokris in *Against Timokrates* is a case in point – while purporting to illustrate his theme by reference to the law of another polis, Demosthenes employs something closer to a folk-tale than to an actual experience. After a preamble on the conservatism of the Lokrians and the wisdom of their laws, Demosthenes recounts that in 'more than two hundred years' only one new law has been enacted, and that this was proposed by an unnamed man, whose sole characteristic is that he had only one eye. Such a story has little link with the real Lokris: it could be set anywhere, and in fact appears in Diodorus attached to the lawgiver Charondas of Thurii.[138]

A law of Sparta is cited by Lykourgos in the same fashion, with no background apart from the insistence that Sparta is the paramount example of a well-governed community. The law which is read, stating that those who would not risk their lives for their country should die, is one which accords closely with the traditional image of Sparta.[139] Praise and blame of Sparta can be found in equal measure, and each is equally vague. Andokides credits that Spartans with untrustworthiness, a motif which emerges in tragedy too, while for Aischines and others the Spartans are the paradigm of good government.[140] Aischines' Spartans are, like Demosthenes' Lokrian, characters in a moral fable, stylised and nameless, not real people. Plutarch's story of the Spartan's ironic comment on Athens, 'everything is fine and good', is complementary to these anecdotes: the Athens of Sparta is stereotyped as vice-ridden and shameless in contrast to Spartan morality. Similarly, Thucydides appeals to stereotypical images to structure thought about different poleis. From his first book he is precise about the features which distinguish the Athenian and Spartan characters, making them complete opposites, and he then uses this as the yardstick to measure the actions of individuals as 'typical' or 'untypical'.[141] Although he is concerned to present historical events accurately, he does not manifest the same concern over a naturalistic depiction of poleis, his own or others, but treats them in terms of large-scale national characteristics.

There are thus two strata of references to foreigners in the sources. Just as personal relations with foreigners could be frowned on at Athens as anti-democratic, unless the outsider were integrated into the polis as a metic, so contact with other states was officially presented in a stylised way. This derives from the idea that a polis should be independent and its inhabitants a closed community: to admit to widespread mobility would be to attack this ideal. Lysias explicitly decribes willingness to travel and settle elsewhere as an attack on the values of the polis:

> Those individuals who are citizens by birth, but who consider that any country is their fatherland, in which they have business interests, are clearly men who would betray even the common good of their polis for their own personal gain, because they consider that wealth, not the polis, is their native land.[142]

The good citizen, by definition, does not travel. It is this perception of the disloyalty inherent in leaving one's polis which accounts for the constant denial of experience of any other community.

Despite the mixing that went on, each polis sought to present a particular and distinct image, and this fed the stereotypes in the characterisation of foreigners. Of all poleis Sparta had the strongest image, and writers constantly emphasise that no one really understood what went on there.[143] Yet there were not only visitors on both sides, but relations of *proxenia* and accounts written by philo-Lakonian writers such as Kritias and Xenophon. Some of the insistence on Spartan strangeness was no doubt coloured by the situation at the end of the fifth century, when Sparta was the old enemy, and familiarity might have implied treachery. But the secrecy which the Spartans themselves sought to cultivate was assisted by the poleis which received it, because the significance accorded to the separation of the Greek poleis was greater than that accorded to the common ties of the Greek world. The emphasis on the religious festivals as encouraging contact and unity among the Greeks allowed the issue of general mobility to be avoided. Under the influence of ideas about the polis, Greek writers sought to minimise this mobility, preferring the idea that the citizen was closely tied to his land and city, even in a polis as open as Athens.

*

The evidence does not support the claim that only the rich travelled. They may have travelled more widely, and had more control over where they went, but there was ample motivation for the peasant to go too, if perhaps less far afield. Those who had least stood to lose most by leaving the polis, but state-sanctioned travel existed through military service, and if involuntary travel by exile or capture is included, then it was far from uncommon to experience life outside one's own polis. The exchange of information between inhabitants of different poleis was expected, and our sources reveal a considerable mobility, allowing individuals to experience at first hand the nature and habits of other Greeks. This provided a background of information which in turn affected political decision-making – personal contacts were used for influence in the political sphere, whether official *proxeniai* or not.

Yet this coexisted with a belief in the independence and autonomy of each individual polis: roads were not constructed to facilitate travel because this would have required a recognition of the interdependence of Greek states. Writers and speakers subscribed to the idea that inhabitants of one polis knew little about any other, and met only in the officially-sanctioned circumstances of warfare and religion, though in fact they could often be very close, both through informal contacts, and involvement in public affairs. Only through institutional systems of communication could inter-polis contact be contained in an acceptable way, and it is to these institutional systems that we now turn.

Official Communications

Why do they bear the honourable name of heralds,
When they are universally hated by mankind,
Lackeys to tyrants and cities?
                    Euripides, *Troades* 424-6

Aristotle suggests in the *Politics* that a polis should ideally be large enough to be self-sufficient, but not so large that all the citizens cannot recognise each other, as this would make the constitution difficult to implement. If a polis is too large, he asks, who could be the strategos, or who the herald, to such a mass of people?[1] The role of the herald is seen here as one of the foundations of the constitution.

The herald, *kêrux*, is perhaps one of the most obvious figures to consider in a discussion of news in ancient Greece: the runner Phidippides and the story of Marathon still hold first place in ideas about Greek news. Inviolable and holding the staff, the symbol of their office, heralds personify news. In drama they regularly appear to report events offstage, and in history no event is complete without the story of how the messenger brought the news.

Contrary to common conceptions, the primary function of the herald was not simply to disseminate news. Heralds were not dispatched as a matter of course from one polis to another with accounts of recent events. In fact there are no cases in which an ancient polis sent out a herald to spread news purely for the information of others. The role of the herald was more complex than this, and the motives that led states to communicate more varied.

The herald, though the most identifiable functionary of the polis in reporting news and making announcements, was not the only one. Envoys were chosen to represent the polis in matters of international diplomacy; although not primarily information-carriers, they could and did bring news from one state to another. Generals also needed to communicate with the polis in an official capacity, as did other officials such as overseers or garrison commanders, both to report events and to receive orders. These characters comprised the official oral communication of the polis, and their roles and responsibilities illustrate the ways in which news was important as a function of the state.

Communication is a two-way process, requiring one body to send information, and another to receive it, and this is true of the polis and its citizens. One should consider not only the information that a city wanted to discover, but also that which it wanted to disseminate. The various means by which a polis communicated with its citizens, and with other poleis, can illustrate what information was considered important, and the reasons dictating the spread of news. Official communication comprises two distinct spheres: within the polis, and outside it: I shall consider these in turn.

1. Heralds inside the polis

The herald in Greece held a clearly-defined and important position within the polis from an early period. In some poleis the office of herald was hereditary, as at Sparta among the Talthybidai, and heralds had both a divine counterpart who protected them (Hermes) and a patron hero (Talthybios).[2] The herald appears as one of the instruments of the constitution as early as the Homeric epics; in the fifth and fourth centuries heralds were, as Aristotle suggests, essential for the running of the polis. They convened and dismissed assemblies, read out oaths, laws and documents in the meetings, announced the results of voting, made announcements of confiscated property, inheritances and heiresses, and made proclamations for specific magistrates.[3] In Aristophanes' *Ekklesiazusai* one of the first arrangements of the new state put in motion by Praxagora is the choice of a herald, in this case a female herald (*kêrukaina*) to reflect the new all-female government, and her task is to proclaim the new regulations concerning citizens' property and public dinners.[4] The proclamations that heralds made were closely involved with polis business, usually part of the assembly procedure, such as the announcement of honours.

As well as such civic roles, heralds were necessary in religion too, for example the *hierokêrux*, Herald of the Mysteries, who was part of a hereditary genos of heralds. In religious ritual heralds spoke prayers and invocations, made libations and participated in the sacrifice.[5] The distinction between civic and religious roles was naturally slight; on the departure of the Sicilian Expedition in 415 a herald led the prayers before the ships put to sea, with all the army and the spectators joining in.[6] The status of the herald as inviolable was of greater relevance outside the polis, in the sphere of international relations, but even in political roles, the social standing of a herald remained high. The herald Kleokritos illustrates this well: after the battle in Piraeus in 404/3, as herald of the Mysteries he made a powerful appeal to those of the Athenians siding with the Thirty.[7] The episode indicates his standing and influence within the city, and not only among those initiated in the Mysteries; Xenophon tells us that those citizens on the side of the Thirty were listening with attention to his speech.

A fourth-century inscription records the appointment as herald to the Boule and demos (*kêrux tês boulês kai tou dêmou*) of first Eukles, and thirty years later, his son Philokles: although the primary qualification remained an ability to speak well, such honorific posts could become hereditary.[8] The herald could sometimes be seen as the symbol or representative of a polis; this idea underlies the negative characterisation of heralds to be found in tragedy. In many cases the role of the herald as proxy for a tyrant is what gives rise to comments such as those of Cassandra at the head of this chapter.[9]

The smaller the community in which a herald served, the greater his role in the dissemination of news. Heralds had a specific place in the smaller units of social and political organisation, the village or deme. Not every deme had an official herald, but the post is attested in inscriptions from seven Attic demes.[10] The main task of these heralds was to proclaim honours voted by the deme, and invite those honored to take their seats at festivals (*proedria*). The role of herald was dispensable – other demes require the demarch to carry out the same functions – but nevertheless it carried a higher status than that of simple public functionary. In Erchia the herald was called on to officiate at a sacrifice to Hermes, and heralds receive honours for their work in several inscriptions.[11] Again, this could be a career as opposed to a short-term appointment; the speaker of Demosthenes *Against Leochares* claims that his father earns a (poor) living as a herald in Piraeus.[12]

In the deme the necessity of the role of the herald to the community can be seen most clearly. Plutarch records the anecdote that Alkibiades, as a boy, ran off to live with his lover, and that his kinsman and guardian, Ariphron, wished to have him publicly declared (*apokêruttein*) a runaway by the herald. This kind of procedure was also used by a father who wished to disinherit a son: the speaker of Demosthenes *Against Boiotos* states that a parent may disown a child by public declaration.[13] In these contexts there is perhaps an element of the herald as town-crier, spreading news among the local community. But a disinheritance is announced because the act of disinheritance is ineffective without publicity. One would not produce a written record to demonstrate that a child or ward had been disowned; the act was achieved through the oral announcement. It is not an act that can be carried out privately, because the rest of the community must modify their behaviour towards the individual concerned. The reason for the announcement was both to inform the community (who could then act accordingly), and to make the decisions effective by giving them public announcement. The same function can be seen in the funerary ritual accorded to Spartan kings: part of the special ceremony is that the news of the King's death is carried to all parts of Lakonia by horsemen. The announcement is not for information only: it illustrates the ritual aspect of the announcement of news.[14]

The herald in the Greek army operated in a similar way, that is, within a small community, announcing orders from the authorities (the general), and bringing matters of public concern to the attention of all. For instance, the herald played a part in military discipline: an insubordinate soldier could be publicly banned from service (*ekkêruttein*), through an announcement made to the rest of the army. The speaker in Lysias *Against Simon* relates that on campaign in Corinth, Simon 'fought with his taxiarch, Laches, and struck him ... and, being known to be most disorderly and worthless, was the only Athenian to be publicly banned by the generals'.[15] This kind of announcement too had an active function. In the military manual of Aineias Tacticus, the herald is not only to give orders to the troops, but also to assist the general in maintaining order – he relates that on an occasion when an irrational night panic arose in an army, the herald was ordered to announce a reward to the man who reported whoever had let his horse loose in the camp, to calm the situation.[16] The herald is here in complicity with the general to allay the army's fear.

Within the polis the best-documented function of the herald is the reporting of military engagements to the polis. This kind of communication is so common in our sources because war forms one of the major themes of history, and because the announcement is a very visible kind of communication. Thucydides and Xenophon provide many examples of messengers from armies, on horseback or in boats, sent to report a military engagement, because they represent the most important aspect of this type of communication, and create the most dramatic scene. Xenophon records the arrival of the news of Spartan defeat at Lechaion in 390:

> While Agesilaos was still sitting, apparently delighting in what he had achieved, a horseman rode up in great haste, on a sweating horse. Many of the soldiers asked him what his news was, and he made no reply, but when he reached Agesilaos, he leapt from his horse and ran up to him, looking extremely gloomy, and told him of the disaster that had befallen the regiment at Lechaion.[17]

Occasionally we see messengers reporting other important events, such as the horseman sent by Alkamenes to Sparta in 411 to report the sailing of the Athenian fleet from the Isthmus. Most of the messengers involved are anonymous, defined only by their role, but occasionally there are indications of the use of known individuals: in 405 after the battle of Aigospotamoi, Lysander sent news of the Spartan success back to the city by 'Theopompos the Milesian pirate'.[18]

In his speech *Against Ktesiphon*, Aischines makes much of his appointment as the messenger to bring the news of the Athenian victory at Tamynai back to the city, because this role was an honour in itself.[19] It is not that the bringing of news per se conferred importance on the representative, but rather that the news needed to be told, and the honour lay in being chosen as the representative of the army. Aischines may be exaggerating here (he is after all looking for popular sympathy), but the role of bringer of news did command some status. Plutarch, discussing how Sparta in the fifth century treated news of victory lightly, comments that even after the battle of Mantinea in 418 the only reward received by the man who brought the news of the victory was a portion of meat from the common mess.[20] This assumes that the bringer of news elsewhere could expect more reward than this.

It is easy to assume from historians that the news of victory in battle entered the city only with the official announcement, as this is the event on which they concentrate. The evidence that we have indicates that news was first given to the leaders of the state, either in an official report, or as soon as urgent news was received. Xenophon emphasises in the example quoted above that the herald would speak to no one before he reached Agesilaos; similarly he represents a herald reporting news of the 'tearless battle' in 368 to the leaders at Sparta 'beginning with Agesilaos and the members of the Gerousia and the ephors'.[21] But there may be reasons for this depiction. Episodes from Sparta in particular tend to emphasise that the news was taken straight to the Gerousia (council) by the messenger, without being spread across the city first; this contrasts to some extent with other states where diffusion was more rapid, and also more haphazard.[22] The emphasis in sources on Spartan messengers reporting only to the authorities is perhaps designed to give the impression that their state is so disciplined that messengers speak only to the Gerousia, who then give out the news as they see fit, or attempt to influence their citizens' response to it.[23]

But although we possess so much evidence for the report of victory or defeat, one should not assume that most information entered the city in this way, or that it was always well-organised. In fact there were both those from outside the city who could bring news in as it happened, and those who received the news from the messenger as he entered the city, before the formal announcement was made. In several cases official messengers are recorded as bringing news of events which could reasonably be expected to be known and communicated by local people – for instance, the legend about the arrival of the news from Marathon. A runner (only later identified with the Phidippides who ran from Athens to Sparta to request aid before the battle) raced from Marathon to Athens with the news of victory over the Persians. He collapsed in the council chamber from his exertions, and with his dying breath gave the message: *chairete, nikômen* (Rejoice, we conquer').[24] In a discussion of the development of the Marathon legend, Frost points out that the battle attracted a story about the man who brought the news, despite the fact that many local inhabitants, on foot and on horseback, would have been in a better position to report the outcome than a runner, a possibility which Plutarch himself entertains.[25]

There is at the root of this, at least in Plutarch, some unwillingness to acknowledge the lower-class, unofficial messenger, but more important is the desire to see problematic news being formally dealt with. News brought to a polis by an official messenger and reported in an orderly way to the authorities, is news under the control of the state. The official herald who goes straight to the prytaneis to acquaint them with the news and allow them to act is a less frightening figure than the stranger who comes to spread alarm among the city at large. News of a disaster could then be formally presented to the citizens, as when the news of the capture of Elateia reached Athens – the herald was brought forward to announce the news at the start of the assembly, even though it was widely known.[26] So the emphasis on the announcement of news by a herald is again a recognition that the correct procedure is being followed.

Thus an official announcement was important in itself, quite apart from its informational value. There was an onus on a commander to send an official messenger with the news, even if there were other avenues by which it would travel – it could not be left to chance. The polis exercises control over news in potentially threatening situations by creating proper avenues for its communication.

2. Control of information

If the authories could control how news entered a polis, they could potentially control how it was disseminated too. The existence of the 'official channel' for the transmission of news made it possible for the state to control the news which it disseminated. This control could work in a variety of different ways, and is interesting because it illustrates the disjunction that could occur between the various arms of the state. The general, though acting as a state official, could nevertheless withold information from other bodies, either at the planning stage, or in response to a particular situation. In 425 when Demosthenes fortified Pylos for the Athenians, the implication of Thucydides' account is that it was a plan prepared between Demosthenes and Kleon, unsuspected either by the other strategoi, or the assembly which gave Kleon his command.[27] The polis authority, equally, could act without concern for the army, as Sparta did in 423 when they began peace negotiations with Athens in spite of Brasidas' presence on campaign.[28]

Similarly, because of the phenomenon of the official report, a general could use a herald to influence who heard news, or even how much of the truth they heard. This kind of control is most easily detectable in the military sphere. At the very least a herald was responsible for the dissemination of an 'official version' of what had happened, and we have examples in which a herald became the instrument of a general or government to disseminate false information.

In 406 the general Eteonikos received news of the defeat of the Spartans at Arginusai, and after hearing the news, he told the messengers to leave the harbour without speaking to anyone, then to sail back in, wearing garlands and shouting that the Spartans had won a great victory.[29] This was designed to prevent panic and loss of morale. In 394 Agesilaos also announced a Spartan defeat as a victory to his men, when the news of the naval defeat at Knidos reached him.[30] The reason Xenophon gives for his action is 'if there were any difficulty, there was no need for the men to share in it'. In each case the army did not find out the truth until the manoeuvre was over. Similarly, Diodoros records the exploitation of a rumour by the Spartan commander Leotychidas at Mykale in 479: the rumour of victory at Plataia sprang up spontaneously among his army, so Leotychidas made a formal announcement of victory, using his authority to lend credibility to the information.[31] None of these generals hesitated to deceive their troops for the good of the campaign.

From the above examples, it may seem that deceiving the troops is a feature of oligarchic government, reflecting the idea of state control of news. Sparta, as we have seen, projected an image of the close control of news and of its citizens' reaction to it within the state, and this control allowed the generals to exploit information for their own purposes, in what appears to be a peculiarly Spartan way. One could perhaps offer Themistokles as a counter-example here; his trickery was double-edged, deceiving the Persian King into attacking at Salamis in the belief that the Greeks would not resist a Persian attack, but at the same time deceiving the Greek army by precipitating a battle without their knowledge.[32] The successful outcome of the battle provided Themistokles with retrospective justification, but in Herodotos' account the right of the commander to act without the knowledge of the army as a whole is not questioned. Themistokles is made to comment to Aristides that it was necessary, since the Greeks were unwilling to join battle, to make them do so whether they wanted to or not.[33]

There does not, then, seem to be an explicit contrast between open democracy and closed oligarchy. Xenophon's *Anabasis* is an interesting example here, since on the whole the Ten Thousand are shown as having preserved the quintessentially Greek habit of rule by democracy, in contrast with the barbarians, choosing their generals and making decisions in council, such as the dawn council when they decided to fight for their safety, or the debate about founding a city near Sinope.[34] But at other points, notably the initial stages of the campaign, secrecy on the part of the generals played a major role. The soldiers were initially assembled on the pretext that Cyrus intended to fight

Tissaphernes, or the Pisidians, and the true nature of the campaign only gradually became clear. Although Klearchos, the Spartan exile, is singled out with the story of the army's growing suspicions that they were in fact being led on a campaign against the Persian King, and of Klearchos' measures to deceive them, when the soldiers were finally told the truth in an assembly at Thapsakos, they accused 'the generals' collectively of having known all along, not only Klearchos, suggesting that Xenophon was concentrating on one figure in the interests of dramatic narrative.[35]

Later, when the army was on the Euxine, the soldiers wished to appoint a commander-in-chief, which they believed would make the army more effective. One of the particular reasons given was that if there was a need for secrecy, this would be more easily achieved with a single commander.[36] Thus although Xenophon is eager to highlight the democratic practices of the Greeks, secrecy and the witholding of information are seen as an acceptable part of this, and even unavoidable under some circumstances.

A similar view is expressed by Andokides in the speech *On the Peace*, namely that it is the duty of a patriotic general to keep secrets from his men in wartime:

> I admit, Athenians, that in time of war it is necessary for a general who is experienced, and has the best interests of the polis in mind, to use secrecy and deceit on the majority of the people, when leading them into danger.[37]

While it is generally harmful for citizens to conduct matters in secrecy, it is admissible for a general to lead his men into danger without telling them what is going on. This may be slightly suspect coming from Andokides, who on another occasion attempted to communicate in secret to the Boule the benefits he proposed to offer the Athenian people.[38] Here he is trying to defend the decision of the negotiators to refer the decision on the peace back to the demos. But the general principle, that a general should exercise control of information, is presented as uncontroversial. Keeping secrets from the demos is levelled as an accusation against Theramenes by Lysias in *Against Eratosthenes*:

> Other men keep secrets to deceive the enemy, but Theramenes would not tell to his fellow-citizens those things which he intended to tell to the enemy.[39]

The anonymous Theramenes Papyrus defends Theramenes against this charge, indicating that it was taken seriously, but the distinction is one of circumstances: secrecy within the polis is in general a bad thing, but in war it is more admissible.[40]

Thus even at Athens there was a recognition that control of information was an important factor in military situations, and that the general could be required to keep matters from, or misinform, his troops. It has been suggested that in wartime the generals could gain in control of decision-making at the expense of the assembly.[41] But in spite of Lysias' words, very few of the examples show control intended to keep information from the enemy, either in terms of plans or resources. Instead, we see manipulation of one's own soldiers made possible by the commander's autocratic position. The appointment of the single commander in Xenophon, and Andokides' aside, point to an awareness of this side of the general's role – a Greek army, at least theoretically, agreed to the necessity of the control of information by one man.

This control of information affected only the troops under the general's command: it was not intended primarily to keep matters secret from the enemy. Accounts of troops being deceived by their leaders, and of generals seeking to deceive the enemy are linked by Powell in a discussion of Spartan guile, as symptomatic of a general Spartan ability at deception.[42] But the main point was the effect on the morale of the army. Andokides recommends deceit simply to make the soldiers fight, and this was the intention of the Spartan commanders too. They could not have hoped to maintain the deceit for long, but the isolation of an army camp made it possible for long enough.

On the other hand, the witholding of information about planned movements from one's own troops could also be an effort to outwit the enemy – Thucydides records that in 413 Nikias at Syracuse was unwilling to have the idea of an Athenian withdrawal debated in a council, in case the enemy should get to hear of it.[43] Should one interpret deceit of the army as a mere side-effect of the attempt to achieve security against external forces? In fact, such measures to keep plans secret succeeded on very few occasions; in Sicily, the Syracusans had a constant idea of what the invading Athenians intended to do, and it seems to have been accepted that it was very easy for one state to find out what had happened in another. During negotiations with the Persians in 479 the Athenians are said to have deliberately delayed answering their envoy at Athens:

> The Athenians delayed giving their answer, realising that the Lakedaimonians would hear that a messenger had come from the Persian King to offer terms, and that once they knew, they would send messengers of their own with all speed.[44]

Surprise attacks depended far more on short-term ruses, not secret campaigns, and these depended on the participation of all, as for instance with Kleomenes' ruse at Sepeia in 494. There all the soldiers had to be party to the plan of the deceptive announcement, and the plan was quickly executed.[45] Thus the deception of an army by its own general is a separate issue, and one connected with morale. The existence of the herald as the formal channnel of information allowed the general to control information in a way which increased his power at the expense of his fellow-citizens, and as long as the official messenger was the only one, the general was able to exercise this power.

3. Failures of communication

Opportunities for control, as we have seen, were not total; on some occasions news entered or left the polis in uncontrolled ways. In communicating with their own citizens, Greek poleis also experienced some serious breakdowns. For example, Thucydides relates that in 431, after the Theban attempt on Plataia, the Athenians wished to give advice to the Thebans on the fate of their prisoners. They therefore sent a herald to the Plataians to tell them not to make any irrevocable decisions about the prisoners. Even before the herald was dispatched, the Thebans had executed their prisoners: 'so the Athenians dispatched their messenger in ignorance of the situation, and the herald, when he arrived, discovered that the men had already been killed'.[46] This episode had no further consequences; the Greeks simply accepted that such lapses in communications were inevitable. At first sight it is hard to see why this should be the case. The Greeks had before them the example of the Persian messenger-system, which illustrated the potential for organised communication. Herodotos writes:

> Nothing mortal is faster than these messengers. The Persian system is devised in the following way: as many horsemen are stationed along the way, as there are days' journey, each man and horse one day's ride from the next, and neither snow nor rainstorm, nor burning heat nor darkness prevents each man completing his assigned stage with all speed.[47]

The Greeks believed that through his network of messengers and spies the King was able to monitor everything that went on in his country; the posts of 'King's Eye' and 'King's Ear' were thought to exist for the gathering of information, and modern writers have accepted the same connection, referring to networks of spies or 'Nachrichtenpolizei'.[48] The Persian King's control over communications among his subjects was assumed to be very great: Herodotos records two stories of secret messages (one tattooed on the scalp of a slave, the other sewn into the belly of a hare) sent in order to foil the guards on the Royal road, who would report any message sent in the normal way to the King.[49] Clearly there was felt to be great potential for effective and well-monitored communications.

Why, then, do we see Greek poleis encountering problems? The main area where difficulties arose was was communication between generals on campaign or envoys abroad and the home authorities. A general, for instance, needed to report his situation and movements to the polis, and the assembly needed to respond with orders, advice and reinforcements. The Spartans in 397, for instance, sent orders to Derkylidas and Pharax to move into Karia; Timotheos in 375 kept sending to Athens with requests for money.[50] Such communication could be sporadic, because of the practical difficulties of the length of time involved. For an army serving in Asia Minor, for instance, communication with the state would have involved weeks of delay, and to fight a war under the direction of leaders at home was impossible.[51] Larger questions of campaign strategy could be asked, but immediate tactical decisions were obviously the concern of the general. Given the lapse between question and answer, and the difficulty for messengers of following an army or fleet, a general could not always rely on contact with the authorities even for strategic questions. Generals seem to have become largely independent once abroad, and some recorded exchanges support the idea of forced independence.[52] The letter of the Spartan commander Hippokrates, intercepted by the Athenians, was a laconic request for advice from the leaders at home: 'The ships are lost; Mindaros is dead; the men are starving; don't know what to do', but this plea came from a second-in-command left in a difficult situation, obviously an extreme case in which advice would be needed.[53] The idea that a general had no choice but to act independently is supported by the fact that this letter was lost in transit; advice was not easy to obtain.

There can be no doubt that ease of communication in some circumstances depended less on the ability of a commander or state to get a message through, and more on the willingness of the parties to listen. Chares was recalled in 355, according to Diodoros, in the face of the threat of action from the Persian King on the mainland.[54] His recall was effected very quickly, even though he was fighting in Asia Minor, because of the seriousness of the threat posed to Athens. In 424, on the other hand, Brasidas' requests to Sparta for reinforcements went unanswered for the first campaigning season, as the government took the opportunity presented by his distance in Thrace to leave his campaign unsupported.[55] Only when it had proved its efficacy by the capture of Amphipolis did the Spartan command start responding to his success.[56] Of course, the opportunity also existed for a general to ignore unwelcome directives from home, and there are signs that Brasidas, and fourth-century commanders too, did just this. The confusion over the truce between Athens and Sparta in 423 is a case in point; the Spartan government had relatively little control over Brasidas, and while they were keen to make peace, for the sake of the prisoners from Sphakteria, Brasidas was still attempting to carry on his campaign.[57]

The conduct of generals, and indeed envoys, abroad tends to confirm the idea that they did not act on a constant stream of instructions. The state's representative was sent out with instructions, but these could be vague, and it was his decision as to how they should be implemented. In Sicily in 415 the three generals discussed their strategy in a way that suggests that strategy had not been predecided; Nikias at one point mentions instructions to attack Selinous, and at another to attack Syracuse.[58] Aischines records the meeting held by the ten ambassadors to Philip in 346, when they arrived at Pella to find an unexpected situation. This meeting was held to reinterpret their instructions, 'The ambassadors are to gain any benefit that they can [for the city]', in the light of the military expedition they saw in preparation at Pella; the envoys voted that each of them, when called on to speak, should say whatever he judged useful to their interests.[59] It is not surprising if initial instructions were vague, because of the difficulty of obtaining current information before the army or embassy was dispatched.

The result of a commander's independence was the attitude of the citizens towards his exploits – if his decision was the right one, then the city shared in his victory and honoured him, but if it proved to have been wrong, he was open to prosecution for disobeying instructions and betraying the city. Demosthenes makes this accusation against Aischines, even though we can see from the speeches that the envoys at Pella had to adapt themselves to the new circumstances.[60] Perhaps also hence the anger against Theramenes over the peace with Sparta, the feeling that he had abused the power he had been granted as envoy by concluding a peace with which the citizens were dissatisfied.[61]

In situations such as these the Greek attitude towards the problems of communication is most clearly seen – although on some occasions there might be breakdown in communication, accidental or purposeful, this was accepted as a hazard of distant campaigns or negotiations, and no steps were taken to rectify the problem. As with Chares, truly important messages usually did get through, and dissatisfaction on other occasions did not lead to changes. When Greek states looked to monarchic rulers or tyrants, they saw people who were skilled at handling information, and institutions designed to regulate its interchange. In particular, kings and spies were linked in the Greek mind, that is, spying on one's own subjects, rather than on outside powers. Aristotle suggests as one of the methods for preserving tyrannies that a tyrant should try to be aware of everything said or done by his subjects: he should have spies like the ôtakoustai (eavesdropper women) in Syracuse, or the potagôgides (talebearers) of Hieron. Further on, he recommends lax control over women and slaves under a tyranny, so that they will be willing to inform on the men.[62] If the idea was current that the better the control of the state over communication, the greater the scope for dictatorial rule, it is less surprising that the Greek poleis never strove to create infallible systems of their own. The independence of the citizen, problematic though it could be for the general or envoy who made a bad decision, was prized above well-regulated communication.

4. Communication outside the polis

Outside the polis, the herald was the essential mediator between states, guaranteed inviolability by the protection of Hermes, and bearer of the universally-acknowledged symbol of his role, the herald's staff.[63] Contact through heralds was necessarily very formal, since each carried a precise oral message, and had no power to negotiate. In wartime the herald became a powerful symbol of the state of war: Thucydides defines the point at which the Peloponnesian War broke out as that from which the two sides communicated with each other only through heralds. The phrase *polemos akêruktos* (literally, war without heralds) denoted a war of particular violence, in which even contact by herald was suspended, and truce was impossible: the abandonment of traditional wartime formalities denoted the most serious of conflicts.[64] The tasks of the herald in war included declarations of war or peace, offers of truce or terms of surrender, escorting foreigners, the request for the return of the bodies of the dead, and carrying messages.[65] Because of the need for communication between the opposing sides, the status of inviolability was clearly of the greatest importance. Acts of violence against heralds, even against non-Greeks, attracted widespread condemnation. Herodotos records the unease of the Spartans over their murder of the heralds sent by Darius in 490; the offence against the Persian heralds was also an offence against Talthybios as protector of heralds, and so the Spartans sought to atone for the crime by sending two of their own citizens to be punished by Xerxes.[66]

The role of the envoy overlapped with, but differed from, that of the herald. All official negotiation between Greek poleis was carried out through the state-selected ambassador, the *presbus*. I described above how contacts between states in the archaic age took place largely between the rich and influential, who formed an 'international class' transcending city boundaries. As the polis developed and power came into the hands of growing numbers of citizens, these individual relationships were transformed into state institutions: the relation of *xenia*, one-to-one friendship, evolved into that of *proxenia*, a relationship between an individual and a state.[67] The envoy, by a similar process became the representative of all the citizens. This meant that negotiation was still carried out on an individual basis, between small groups of often powerful men, even though these men were acting on behalf of the state rather than on behalf of themselves and their families.

The role of the envoy in international relations was not to disseminate news of relevance to another state, but to carry out one predetermined task of communication – to ask for a treaty, negotiate, complain or swear to an agreement. This point is illustrated by the betrayal of Athenian interests by the Phokians under Phalaikos in 346; although the government at Phokis changed and the new rulers were not favourable to Athens, the Phokians did not communicate this fact, and it was not until Proxenos reported his failure to take over the forts that the Athenians were made aware of events:

> Instead of handing over the forts to Proxenos, the Phokian tyrants arrested their own ambassadors who had promised to hand them over to you .... On the same day that you were debating the peace [with Philip], you heard the letter of Proxenos, in which he reported that the Phokians had not handed over the forts, and the heralds of the Mysteries reported that the Phokians alone of all the Greeks had refused the sacred truce, and had arrested the envoys who had been here.[68]

It was not regular to report changes or events of this kind outside one's own state, unless for a specific purpose.[69] Ambassadors could even be seen as a threat to security: Xenophon records that the Athenian ambassadors to Persia in 407 were detained by Pharnabazos for three years, at Cyrus' request, to prevent them carrying news of the situation in Asia back to Athens.[70]

Given what has already been said about the herald or envoy's lack of involvement in simple news-spreading, one should examine the motives that would lead a polis to make announcements outside its borders. There is obviously no one answer to this – different kinds of announcement had different motives. The easiest place to start is a consideration of the reasons why a state might want to communicate with others. Between equals, a state might want to protest, suggest collaboration of some kind, pay honours, make peace or declare war. An imperial power would want to send directives to subject states, or make claims on them. States with religious powers needed to inform others of dates of festivals or meetings, or declare sacred truces. These are all tasks one finds heralds, envoys or other state officials carrying out.

In its simplest form communication between poleis was achieved by sending a herald to an individual state to address the government or assembly. For one-to-one communication such a system was obviously workable within the convention of the herald's inviolability. But for wider dissemination, a different approach was necessary. The Athenian empire was divided for administrative purposes into four regions, and it became standard to send out a herald to each region to announce, for instance, the making of new tribute assessments. The decree of 425/4 on this topic prescribes that two heralds be sent to Ionian and Caria, two to the Thraceward cities, two to the Islands, and two to the Hellespont.[71] The route of the herald would be prescribed beforehand, as is shown in inscriptions, and became standardised. The same is true of those heralds sent to proclaim a sacred truce; this was done regularly, and so an element of consistency entered into it. In the third century, when the Magnesians were trying to get states to join their newly-instituted festival, the groups of envoys they sent covered definite geographical areas, as the inscriptions show.[72] One group visited north-west Greece (Apollonia, Epidamnos, Corcyra, Same and Ithaka), another central Greece (Athens, Eretria, Chalkis and Phokis), and a third the Peloponnesian states. It is perhaps this kind of contact that Starr had in mind when he referred to 'a flow of heralds bearing messages and decrees'.[73]

For the most part official messages carried by individuals went either by foot, or in the case of the army, on board ship. The kind of vessel used depended on the nature of the message: for duties such as scouting, ferrying supplies or carrying messages, it was often more reasonable to use a smaller vessel requiring less manpower than to press a trireme into service.[74] Obviously, if a command needed to be executed quickly, a trireme would be the fastest-sailing alternative, as can be seen in the Athenians' use of triremes to report decisions of the assembly to the army at Mytilene, or the transporting of the Spartan envoys from Pylos to Athens and back in a trireme in 425.[75] In our sources the use of the flagships of the Athenian fleet, the *Paralos* and *Salaminia*, is noted only in serious situations, and those concerning internal political matters, as in 411, when the *Paralos* was used to carry messages between Athens and Samos in the difficult days of the revolution, or in 415, when the *Salaminia* was sent to recall Alkibiades from Sicily to stand trial.[76] This indicates that such speed was considered important only in unusual cases. This is emphasised by the provisions of the decree of Kleinias calling for the tightening of tribute collection from 448/7.[77] In this four heralds are to be sent out, two to sail to Ionia and the Islands 'on a swift trireme'. The other heralds are apparently not afforded this transport; a fast warship used for heralds was out of the ordinary.

The most important question, however, is not how Greek cities communicated, but why. The communication between Greek states was not always straightforward, any more than was that between the state and its citizens. One finds cases of deliberate disinformation, where envoys or observers were fed wrong information to influence their city's decision. This happened at Egesta in 415, when the Athenians sent envoys to discover how much financial aid they could expect from the Egestans in the war against Syracuse, and the Egestans successfully deceived the envoys by making a show of relatively cheap silver treasures, and circulating a number of silver and gold vessels among the hosts who entertained the envoys. The envoys duly reported that the Egestans were extremely wealthy, and the deception was not discovered until the Athenian expedition reached Egesta themselves.[78] The Spartans clearly suspected a similar deception in 411, when Chian envoys came to Sparta to request an alliance and military aid; the Spartans sent one of the *perioikoi* to check whether the Chians were telling the truth about the number of available ships, and the strength of their city. Spartan scepticism was also revealed in 395, when they received official ambassadors from Phokis, asking for help against a threatened Boiotian invasion, and, according to the Oxyrhynchus *Hellenika*, considered the ambassadors' report untrue.[79] But news could inhabit a spectrum between true and untrue, according to the reasons for its dissemination.

The two examples above contrast in the nature of the information carried. For the member states of the Athenian empire the news that there was to be an assessment, or the imposition of a decree about coinage, was news and needed to be told to them; some reaction was expected (sending a representative, for example) and the herald was the means by which news was spread. The case of the sacred truce was slightly different. Those organisations or states which controlled a religious shrine or celebration would periodically send heralds to the poleis to declare the sacred truce, *hieromênia*, to allow participants to travel to the shrine.[80] This also was not news-carrying in a strict sense, since the content of the message was invariable and of little informational value. The sacred calendar was based on similar principles all over Greece, and most Greeks would know when the games were due to be held, and when the *hieromênia* could be expected to come into force. The announcement was not so much for the sake of information as for affirmation – the truce could not become active until it had been formally announced by the presiding state and accepted by the participants. The ritual of announcement and acceptance was far more significant than any exchange of information. In 388 the Argives attempted to head off a Spartan attack by sending two garlanded heralds to claim a sacred truce; Agesipolis simply refused to accept the truce on the grounds that it was unjustly claimed.[81] Clearly the announcement formed part of the ritual.

I claimed initially that the official spreading of news from city to city for its own sake was virtually unknown in Greece. The contact between Athens and Thebes after the battle of Leuktra in 371 is a case in point. After the battle the Thebans sent a messenger to Athens with news of its outcome:

> Immediately after the battle the Thebans sent a messenger to Athens crowned with a wreath, and at the same time announced their great victory and demanded the Athenians' aid, saying that now it was possible to punish the Lakedaimonians for all their ill-deeds.[82]

This is one of the rare occasions on which one of the participants in a battle informed a third party of the outcome by sending an official herald. However, the Theban herald had a dual role, to bring the news and to ask the Athenians to join Thebes in their campaign against Sparta. The Thebans had been isolated at the recent Common Peace agreement because of their insistence on swearing oaths on behalf of the Boiotian states as subjects, and the thinking behind the announcement was clearly that so overwhelming a victory gave Thebes considerable leverage in negotiation with Athens. The sending of the herald was not for the sake of information alone, but to influence the Athenians through the receipt of the news. This is doubly emphasised by the hint in Xenophon's account that the Athenians were not hearing the result of the battle for the first time: the Boule was in session on the Akropolis when the herald arrived, although the usual meeting place was the *bouleuterion* in the Agora, suggesting that they knew already that they faced a serious situation.

This practice of spreading your own news is paralleled in wartime: Xenophon gives two examples where a state ensured that its own allies heard about its latest successes. After the Spartan victory at Nemea in 394, Agesilaos sent out Derkylidas to spread this news among the allies in the Hellespont, whose chance of hearing it quickly was apparently slim, in order to encourage them in their efforts.[83] After the successes of Konon with the Persian fleet in the same year, Pharnabazos and Konon together sailed around the cities of Ionia to tell them the news and drive out the Spartan governors.[84] In these examples the real motive behind the announcement was the dissemination of news of success in order to influence the recipients; news of defeat would not receive the same treatment.

The element of announcing favourable news for propaganda purposes was always present in some measure in communications between states. Announcements required a considerable investment of manpower, even if only one herald was sent around each state of any importance, and it was more usually two or three. Aristophanes' *Acharnians* demonstrates the emphasis placed on the money paid to such persons, and long absences from the city entailed larger payments.[85] So the city usually had a particular investment in seeing that a piece of news was widely (and officially) broadcast. In the example discussed above, the city of Magnesia sent heralds to all the Greek cities (and some Persian ones) in 207/6 to request recognition of, and attendance at, their new festival to be instituted in honour of Artemis Leukophryene, and these groups of envoys brought their news partly for information, but at least partly for propaganda too – making sure that everyone knew about the theophany, the festival, and the enhanced status of Magnesia.[86] This is reflected in their collection of the decrees relating to the announcement, and inscribing them in the temple of Artemis at Magnesia.

More explicitly, in 340 the Corinthians made an announcement of their liberation of Sicily, combined with a request for colonists to join their resettlement of the island. Plutarch records that this announcement was made at the sacred games and the greatest festivals, as well as in Asia and the islands:

> First they sent heralds to the sacred games and greatest festivals in Greece, and announced that the Corinthians had overthrown the tyranny in Syracuse, and had driven out the tyrant, and they invited the Syracusans and any other Sicilian Greek who wished to settle in the city .... Afterwards they sent messengers to Asia and to the islands, where they discovered most of the scattered exiles were living, and invited them all to come to Corinth [to be convoyed to Syracuse].[87]

The ostensible motive of the Corinthian heralds was to encourage colonists to join the Corinthians in resettling Syracuse, but the wording of the announcement shows them far more keen to broadcast their triumph in conquering the country, and to spread this news over as wide an area as possible. Dissemination of news by the city concerned could, in some cases, put the desired 'slant' on some information that was already widely known. What is significant is not only that the news gets through, but how it is understood by those who receive it. Corinthian conquest in Sicily was news important enough to have been received from other sources, yet one can perhaps see a more sophisticated response to this one the part of Corinth itself: by inviting the participation of all the Greeks, they tried to show that despite Corinthian success, justly to be praised, their motives should not be considered suspect.

5. International announcement

The circumstances of the Corinthian announcement suggest a further opportunity for the dissemination of news – by making a general announcement at the international games and festivals. Where it was not a case of reciprocal business, as with envoys, publicity could be achieved simply by sending a herald to make an announcement at the public centre of each city. This necessitated a certain investment of time, but time was not normally a pressing concern, except in military matters.[88] But there also existed the possibility of addressing a mass audience. The Greek states, just as they had sanctuaries in common, had occasions in which they participated as a group, both officially, by sending representatives, and unofficially, as individual citizens. These were the religious festivals. There are some interesting preconceptions to be found among historians about the way the major panhellenic festivals functioned in the spreading of news. Riepl emphasises the importance of the festivals as *Sammelpunkte*, central gathering points, in the Greek world:

Bei den olympischen, pythischen, istmischen, nemeischen Spielen bot sich fast die einzige Gelegenheit, die zersplitterte hellenische Welt an einem nationalen Zentralpunkt versammelt zu sehen.[89]

According to this view, announcements were made at the Olympian and Nemean festivals because these were the *Sammelpunkte* for the population of Greece and the most convenient places to address a large number of people. Livy emphasises the importance in 196 of the geographical position of the Isthmian festival in this respect:

> Since its situation was favourable for supplying to humankind all kinds of commodities brought from two different seas, the Isthmus was the market and meeting-place for Greece and Asia.[90]

It is certainly true that the festivals were used as centres for the dissemination of information. They were the central meeting places for the Greek world, and each participating state sent official representatives, *theôroi*, as well as competitors and spectators. We have testimony of different kinds of announcements: there are direct official proclamations, such as the Exiles' Decree of Alexander the Great in 324, or the proclamations of the 'Freedom of the Greeks' made in 196 and AD 67, political speeches made by orators, and non-political speeches. Lucian lists Empedokles, Prodikos of Keos, Anaximenes of Chios and Polos of Akragas giving readings of their own works at the Games, while Dio Chrysostom writes of numerous sophists, poets and painters all competing for the attention of the spectators.[91]

Nevertheless it is important to be clear as to how exactly the festivals were being used. For instance, as far as oratorical performances are concerned, the practice of displaying one's work at international festivals was not intended simply to reach a mass audience. The claims of Lucian in the *Herodotus*, that philosophers, historians and sophists all went to perform at the festivals, as the easiest means of reaching the widest possible audience and gaining an international reputation, are based on the idea of addressing all the important and influential Greeks at the same time.[92] The *Herodotus* was itself written to be delivered at a Macedonian festival, and consequently Lucian is at pains to emphasise the nobility and importance of his audience, calling them 'the leaders of Macedonian society'.[93] But it is clear that where a reputation among the mass of the people was established as a result of festival performances, this was not the primary aim of the performance.

We have seen that the circumstances of an announcement of news could be as important as the news itself; news could also be exchanged at festivals in more figurative ways. There are many instances of international reputations being formed or recognised at the panhellenic gathering. Alkibiades used the Athenian public vessels in a display designed to add to the myth of his personal wealth in 416, and both

Themistokles and later Philopoimen are said to have received ovations from the audience in the theatre, at the Olympia and Nemea respectively.[94] The winning of a prize at one of the four games of the *periodos* itself guaranteed international fame of a more evanescent kind. Great prestige surrounded the winner of an event, and his city, but even at this level the prestige element was quite complex – tyrants could be 'given' a win by an athlete of another city in return for material benefits. The famous Crotoniate runner Astylos twice had his victories announced as Syracusan in order to gain favour with the tyrant Hieron, while Kimon had his victory at the Olympia of 532 announced as that of Pisistratos in return for a recall from exile.[95] Thus the prestige was not linked solely to sporting prowess, but resided as much in the announcement of the name.

The main way in which festivals served the Greeks as news-centres was by providing the opportunity for individuals to travel and meet. I discussed in my previous chapter the importance of this for the exchange of news among citizens of different poleis; on an official level too, festivals could lead to the discovery of news. The clearest illustration of this is the Athenian discovery of events at Chios at the Isthmia of 412. The Spartans planned to help the rebellion of Chios against Athens, and the Spartan fleet had been gathered at the Isthmus in order to sail. But the Corinthians insisted on celebrating the Isthmia before the fleet departed, and the Athenian officials, attending the festival as theoroi, were able to discover the plan.[96]

Festivals provided a neutral ground for treaties and similar agreements to be discussed, but such negotiations remained private, between the ambassadors of the state concerned. Because of the non-political nature of the festival authority, there was no opportunity for any one state to make its own announcements. An early example from Herodotos helps to illustrate this. Kleisthenes of Sikyon is represented as announcing the competition to choose a husband for his daughter Agariste at Olympia in 582, but the context of the announcement is made clear by Herodotos. When Kleisthenes had achieved his victory and was having it proclaimed by the official herald, he was able to use the circumstances to make a proclamation of his own.[97] He was able to do this precisely because those with whom he wished to communicate would be there – he was addressing the members of prominent houses of sufficient status to aspire to marriage into his family. Such announcements were personal and unofficial.

Two kinds of announcement appear to be exceptions to this theory. First, there are the decrees from cities in the Hellespont, quoted in Demosthenes' speech on the Crown, and second, the major political announcements mentioned above. We shall see that the announcement of an honour in the state was as much, if not more, to do with the honour of the act of proclaiming, as with telling the citizens. An honour became greater if announced in a place where there were more listeners, and announcement in the assembly or theatre was an extra form of favour. Demosthenes cites a decree which appears to take the honour a step further. Honours were awarded to the Athenian people by the citizens of Byzantion and of the Chersonese, in recognition of their aid against Philip in 340.[98] The decree of the Chersonesites contains the provisions which one might expect: the people decree a crown of sixty talents to the Athenians, and are to erect an altar to Charis and the Athenian Demos. Such honours are again essentially a private affair between the two cities – the decree was made known through the assembly at Athens (hence the existence of a copy for Demosthenes to quote), and the altar built in the Chersonese. The decree from Byzantion, however, is different. It grants to the Athenians both civic rights and privileges at Byzantion, and the erection of three statues there, but as well as this, the honour is to be proclaimed at all the panhellenic festivals:

> Let deputations be sent to the festivals of Greece, the Isthmian, Nemean, Olympian and Pythian festivals, and let the crowns with which we have honoured the Athenian people be proclaimed, so that all the Greeks know the valour of the Athenians and the gratitude of the Byzantians and Perinthians.[99]

This would then mirror the provision for Athenian decrees in some cases to be read out in the theatre – by having the gratitude of the Byzantines proclaimed at all the Games, the Athenians will be honoured in the eyes of all the other states. But these decrees cannot be taken at face value. They are generally considered to be spurious, being either composed deliberately to fill the gaps in the speech, or real decrees taken from the archives and added in the wrong context.[100] There is no precedent for announcements of this nature at festivals; one has to wonder when they could be made, as they do not form part of the religious ceremonial, and fit uneasily into the games and competitions. It seems more likely that a later idea, that of 'all Greece' being addressed at the panegyris, has been anachronistically applied by a later commentator.

The Exiles' Decree, and other official proclamations, are different again. In 324 Alexander the Great sent his envoy Nikanor of Stageira to read his letter at the Olympia, providing for the recall of all exiles from the Greek states.[101] This is of the same kind as the announcement by T. Quinctius Flamininus in 196 of the 'Freedom of the Greeks'. After the defeat of Philip V of Macedon by the Romans, Flamininus chose the Isthmian Games to announce to the Greek states that they were now free of Macedonian rule. The joy of the listeners was such that the herald was recalled to make the announcement a second time.[102]

These announcements clearly utilised the festivals in exactly the way perceived by Riepl, as gathering points. But the motivation behind them was different. To take the Exiles' Decree first, it is obvious from Diodoros that the proclamation as it stands is specific to the occasion, addressing the exiles directly and referring to their situation: 'King Alexander to the exiles from the Greek poleis. We are not to blame for your exile ....'[103] The sources record that the proclamation was heard by twenty thousand exiles, a large proportion of the Olympic stadium's forty thousand capacity. Diodoros states that the exiles had assembled specifically to hear the pronouncement, and this was not the first time that the decree had been made public, having been previously announced at Susa.[104] Many of the mercenaries who had left Alexander's army after the disbandment of satrapal armies in 324 had gathered at Tainaron, forming a stateless and threatening group, and it is significant that Olympia is the largest panhellenic centre accessible from Tainaron. This has parallels with the circumstances in which the 'Freedom of the Greeks' was proclaimed. Livy describes how the Greeks knew in advance that the proclamation was to be made, and attended the Games specifically to hear it:

> On this occasion, then, the Greeks assembled from all parts, not in their accustomed fashion, but in the expectation of finding out what the future state of Greece was to be.[105]

This suggests that in both cases the announcement was something out of the ordinary and not a normal part of the festival.

The significant element in the Exiles' Decree is that it marked a shift in Alexander's relations with the Greek states which was complete by 324. Alexander was no longer first among equals in the League of Corinth; he was now a monarch, delivering a direct command to his subject states. The Synod of the League was not the place to issue a command, because there was to be no opportunity for debate. For a Common Peace, one sent around the cities and invited them to send representatives to a conference. Alexander had no need to do this: making his command public at Olympia was more appropriate for the ruler of Greece.

The Decree was known before it was announced (August/September 324) because it had been proclaimed in Asia at the time that Alexander's veterans were discharged at Opis.[106] In the months intervening between this and the Olympic festival there was considerable debate in Greece about the repercussions of the decree.[107] The exiles gathered to hear it because the act of proclamation made it law – they were, once it had been pronounced, allowed to go home. Again, it was as much the affirmation of a decision known already as the delivery of information. The details had to be agreed in each state, and it took time for them to be settled; the passage of the decree itself was only the first step.[108] Its public airing, however, allowed Alexander to impose his will and gain recognition of his clemency.

These examples illustrate that when the need had arisen for an external power to make announcements to the Greeks as a whole, and for the Greeks to gather to hear the news, the existing festival system was put into use to achieve this. The system of religious gatherings at the major shrines was well-suited to this need, particularly because of the avoidance of political affiliation at the panhellenic centres. Philip had already turned to the (largely) unaffiliated religious organisation of the Delphic Amphiktyony to carry out his early settlements in Greece. In Roman times the politically negligible Olympia became the capital of the Greek world, and the view of the festivals as international information centres reflects the circumstances of the domination of Greece by an external, centralised power.

In classical Greece, in contrast, there was only a limited sense in which the Greek poleis had any international political affairs. Each polis had its own government and laws, and they interacted by and large only in the military sphere. No centralised Greek authority apart from the religious was ever formed by the Greeks themselves. Thus it seems that this use of the festivals as centres for the dissemination of official news could not develop until the late fourth century, and was the result of an expansion of perspective in the Mediterranean world – after Philip, Greece was considered as a political unity. The festivals were of most use to the Romans, who needed regional centres from which to govern and make announcements. It is noteworthy that when the festivals were used in this way specific groups would gather to hear specific things. This is the festival as affirmation rather than news – one comes to hear the announcement, but it is not news in an absolute sense.

Questioning the motivation for such announcements under these circumstances brings one back to the issue of propaganda. Under Macedonia and Rome these decrees were not proclaimed in isolation, but were also published in the major cities either in letter form or as inscriptions. Nero is supposed to have emulated Flamininus at the Isthmia in the 60s; according to Suetonius he competed in the Olympic and Isthmian Games, and as a climax to his performance re-proclaimed the freedom of the Achaians. Nero's speech was inscribed and set up in cities across Greece (it has survived from Boiotia), suggesting that the propaganda value of the announcement was paramount.[109] Such a motive, as I said, was rarely absent from Greek proclamations of news, but even under Rome, when there was a need for widespread dissemination, this concern tended to dominate the use of the panhellenic festivals.

*

The same principle holds true for all official dissemination of news, not only in the international sphere: the news itself was not the primary motivation for making an announcement. In most of the examples I have discussed, the value of the message or announcement as news was small, and other motives were of greater significance. News was announced to demonstrate the control of the disseminating authority over the information, and to affirm the standing of that authority. Where poleis did send messengers with their own news, it usually occurred because they saw a particular advantage in the news being heard. Ritual aspects were also important: some news had to be seen to be announced, and some decisions could not become effective until they were announced. The news a Greek citizen heard from official sources was governed largely by expediency; a city or government told its citizens or outsiders what it considered useful or appropriate for them to know.

To see the dissemination of news by Greek states in terms of heralds continually moving from city to city to provide the latest news is wrong. The desire to inform, while not entirely absent, was not sufficiently great to encourage the development of efficient systems for gathering and disseminating news, nor of methods of mass dissemination. This is partly because of the problems associated with control of such systems (control of news being a means of power), and partly because of the concern to maintain the separation of each polis, which was as strong among polis institutions as it was among individual citizens. In demonstrating these associations, this chapter has hinted at other channels for news beyond the official. Events reported by heralds or messengers were often already known to the polis at large, and we have noted the function of the official herald as providing a means for the mediation of troublesome news. It is to the second half of the relationship, the unofficial messenger, that we now must look.

Unofficial News

Though it be honest, it is never good
To bring bad news. Give to a gracious message
An host of tongues; but let ill tidings tell
Themselves when they be felt.
                    Shakespeare, *Antony and Cleopatra*

Among Theophrastos' *Characters* is the *logopoios*, or newsmonger. This man accosts his friends with concocted stories, claiming to have the latest news from Macedonia, and spends all his time seeking new audiences for his tales. His sole motive is the pleasure of being first with the story, and he invents freely to impress his listeners.[1] The *logopoios* is an extreme example of the unofficial newsbringer, and of the problems he or she could cause.

Official news, as we have seen, accounted for only a part of the information entering the polis. Much news in ancient Greece was spread, either purposefully or by chance, by individuals moving from one city to another, not by heralds or official messengers. Finley, commenting on the role of Demosthenes in the assembly in 339, says:

> Presumably the messenger who brought the news from Elatea was more or less official and trustworthy, unlike the orator's private informant on another occasion

but does not elaborate further on the distinction between these two individuals.[2] In fact there was in the Greek polis a clear division between official news, carried by those in the service of the polis, and unofficial news, brought by traders, travellers or ordinary citizens. News arriving by chance and brought by unrecognised individuals was immediately open to question, and all poleis reveal problems in handling and responding to news of this kind.

Unofficial messengers are of course not an homogeneous group; the motives of informants and the degree of involvement by the polis varied, and this in turn influenced the reception of the information. I shall illustrate this with three examples. In 396, as we have seen, news arrived at Sparta about the fleet being raised by the Persian King, brought by 'a Syracusan called Herodas'. He had seen the Phoenician ships gathering in Phoenicia, and heard about the size of the planned force, and so embarked on the first ship for Greece in order to warn the Spartans.[3] He gave the Spartans a clear and precise account, which was accepted and acted upon, the Spartans mobilising their allies and preparing for a campaign in Asia.

While Themistokles was at Sparta in 478, postponing his negotiations in order to allow the Athenians to build the Long Walls, Thucydides tells us that travellers were constantly bringing reports to the Spartans about the building of the walls:

> but others were constantly arriving with clear accusations that the wall was being built, and had already reached a significant height, and the Spartans did not know how they could disbelieve this.[4]

The Spartans were unsure whether or not to believe what they heard, because they trusted Themistokles, and had only the uncorroborated reports of strangers to contradict him. Themistokles advised them to send investigators of their own to discover the truth, which they did. Clearly in this case the Spartans had no means of evaluating the two competing accounts of events they were offered, until they decided to find out for themselves.

A decree of 386 records the Athenian grant of proxenia and other honours to Phanokritos of Parion, in return for his services to the state. It is unusual in that the remains of the decree grant Phanokritos the title of *euergetês*, and hospitality, while the grant of *proxenia* appears in a rider together with a description of Phanokritos' meritorious act. It states that Phanokritos had brought news to the generals about *tôn neôn tou paraplou*, 'the passage of the ships', which, if the generals had believed him, would have led to the capture of the enemy ships. The rider contains an implied criticism of the generals, and the fact that the honours were proposed as a rider suggests that there may have been an attempt to cover up the generals' error. The award in the decree of a public dinner shows at least that Phanokritos was present in Athens at the time, possibly to claim recognition for his deed.[5]

It is clear from these three examples that news of considerable importance to the interests of a polis could come through unofficial channels. The poleis concerned, so far as we can tell, had no other source of information on these matters, and had made no attempt to find out for themselves before the messenger brought it to their attention. There are also significant differences between the three stories, which illustrate some of the problems of handling such information. In the first example news is brought by a named individual, in the second by unnamed 'others', and in the third by an individual who was possibly known to the generals, possibly influential, but an outsider. A messenger always had to be judged on his (or more rarely, her) own merits, and some would arouse more suspicion than others. The Spartans were unsure whether they should believe the news about the Long Walls, but accepted and acted on Herodas' news, while the Athenians rejected the information offered by Phanokritos. What the three examples have in common is that on each occasion the information offered was true, and of value to the polis concerned; this was not necessarily always the case.

1. Problems with news

The problem faced by a Greek polis receiving unofficial news was how to evaluate information from such a source. It could not be taken at face value; the prytaneis, ephors or generals needed to find out the source of the news and decide whether or not the messenger was credible, before they could act on the news they had received. The sources illustrate that even important information could be received in this apparently haphazard way, and that it could provoke the wrong response, either through failure to act on genuine information, or action in response to false news. The main problem was how much credibility an unofficial messenger should be afforded.

Adventitious news immediately raised questions about the trustworthiness of the bearer. An official messenger, if not from the city itself, would come and present his credentials to the Boule, but an adventitious messenger had to prove who he was and why he should be believed.[6] In the case of Phanokritos, discussed above, decrees reveal the Athenian generals practising unecessary caution, with the result that their campaigns were less successful than they could have been. Another decree, *c.* 355, records that Philiskos of Sestos was made a *proxenos* and benefactor of Athens in return for some information about the fleet of Byzantion which he supplied to the generals.[7] The decree relates to the naval battle fought by the Athenians in the Hellespont during the Social War; their failure to capture Byzantion suggests that Philiskos' information was either not believed or not effective.[8] In 428 too, when news of the threatened revolt of Mytilene was brought to Athens, the information received in the city was treated with scepticism.[9]

One of the reasons for such caution is the significance of the role played by deceit in Greek warfare. While secrecy, in the sense of concealing numbers, equipment or battle plans, was hardly ever important in warfare, attempts to mislead or deceive an enemy were widespread and effective.[10] One thinks first of the strategy of Themistokles at Salamis, or the Spartan use of Sicyonian shields to deceive the Argives in 392.[11] Since this was so, an unknown member of a hostile state coming forward with information would tend to suggest a trap – that the information was being passed on for the benefit of the enemy rather than polis receiving it. It is not hard to think of occasions when a foreigner bringing information was in the service of the enemy. The slave Sikinnos, for instance, was chosen by Themistokles to carry his false message about the Greek retreat to Xerxes, to draw the Persians into attacking at Salamis.[12] In Sicily in 415 Nikias used a man from Katana to draw the Syracusans into making an attack on that city. They chose for the purpose a man who was known to the Syracusans, and who used the names of fifth-columnists in Katana as a proof of his credibility.[13]

Very probably a fear of this kind explains the Athenian generals' apparent failure to act on the information brought to them by Philiskos the Sestian – as a Sestian, citizen of a state which had recently revolted from the Athenian Confederacy in 357, he may have come under strong suspicion of passing on false information in order to lure the Athenian fleet into a disadvantageous situation.[14] The burden of proof of good intentions in cases like these was on the messenger. False news could also be circulated without an ulterior motive, in the belief that it was true. This is harder to exemplify, because news reported but found to be inaccurate rarely finds its way into historical sources. One case of which we do know is reported by Lykourgos in his prosecution of Leokrates: he accuses Leokrates of telling the news of the defeat of Athens to the merchants at Rhodes, with the result that it was spread all over the Greek world.[15] The merchants in this case did spread news of an important event, namely the fall of Athens after the battle of Chaironeia, but it was not in fact true. They had been deceived by the account of a deserter who was himself an unreliable source.

Notoriously, the barber who received the news of the Athenian disaster in Sicily and attempted to spread it in the Agora was tortured, because he could not give a clear account of his source for the news, and was thus suspected of being a *logopoios*:

> But when he was asked from whom he had heard the news, he could not give any clear answer, and so was judged to be a *logopoios*, trying to stir up unrest in the city; so he was put on the wheel and tortured for a long time, until some messengers came with a full report of the disaster.[16]

He was thought to be trying to stir up the city, that is, to cause confusion and unrest. This represents another kind of adventitious news, that invented by a *logopoios*. The idea that news might be invented is one that recurs in the historical sources; suspicions of this kind appear as a response to news twice in Thucydides, in Demosthenes, and in Lysias.[17] What needs to be understood is why people would want to make up news, and how it could benefit them.

The confusion generated by the xenos in Plutarch's tale was a threat under the wartime conditions at Athens, if only from the point of view of undermining morale. A similar motive is attributed by Athenagoras to those who put about the news of the arrival of the Athenian Expedition in Syracuse in 415. This gives some detail of the motives of those who are inventing the stories of invasion:

> There are here in the city men inventing tales of things which are neither true, nor likely to become true; I have not recently discovered these men, but I have known of them all along. These people wish, by means of stories like these or even more criminal ones, rather than by deeds, to frighten you, the majority, and so rule the city themselves.[18]

According to Athenagoras, such plots were not unusual in Syracuse, were the cause of continual internal strife, and had previously resulted in dictatorships or coups. In this context the spreading of rumours is seen as a powerful tool of agitators, and something which needs to be guarded against. In 411 in Athens it was precisely this kind of situation, news of disaster, which proved to be the catalyst for revolution. Such stories could not be ignored in case they were true. On three occasions in wartime Athens was thrown into panic by a reported Spartan attack on the Piraeus: in 428 and 411, this was simply panic arising from ill-digested news, but in 387, in the case of Teleutias' raid, it was true.[19]

A similar ulterior motive is ascribed to traders who concoct false news. It is clear from our sources that on some topics traders had a near-monopoly of news, and that this could be economically useful to them. Lysias' speech *Against the Corn-dealers* accuses the corn merchants of fabricating stories of shipwrecks and disasters in order to raise corn prices; he states that they are in a position to do this because they regularly hear news of this kind first.[20] Similarly Dionysodoros in Demosthenes' *Against Dionysodoros* is accused of being part of a conspiracy with Kleomenes in Egypt. The latter had men in Athens to inform him when the price of grain was high, so that it could be shipped there, and when it was low, so that the ships could trade elsewhere.[21] Demosthenes is keen to blacken the character of the accused, and states that the price of grain rose 'as a result of such letters and conspiracies'. Merchants and traders were in a particularly good position to hear economic news, being part of an international community with an interest in finding out and disseminating this kind of information, and because of the control they exercised over information, they were able to manipulate prices by creating unverifiable rumours. Moreover, the dissatisfaction among citizens over the access to, and control of, information that traders had could be exploited by speakers. Aristophanes' *Knights* depicts the exploitation of information in this way for comic effect, when the Sausage-seller suggests to the Boule that they should use his news that sardines are at a record low price to rush to the Agora and prevent anyone else buying them.[22] The idea seems to be that specific information would allow one to corner the market. It is clear from these examples that there was seen to be no defence against such inventions – the price of corn was open to influence, and if you had only news from traders, you laid yourself open to exploitation.

Other *logopoioi*, like Theophrastos', had more obscure motives. In his *First Philippic*, Demosthenes says that Athens is full of rumours invented by newsmongers as to what Philip's intentions are, but that all these rumours are idle, as no one could really have such information.[23] Demosthenes accuses the Athenians in this speech of allowing such rumours to distract them from their campaign against Philip, as he claims happened during the siege of Heraion Teichos, when a rumour of Philip's illness and subsequent death prevented the dispatch of an expedition.[24] Newsmongers of this kind, he claims, are harmful, but this is precisely because their activities throw into relief the problems of gaining accurate information about foreign affairs.[25] The city is at the mercy of such people because all its information is open to doubt. In such circumstances it is not surprising if news and rumour were hard to act upon.

The unifying factor behind these three motivations for inventing news, causing political instability, profit and entertainment, is that they were all particularly easy to accomplish, as it was difficult to distinguish true news from invention. Some news-mongering was the natural result of a culture which constantly looked to hear the latest news, as Demosthenes depicts (the phenomenon of news created to fill a demand is not solely modern). The *logopoios* is the creation of a society which wants to hear news for its own sake.[26] The invention of news involved the manipulation of information for personal benefit, because the instability of information bestowed power on those with access to it. Hence the suspicion with which messengers could be treated – the awareness was that there could be harm to the state if deceitful news were believed.

2. Criteria for evaluation

The evaluation of the news itself and of the messenger was thus of paramount importance for those whose responsibility was to decide what action to take. I will examine four criteria on which evaluation was made: whether the identity of the messenger could be vouched for, their status, whether or not they were an eye-witness, and their motives in bringing the news. These criteria were not exclusive, but combined to provide grounds for the acceptance or rejection of a story.

(i) Identity

One of the simplest ways to establish one's credentials was through a personal acquaintance – by finding a citizen of the state concerned who could vouch for your identity. This would, at least in part, bridge the divide between citizen and outsider, and allow the chance messenger to be partially co-opted into the polis. It afforded the city some possibility of retribution if the information proved to be untrue or harmful. This mediation between the city and the outsider was of course one of the primary roles of the *proxenos* – any citizen abroad could go to the *proxenos* of his or her state, who could then vouch for him or her in legal and other such matters.[27] Demosthenes *Against Lakritos* describes in some detail the procedure used by bankers, calling witnesses to the identity of foreign clients. Androkles, the speaker, lent money to Lakritos, who was introduced to him by two of Androkles' close friends, Thrasymedes and his brother Melanopos, both of the deme Sphettos.[28] It follows that one of the criteria for the selection of an ambassador was that he had a personal contact with a member of the negotiating state; apart from the goodwill and trust existing in the relationship, it provided a means of validating the information.[29]

The belief that the stranger who could not be identified in this way was suspect is illustrated by an anecdote from Polyainos: when Chares suspected that there were spies present in his army, his method of exposing them was to have each man in his army identify himself to his companions, which quickly discovered the enemies.[30] It seems most likely from Xenophon's account that the Syracusan Herodas was known to the Spartans – hence the use of his name, and the matter-of-fact way in which Xenophon reports the episode.[31] Such knowledge is also implicit in the episode of Epaminondas' planned attack on Sparta in 362, when news of the Theban advance was brought to Agesilaos and the Spartan army by an unnamed Cretan; the nature of Xenophon's reference to the man suggests that he was known to Agesilaos.[32]

The most important example of the use of personal acquaintance to verify a messenger is in the account of the news brought to Athens about Mytilene in 428. Thucydides tells us that news of the impending revolt was brought by some Tenedians, Methymnians and the Athenian *proxenoi* in Mytilene. The Athenians at first were sceptical about the news, because they were already in great hardship and did not wish to believe more bad news. They subsequently sent an embassy of their own, and were convinced of the impending revolt.[33] After the first battle, both sides were eager to agree an armistice, and the Mytileneans sent a delegation to Athens to persuade them of Mytilene's goodwill. This delegation contained one of the original informants, who had changed his allegiance, but it did not achieve its objective.[34] Thucydides obviously felt the fact that the embassy contained one of the original informers to be worthy of mention, since the Mytileneans were using this man to convince the Athenians of their good intentions. He had originally brought valid information to Athens, and had been proved to be acting in their interests, so his information would be more trust-

worthy the second time. It need not be assumed that this design was a
failure because the embassy was unsuccessful – Athenian hostility
towards Mytilene was such that the Mytileneans themselves held out
little hope that the embassy would do any good.[35]

The same consideration of personal knowledge affects our view of the
grants of *proxenia* to Phanokritos and Philiskos. The *proxenos'* role was
to protect the interests of the polis and its citizens in another state, and
we have examples of *proxenoi* passing on useful information to the polis
to which they owed loyalty.[36] The extent and nature of this communication is a problem. Gerolymatos, in a study of the *proxenia* in the fifth
century, asserts quite correctly that there was a need among the Greeks
for an intelligence system, for use specifically in war, and goes on to
argue that, perceiving this need, they began to employ the *proxenoi* as
an intelligence-gathering service from the fifth century.[37] The evidence
he offers for an organised system is poor, and it seems that although
the need undoubtedly was perceived, it was never satisfactorily re-
solved; information received through *proxenoi* remained haphazard.
One only needs to consider the episode of the Phokian coup in 346 to see
the failure of such a system to work in practice: a change of government
at Phokis was not reported to the Athenians by any Phokian, but was
unknown until the Athenian heralds of the Mysteries returned with
news of what had happened.[38] The system of *proxenia*, though well
established at this stage, was clearly not a foolproof means of learning
information.

Xenophon records an episode at Sparta in 374 when the Spartan
proxenos Polydamas of Pharsalos came from Thessaly to warn the
Spartans about the ambitions of Jason of Pherai for the conquest of
Thessaly. The speech which Xenophon gives Polydamas shows him
justifying his actions:

> Since I am your *proxenos*, Spartans, and your benefactor, just as all my
> ancestors of whom we have record, I think it right to come to you, if I am
> in any difficulty, and to warn you, if anything contrary to your interests
> arises in Thessaly.[39]

There is, however, more to the incident than a *proxenos* passing on
useful information; it is governed by self-interest. Polydamas was a
man of substance in Pharsalos and stood to lose all his position to Jason
if Sparta failed to send aid. Polydamas claims that Jason encouraged
him in his mission to Sparta in the hope that they would refuse help,
and the Pharsalians would then submit voluntarily.[40] The position of
Polydamas illustrates the problems attendant on a *proxenos* who acted
as a spy: he was well known in Pharsalos as both an influential citizen
and a self-confessed pro-Spartan. A grant of *proxenia* was not something to be hidden. His mission to Sparta was also not secret, and would

have been hard to keep confidential: Demosthenes' concern to defend himself against the charge of spying for Thebes demonstrates that the *proxenos* would be the first suspect for passing on information.[41] Sympathisers and *proxenoi* were a constant leak of information to be plugged in wartime, as Alkibiades did in 411/0 (by putting all boats in the harbour at Prokonnesos under guard), but they did not and could not provide a constant and reliable flow of information.

Gerolymatos suggests that the award of *proxenia* to these men was not simply an honour, but had a practical relevance, firstly that they would have an obligation to pass on information to the Athenians in the future, since this was one of the roles of a *proxenos*, and secondly that it would be made easier for them to carry information.[42] Not only would a *proxenos* have more reason to visit Athens and communicate with its citizens, but the *proxenia* would also ensure that their information carried more weight and would be likely to be believed. This view, as I have said, somewhat overemphasises the importance of the intelligence-gathering role of the *proxenos*, as this was certainly not the only function attached to the award, but the element of identifying an informant for the future was certainly present.

Records of similar awards of *proxenia* in return for information at other states in Greece reveal the value that was placed on such informants, even if they were unlikely to be believed the first time – at Troezen, for instance, in 369 *proxenia* was awarded to Echilaos of Plataia, who had come to Troezen 'concerning the safety of the country', which appears in the context to refer to information.[43] This may go some way towards explaining the continuing importance of the *proxenia* in the fourth century, despite the suspicion that attached to it as a sign of shifting loyalties during the Peloponnesian War because of the frequency of treachery and betrayal. As well as lending credibility, the grant of *proxenia* was also an effective means of ensuring the protection of an informant, carrying as it did rights of *asylia* and protection in case any of his actions alienated him from his own state. Passing on information could entail a risk from one's own countrymen, and a grant of *proxenia* made an individual much harder to attack.

Establishing one's identity could be more difficult for some groups than others. Attaching importance to personal contacts necessarily favoured the wealthy and influential – a noble or rich traveller would usually have a friend or host in the city he was visiting, but a poorer traveller would find it much harder to produce a citizen to vouch for him. Similarly, traders suffered from a disability in this respect, because in some ways they formed a separate community. A trader was often separated from his native city and lived instead as part of a self-contained trading community, which centred on the larger ports such as Athens, Byzantion and Rhodes.[44] Within a polis the trader inhabited the port, and even if he remained in his native polis, by his frequent absences became less identifiable as a citizen. At Athens the separation of the port from the city was deliberately emphasised, leading to a lack of contact between citizen and trader.

Finding a respectable citizen to vouch for you, then, was not so easy. As Mossé emphasises, the world of the emporion was, in Athens, a marginal one, distinguished sharply from that of citizenship and politics, and orators try to induce an attitude of scorn and distrust for the inhabitants of the Piraeus. Androkles, for instance, in Demosthenes *Against Lakritos*, seeks to emphasise the fact that his opponents are Phaselites, with no claim on the goodwill of the jury, unlike himself.[45] In the *Politics* Aristotle sets out his prescription for the ideal state, and in this he accepts that trade is a necessary evil for a city, but states that the market and city should be kept separate as far as possible; Plato concurs with the view that foreign traders may corrupt the citizens and introduce 'subversive innovations' in the *Laws*.[46] In the speeches of Demosthenes those who associate with merchants, either providing bottomry loans or actually engaging in trade, seek to dissociate themselves from this embarrassing contact and to emphasise their citizenship, to show that they belong to the respectable world of the polis.[47] Thus those who inhabited the port and carried on trade were distinguished from the citizenry proper, and may have been at a disadvantage in matters involving the proof of credibility.

At this point some interesting parallels can be drawn with the treatment of messengers in tragedy. It is obviously unsound to treat drama simply as a historical source, and the messenger in particular was a standard figure in tragedy, designed to allow offstage events to be reported to the audience.[48] Nevertheless a disjunction can be observed between dramatic conventions on messengers, and their treatment in the plays, and some dramatists use this disjunction to create tension or comment on their characters. There are indications that even a messenger in a play, with a clearly-defined role within the drama, could not escape some of the same doubt as surrounded a real messenger. This is particularly noticeable with non-standard messengers. Tragic messengers are generally assumed to be servants or attendants of the characters, or simply to be defined by their role – they are Messengers.[49] Some, however, who arrive unexpectedly, and for whom news-carrying is not their primary role, are asked to prove their credibility, or begin their speeches with explicit claims to be known by the characters they address.

In the *Phoenissai*, when a messenger comes to Jokasta with an account of the battle, he is explicitly recognised by her as the shield-bearer of Eteokles, incidental though this characterisation is to the plot. Similarly in the *Troades* Talthybios, on his first entrance, confirms his identity and role to Hekuba.[50] This confirmation, that the messenger is someone who can be recognised, is intended to reinforce the credibility of the news. In *Herakleidai* and *Elektra* this idea is taken even further – the character addressed by the messenger asks who he is and why he should be believed, before they accept the news that is brought. Elektra asks who the old man bringing news of Aigisthos' death is, and he says that she should recognise him as an attendant of Orestes; Jokasta in *Herakleidai* asks the messenger (designated simply as *Therapôn*, 'Attendant') who he is, and is told he is a servant of Hyllos.[51] It is probably not coincidental that in these four cases the messengers are justifying themselves to, or are asked to justify themselves by, women, who are either nervous or suspicious of the stranger's approach.

These problems of credibility become most acute when a character in a play disguises himself or herself in order to bring news to another character. In all the cases we have, the audience is prepared beforehand for the disguise scene by a scene of planning, describing the way in which the disguise will be effected, and one of the elements of the disguise is the claim to be known to a friend of the deceived person.[52] In *Choephoroi*, Orestes tells Elektra and the Chorus that he and Pylades will pose as Parnassians, using the Phokian dialect to avoid detection, and will claim to be *doruxenoi* (friends and allies) of Aigisthos and Klytaimnestra. In Sophokles' *Elektra* Orestes states that the Paidagogos' story will be trusted if he claims to be from Aigisthos' ally Phanoteus, and confirms it with an oath. This is the first question that Klytaimnestra asks when the Paidagogos reaches the palace.[53] Furthermore, the plans in both *Choephoroi* and *Elektra* establish a defence against questions, suggesting that the messenger will have his credibility called into doubt, even though this is in fact absent from the subsequent scene.

By raising questions about credibility characters in tragedy react to messengers in a manner at odds with the convention, in a way which seems to reflect contemporary concerns. These dramatic effects could be achieved only against a background of preconceptions about the reception of a messenger, one of which was the need to establish an identity in order to be believed. The best messenger, then, was one already known to the recipients of the news, or who could prove his identity. Some of the structures of the polis, such as the *proxenia*, were designed to facilitate this kind of indentification. But if a messenger could not be vouched for, the story then needed to be judged on other criteria.

(ii) Class

Many Greek historians, including Herodotos, Thucydides and Arrian, are concerned to emphasise the status of their informants, in support of their credibility. Arrian, for instance, refers in the *Indika* to Nearchos and Megasthenes as *dokimô andre*, distinguished men, and refers in

the introduction to his *Anabasis* to Ptolemy's kingship as a proof of his
trustworthiness as a source:

> But I judged Ptolemy and Aristoboulos to be more trustworthy in their
> accounts, Aristoboulos because he accompanied King Alexander on his
> campaigns, and Ptolemy first because he too was present on the cam-
> paign, and secondly, since he was a king it would be more dishonourable
> for him to lie than for anyone else.[54]

Herodotos reveals the same preoccupation with his informant for the
banquet of Attaginos, Thersander, whom he calls 'one of the most
distinguished men in Orchomenos'. He is also keen to emphasise the
official nature of the information he gained from the Egyptian priests
in his second book, and appears to be dismissive of the account of the
source of the Nile given by the scribe of Saïs precisely because he
thought of the man as only a scribe.[55] Thucydides, describing his
working methods, says 'I did not think it right to take my account of the
war from the first witness I chanced upon ... (*ouk ek tou paratuchon-
tos*)', a statement which is difficult to interpret. Gomme sees Thucydides contrasting his methods here with those of Herodotos – whereas
Herodotos simply wrote down the first report he was given, Thucydides
has collected several reports and sifted them to get closer to the facts.[56]
But it has also been suggested that the phrase carries an air of social
snobbery: not from just anyone who was there, but from reliable and
upper-class informants.[57]

Thus one can detect a belief among historians that the noble or
high-status were more likely to be reliable witnesses, while the testimony of those of lower status could not be counted on. Just as ordinary
informants often lie behind orators' unsubstantiated facts, so it seems
that upper-class people are more commonly named as historical
sources. This is also true of those informants documented in historical
writing – those of lower status are identified only by toponym, such as
the Histiaean in Herodotos, or Xenophon's Cretan, or dropped from the
text altogether. One can only guess at the informant in many cases
where news is said to have been brought.[58]

At an abstract level one can see a more general discrimination
against the poor or low-status man, in that he was thought to be of lower
moral character than the nobleman. Brunt has collected passages
where this idea is clearly expressed; the prevalent idea among sixth-
century sources is that poverty will drive a man to lie or steal, and is a
corrupting influence on the character.[59] Among writers in fifth-century
Athens this idea was becoming outdated. The rise of wealthy but
non-aristocratic men at Athens in the fifth century, men like Kleon and
Hyperbolos, led to a questioning of the reliability of wealth as a guide
to character, and in Athenian literature a greater variety of responses

can be discerned. Euripides was famed for his depictions of beggars and his questioning of the definition of virtue, but even so his plays do not offer one consistent line. In the *Andromeda* (and other fragments) his characters follow the view that nobility is conferred by wealth; elsewhere he suggests that nobility is different from wealth, but wealth is the more important; and elsewhere again he advances the exalted view that true nobility is of the soul.[60]

But even in the *Elektra*, where the character of the Autourgos is introduced to make a point about the nobility of the soul, there are plainly a number of preconceptions at war in the text. Orestes' view, that poverty cannot be noble, is not seriously undermined by this one example, which he sees as an exception, and while the farmer may be noble in spirit nevertheless he cannot be a suitable husband for the princess Elektra. The Autourgos himself has to make the point early on that he is not truly poor, but of noble birth and impoverished. For Elektra, poverty is something degrading in itself and which a noble spirit cannot simply overcome.[61] The idea of poverty as productive of low moral character is still present.

Aristophanes' *Wealth*, produced in 388, also offers conflicting ideas about virtue. In this utopian fantasy, all the main characters are initially poor, and see wealth as the rightful reward of the good – in a perfect world only the worthy would be rich (and the characters are of course by definition worthy!).[62] One might expect that the character of *Penia* (Poverty), when introduced for the agon, would receive an unsympathetic portrayal in contrast with Wealth, but this is not the case. A clear division is made between the state of poverty (*penia*), having just enough to live, and destitution (*ptôcheia*), and Penia claims for herself responsibility for all the old-fashioned virtues of hardiness and industry, as well as for improving men's characters; it is destitution which has a corrupting influence.[63] Her opponents in the agon argue the view that poverty corrupts a man's character and leads him to crime, but Penia obviously has the stronger case. There is a tension which remains unresolved in the second half of the play as the benefits of wealth for the worthy are illustrated, but the warnings of Penia about its evil consequences are not. The concept of 'virtuous poverty' was clearly acknowledged by some at Athens, even if the main thrust of Aristophanes' fantasy was that everyone who deserved it should be rich.

The complementary idea that luxury can be equally corrupting appears in the *Wasps*, and in the works of the Spartan-inspired Xenophon.[64] Plato combined the two ideas in the *Republic*, arguing that poverty and wealth represented the two extremes, and each corrupted a man's character in different ways. Poverty caused degeneracy as a result of the occupations, living conditions and social position that a man was forced to endure; wealth corrupted through idleness and overindulgence.[65]

Such contradictory beliefs coexist in many other writers, and it is likely that the Greeks themselves had inconsistent attitudes on the topic. Nevertheless, the practical view, that a poor man was less trustworthy, is strongly expressed in Athenian forensic speeches. To an extent this is a result of the speechwriters' willingness to exploit any line of attack – if the defendant is rich, he is likely to be corrupt, while if he is poor he is depraved. But this kind of attack does rely on the belief that poverty affected a man's character for the worse, and the recurrence of the antithesis 'poor but honest' in speeches defending less wealthy men certainly indicates a need for emphasis on the virtue of a poor man. Euxitheos in Demosthenes' *Against Euboulides* protests that he and his family should not be believed to be malefactors just because they are poor: 'If we are poor, that is not our crime; we have done wrong only if we are not citizens.'[66]

Greek juries and litigants placed much importance on the character of those concerned in the case, litigants and witnesses, as affecting the testimony they gave, and character was assessed by social and economic status.[67] It was standard practice in an Athenian trial to attempt to discredit one's opponent and his witnesses by undermining their credibility. The main ways of doing this were accusations of previous convictions for perjury or prostitution, or a general reputation for untruthfulness, but Volkmann adds to the methods of discrediting litigants 'ob er arm ist' (whether he is poor), because a poor man could easily be bribed to give false evidence.[68]

The poor witness always needed to defend his moral character before anything else, because it was felt to affect his testimony. Euxitheos, above, asks the jury not to show bias against him because of his family's poverty, even though the case is one of disputed citizenship. He agrees that poverty leads men to crime, offering excuses for his impoverishment, and obviously fears that it will prejudice the jury against him.[69] The extreme of this attitude can be found in the treatment of slaves in Athenian courts: the evidence of a slave was only admissible if given under torture.[70] It is the estimation of the moral worth of a slave that is important here, not the character of the individual slave; the testimony of any slave is considered questionable, since the Greeks believed that servility equalled dishonesty.[71] The root of the belief was that slaves had nothing to lose, physically or morally, by lying, and that all slaves would lie to further their own interests. The concept of a slave's lack of shame relates to the idea in Arrian about the trustworthiness of kings; the more *timê* (honour) one had to lose if detected in deceit, the less likely one was to lie.[72]

Low-status or poor informants were thus less likely to be believed. This probably contributed to the Persian choice of Alexander of Macedon to communicate with the opposing Greeks in 479 – as King of Macedonia he was not only more recognisable, but also more trustworthy.[73] Related to this kind of thinking is the fact that low-class messengers were more likely to be treated harshly by the authorities, the most obvious example being the barber who was tortured to find out what he knew when he failed to substantiate his information. They were more often held overtly as hostages while their news was substantiated – as the Persians did with the man from Histiaia who brought news of the Greek withdrawal from Thermopylai to the Persian fleet at Aphetai in 480. The Persians were reluctant to believe the information, so put the man under guard until they sent some fast ships to find out for themselves.[74] In 369 when the Thebans invaded Lakonia they were helped by some men from Karyai, who gave them information about the position of the Spartan army, and offered themselves as hostages, to be killed if the information proved to be false.[75] The Thebans, we are told, were even so not disposed to believe them straightaway, and needed to hear the same story from all sources before they were convinced. Similarly in Herodotos' account of the miraculous appearance of a divine boat to the Corinthian commander Adeimantos during the battle of Salamis, the occupants of the boat offered to Adeimantos that he take them with him as hostages and kill them if their story turned out to be false.[76]

There is often an inexplicit contrast between the official and unofficial messenger in terms of class: in the passage I discussed initially, the men the Spartans sent to Athens to check Themistokles' story were *chrêstoi*, worthy citizens, suggesting a choice of upper-class informants to check the stories brought by lower-class travellers.[77] A polis which usually chose the wealthy or noble to act as envoys would find it all the harder to believe the account of the chance messenger if he were low-status.

(iii) Autopsy

The Greeks, like all cultures, attached great importance to the first-hand account of news. In 373 Iphikrates was sailing round the Peloponnese to help the Corcyreans, who were under siege by the Spartans under Mnasippos. During a battle outside Corcyra Mnasippos was killed, and this news, Xenophon tells us, had reached Iphikrates. Nevertheless he approached Corcyra with his ships in battle formation, as the news he had received was not from an eye-witness, and so he feared that it might have been made up by the Spartans themselves to deceive him.[78] Xenophon states further that once Iphikrates arrived at Kephallenia he received reliable information, without indicating the nature of the source, but under the circumstances it seems to have been both someone closer to the action, and known to be an Athenian sympathiser, since Kephallenia was favourable to Athens. On reaching Corcyra, he heard about Sicilian ships which were on their way to reinforce the

Spartans, and this also seems to reflect information from partisans being more readily accepted.

The distinction between the eye-witness report and hearsay is one which appears early on, and a further criterion influencing the response to a messenger was whether or not he was an eye-witness. This is first found in Homer, with emphasis on seeing with one's own eyes.[79] To the Ionian historians the literary work in which they were engaged was literally *historiê*, enquiry, finding out for oneself, and they privileged direct experience over reports from others. Herodotos claims first-hand knowledge where he can, and emphasises that he cannot guarantee the accuracy of information gained at second hand.[80] This distinction was developed by Thucydides, who asserted that contemporary history was the only kind of history it was possible to write with accuracy, making direct personal experience the foundation of historical writing. Second in historical status to this is the use of witnesses as close to the original events as possible.[81]

The early belief in first-hand accounts is attributed to Heraclitos, in a fragment cited by Polybios – 'eyes are surer witnesses than ears'.[82] The verbs 'to see' and 'to know' in Greek have a common root (*eidô/oida*), and in some sources, especially tragedy, seeing and knowing are equated. In tragedy the idea is expressed by both characters and choruses, often with the sense of a cliché; the chorus in *Medea* say: 'I have seen it myself, it is not a story I heard from others.' Autopsy is produced as a guarantee of truth, by messengers in *Persai*, *Seven Against Thebes*, and *Supplices*, and by Andromache in the *Troades*.[83] By the time of *Helen* the idea seems to have enough credit to be parodied in an exchange between Helen and Teucer, who is claiming to have seen Helen, when in fact what he saw was an *eidôlon* (phantom):

> Helen: Did you see the unhappy woman, or is this hearsay?
> Teucer: I saw her with my own eyes, as clearly as I see you now.[84]

If one can indeed see a generally-held idea about sources, this should then hold true in Greek reaction to messengers in real life. It is possible to find historical examples in which emphasis was put on the eye-witness report. Xenophon tells us that Agesilaos stressed this, when he dispatched Derkylidas to carry the news of the Spartan victory at Nemea to the allies in Asia Minor. No messenger could be better than Derkylidas, he says, because he was actually present at the battle.[85] In other examples, the emphasis is usually on first-hand information, seeing for oneself, as opposed to gaining a better report. The Spartans received many reports from 'others', but sent their own investigators; the same preoccupation is attributed to the Persians in Herodotos.[86] When the Athenian expedition arrived in Sicily in 415, the Syracusans sent investigators to Rhegion, where the Athenians were stationed, to find out the truth of the rumours they had received. The reaction to the information of these investigators demonstrates the difference in status of the information – previously, when the news had come as rumour, reaction had been slow, but now preparations were stepped up, garrisons and troops dispatched, and the army prepared for war.[87] The *logopoios* in Theophrastos' *Characters* is eager to substantiate his false news by appeals to sources, and emphasises that these sources are first-hand:

> And he has a soldier, or the slave of Asteios the flute-player, or Lykon the contractor, who has come from the very battlefield, from whom he has heard the news.[88]

Information from a stranger was far more convincing if at first hand.

(iv) Motive

A fourth means of deciding on the validity of the news of a chance messenger was a consideration of his or her motive in bringing the news. I discussed above the possibility of deceit, and of causing political unrest, but other motives could make a messenger equally suspect. Merchants as a class were particularly affected by this kind of attitude. The speeches of Demosthenes reveal a general opinion that merchants were untrustworthy, because they were only in search of a profit. This idea has already been shown to apply to the corn-dealers, and is applied to all merchants as part of the citizen/trader opposition. The fact that merchants went by sea all over the Greek world, and were often without loyalty to any particular state, was also perceived to give them the opportunity to become spies. There are some historical indications of this role, such as the spy disguised as a merchant in Plutarch *Pelopidas*. In certain instances, when news was being carried by partisans, they relied on merchant shipping for travel, as in the warning taken from Mytilene to Athens in 428.[89] Merchants were at least complicit in this type of traffic, and could obviously benefit from it.

The motive of bringing news for financial gain is attributed to messengers in literature. In the *Philoktetes* the sailor sent by Odysseus to carry out his plan is disguised as an *emporos*, and he enters into self-justification with Neoptolemos, in order to deceive Philoktetes, giving an explanation of his motives for coming to inform Neoptolemos: 'I decided not to keep silence and sail onward, before I brought the news to you, and obtained a just reward.'[90] Similarly, motives are examined in *Trachiniai*, in a scene between two messengers: Lichas, the official herald, and the old man, a chance messenger. Lichas does not have to establish his credentials, since he has already been introduced as Herakles' official herald, but the second messenger, the old man who is

to contradict Lichas' story, has to account for his knowledge. Deianeira
asks him how he heard, and why he has come instead of Lichas, giving
the chance messenger (ironically) less credibility than the herald:

> Deianeira: From what citizen or foreigner did you learn what you report?
> Messenger: Lichas the herald is proclaiming it to a great crowd, in the
> meadow where the oxen feed in summer. I heard it and came here, so
> that by being first to bring this news to you, I might gain some profit
> and earn your favour.[91]

The claim of the old man, that he hoped to win some favour by bringing
the news, is the claim which distinguishes the adventitious messenger.

Underlying the expectation of reward for bringing news is the idea
of news as commodity. An item of news has a value to a given group, a
value which can be converted into material form. The messenger with
news can sell it to an interested party, and its value can be increased
by seeking a specific market. This was the intention of the chorusman
in Dionysius' tragedy when he made strenuous efforts to be the first to
report to the tyrant news of his play's victory at the Leneia.[92] Being the
first with a piece of news was important in the abstract, but it was also
essential in material terms. The value of news depends on its newness,
and news is saleable only so long as it is new – its value can be collapsed
without warning by the disclosure of the information by another source.
This provides another reason for the problematic nature of *logopoioi*: by
inventing and spreading false news indiscriminately the *logopoios*
undermines the commodity value of all information. The practice of
offering rewards for good or useful news was meant to encourage those
well-disposed to a polis to bring information, but it naturally also set up
the possibility of exploitation.

Motive could also influence the story which an informant told. De-
serters or traitors are likely to say what they feel their hearers want
them to say, in the hope of acceptance by the opposing side.[93] If they
often hoped to receive some material reward for their action, this too
could lead to distortion. Themistokles, for instance, claimed favour from
Xerxes on the grounds that he had prevented the destruction of the
Hellespont bridge, even though this was not in fact true.[94] Clearly the
idea of betraying a polis or army for personal gain is unlikely to figure
among the motives offered by fifth-columnists themselves; it is far more
attractive to think of oneself as a partisan or idealist than a self-seeking
traitor.

Equally, the motive is easily imputed to traitors by others – Philip of
Macedon notoriously said that any polis could be captured if there was
a way for an ass loaded with gold to be sent up, while Demosthenes sees
all pro-Macedonian factions as motivated solely by the desire for Macedonian gold.[95] The habit of awarding honours or recognition to those

who brought valuable news made news-bringing a means of achieving such rewards, and allowed poleis to foster would-be informants, as is explicit in Demosthenes' speech *Against Leptines*. Demosthenes refers to Archebios and Herakleides, who betrayed Byzantion to Thrasyboulos, and were subsequently exiled from their polis. These men received grants of *proxenia* from Athens, and Demosthenes' argument is not only that they deserved such a recompense, but also that the polis must be seen by others to reward its benefactors.[96] The betrayal of cities from within is one of the features of Greek warfare of the fifth and early fourth centuries, and the need to encourage betrayal meant that even unsuccessful attempts could result in the 'fifth column' receiving rewards from the enemy city, making the role of newsbringer an attractive one.[97]

3. Analysis and response

There were thus several ways to test the credentials of a messenger. An individual known to the polis, or who could make himself known, was more likely to be believed than a stranger; some attempt was made by Greek poleis to integrate such unknown messengers into the structure of the polis. A noble or wealthy individual was considered more credible than a poor or low-status one, and an eye-witness was more convincing than a messenger with a second-hand account. Proof of a disinterested or benevolent motive, as opposed to a purely mercenary one, also raised the credibility of a messenger. A range of responses to adventitious news on the part of the state existed. Broadly, three reactions were possible – to reject the news as untrue, to make attempts to verify it, or to accept it as true and act on it. By far the most common reaction to an adventitious messenger was to seek further information, sometimes keeping the original informant as a hostage. If a situation did not require immediate action, this could be easy enough – the Spartans on their way to Mytilene in 427 distrusted the news they heard, that Mytilene had been captured, and so simply sailed on their way until they heard it from a source they believed.[98] But it was not often that a situation could be treated in this way; news more usually necessitated a quick response.

At Syracuse in 415, if the news of the approach of the Athenian fleet were true, it called for the mobilisation of defences, and a change in policy towards other Sicilian states. What we see in Thucydides is a twofold response; although the debate at Syracuse ends in compromise, with no decision made as to the authenticity of the news, one of the generals makes the proposal that Syracuse should ready itself for war, even if it is in the short term unnecessary, as such preparations are always a good idea.[99] Later on the Syracusans also sent out their own men to find out more about the situation, and once they had more

definite information their military preparations were stepped up.[100] A
similar response can be seen in Plutarch's *Solon*, where a report of
threatened military action against Megara led to both the mustering of
an army, and the dispatch of a ship to find out whether the news was
true.[101] If one heard news of an attack it would, as the Syracusans are
made to say, be foolish to ignore it when preparations would probably
be valuable anyway. This idea lies behind the ruse reported in both
Aineias Tacticus and Polyainos, of announcing a fictitious attack on the
enemy in order to forestall their attack; no general could afford to ignore
news of this kind.[102]

In situations where immediate response was not required, the sending of messengers could be a temporising measure. Representatives
were sent by Athens to Mytilene in 428 to investigate the state of the
island, in part because the Athenians felt they had enough on their
hands without war with Lesbos. Similarly in 395 the Spartans sent
ambassadors to Thebes, requesting them not to invade Phokis, rather
than going to war on their allies' behalf immediately.[103] This has
similarities to the situation Demosthenes describes in 352, when the
Athenians voted an expedition to relieve Heraion. The expedition was
dispatched, much reduced, three months later, because rumours had
arrived at Athens in the meantime that Philip was either ill or dead.
Demosthenes accuses the Athenians of making such rumours their
excuse for inactivity, but it is fairer to say that they were forced to act
slowly because the information they received was dubious.[104]

The two instances in which chance news is apparently accepted
without consideration are the two concerning Agesilaos. These incidents are parallel, in that information is brought by an individual about
whom little is said in the source, yet the information is accepted and
acted on. Xenophon's description of 'a Cretan' coming direct to Agesilaos
seems to indicate that he was expected, while his account of Herodas
contains details which have led some historians to see Herodas not as
a chance messenger, but as an individual with some kind of official
standing. If he was personally known to the Spartans, it is hardly
surprising if his news was believed. Thucydides comments that the
Syracusans showed a lack of judgement in accepting the man from
Katana at face value, even though this was a messenger with a very
convincing story, suggesting that one would always expect such messengers to be received with scepticism.[105] Information which was believed to be suspect could simply be rejected, but the inscriptions for
Phanokritos and Philiskos show the dangers of this. In wartime, if the
news was disbelieved and neglected by a few men in a position of power,
this could later be brought to light, and those who had rejected it held
responsible.

It is clear from Thucydides that internal factors could have equal
influence on the reception of a messenger, and were sometimes para-

mount. The account of the episode in 428 concerning Mytilene is very interesting in this context. Those who brought the news of the impending revolt to Athens were eminently trustworthy, being the Athenian *proxenoi*, and thus known to the Athenian authorities. Yet the information which they brought was initially ignored by the generals, not because it was in itself incredible, or because they had other sources of information, but because, according to Thucydides, of wishful thinking, because the Athenian position was bad enough as it was.[106] It is of course possible that Thucydides is presenting a biased version of events, but this seems to reveal a certain flexibility in the Greek attitude towards news. Thucydides records that there was also a rejection of the news of the Sicilian disaster at Athens: the city as a whole, we are told, was unwilling to believe the news even when it arrived from informants with first-hand accounts.[107]

It is surprising that the news from Mytilene could be ignored so easily – if the informants presented their news to the assembly as well as the Boule, it implies that an opinion based on wishful thinking could direct the actions of the whole city. Further, the willingness to believe news could be affected by its political advantageousness: in a situation in which a polis was looking for an excuse for aggression towards an enemy, even an unlikely story would be believed if it provided the necessary reason for action. Equally, a polis seeking to avoid war would develop a more cautious approach to messengers. The reception of Herodas' news was influenced by the readiness of Lysander and Agesilaos to embark on a campaign against Persia at this time, while Xenophon is explicit about the motives that led Sparta to accept the embassy from Akanthos, and attack Olynthos, in 382 – the Akanthian envoy claimed to be informing the Spartans of a dangerous situation of which they were unaware, but all Sparta's allies realised that they simply wanted an excuse to attack.[108] Demosthenes, in contrast, relates that when the Athenians were reluctantly making preparations for the defence of Heraion Teichos against Philip in 352, it was reported (falsely) that Philip was either sick or dead, and the campaign was immediately abandoned.[109]

Adventitious messengers remained problematic once their news had been passed on, since it was harder for the polis to control the further dissemination of their story. Official messengers could be removed from the city quickly, and could be required, at least in theory, to keep news secret. The unofficial messenger, citizen or stranger, was more likely to encounter censorship. In ancient Greece, censorship was most commonly achieved by the removal of the individual from the community, rather than by censorship of books or other media.[110] The working of censorship is most easily seen in the case of Plutarch's barber: the man was taken away by the prytaneis to give him no opportunity to spread his disturbing news further.[111] There was of course more danger for the man who brought bad news, from the citizens as well as from the authorities; the death of the messenger at the hands of an angry mob became a commonplace idea. Herodotos tells the story of the sole surviving Athenian soldier who returned with news of defeat by Aigina: he was stabbed to death by the wives of the dead when they heard his news.[112] Beyond the arrest or removal of an individual, there was little that could be done to control the unofficial news-bringer, hence the comments of Demosthenes and Lysias about the dangers presented by *logopoioi*. The polis was at the mercy of individual news-bringers precisely because it needed to rely on both official and unofficial sources for the information it required.

*

It appears from the above that chance news could rarely be accepted at face value. All of the reactions show a perception of the inadequacy of news brought in this way. Where possible, news from an adventitious messenger was reinforced by being confirmed by a 'real' messenger, a representative of the city. The *proxenia* inscriptions provide evidence for a wish to avoid this kind of communication in the future, by rewarding the messenger with a grant that would give him an identity within the city. The grant of *proxenia* converts the unofficial messenger into an official one, allowing the state to exert some control over its information system.

A problem arose with messengers who reported to an individual rather than to the prytaneis, ephors or other authorities, as is suggested by Finley in the passage with which I began.[113] For a general with autocratic command, this need not be so serious – I have already demonstrated the Greek willingness to accept secrecy in this context. For individuals acting within the city, on the other hand, the status of a messenger reporting to them is more difficult. This is perhaps at the root of the unease felt by orators in naming their sources in the assembly – while a modern historian may find it normal for a politician to have 'personal associates and lieutenants' to pass on information, for the polis the status of such informants was confusing. They were not the kind to whom the procedures designed to judge credibility could be applied, and this is one of the reasons for Demosthenes' emphasis on the worthiness of his Macedonian source in the *Second Olynthiac*: 'a man incapable of lying'.[114] It is also true that in such cases information was being treated as a private rather than public commodity, and an analysis of events being offered to the assembly, not information allowing them to judge for themselves. The uncertainty which surrounded the adventitious messenger came to the fore when information from such a source was presented to the people.

5

The Assembly

Society is held together by communication and information.
Boswell's *Life of Johnson*, 15 April 1778

So far I have argued that most news arrived in the Greek polis through unofficial messengers and means, and that there was resistance to the idea of creating official channels for news. How can one place the political assembly in this interpretation? The ancient polis did not possess channels to broadcast news as news, in the way that government decisions or important events are reported by the press conference or press release in modern states. The popular assembly was the centre of political life in the democratic polis – it was a place where the citizens gathered regularly, and where polis business was discussed and decisions taken. The assembly has therefore long been characterised as the focus of news in the polis.

Because of its prominence, those examining the means of transmission of information in ancient Greek poleis have tended to assume that the political assembly in democracies, or other types of public assembly in other constitutions, had a primary role in both gathering and disseminating information. Hansen comments:

> The assembly was the obvious forum for notifications and announcements. Forty times in a year the ecclesia was attended by no less than a fifth or so of all adult male citizens.

Starr, similarly, in his interpretation of political intelligence in the Greek city, concentrates on the role of the politicians and generals in handling information.[1]

To understand how misleading this assumption can be we must first consider the nature and purpose of the assembly. Assemblies did not act as neutral centres for the general transmission of news. The news they disseminated, and the audience that they reached, were limited by the nature of the assembly itself, and I will demonstrate that the place of the assembly in the pattern of information flow within the city was at the same time less central, but more influential, than has previously been claimed. Most of our evidence, and all of our detailed evidence, concerns the Athenian assembly; discussion of Athens can nevertheless

indicate some fundamental attitudes, which are of relevance to all
states, and which have consequences for our understanding of the role
of the assembly in other kinds of constitution.

1. Symbolic functions of the assembly

At first sight, the purpose of the assembly appears to be transparent.
Matters relating to the military, economic, religious and political management of the state were discussed at the assembly, and news and
information on a variety of topics offered to the citizens, either directly
or indirectly, by announcements, speeches by politicians, magistrates'
reports and foreign embassies. We have several accounts of the organisation of the assembly in Athens, which give details of the matters
prescribed for discussion, and the topics on which politicians spoke. The
framework is outlined in the *Athenaion Politeia*: four assemblies were
required to be held in each prytany, and certain topics were prescribed
for discussion in each of these.[2] In the principal assembly (*ekklêsia
kuria*), there is to be the vote of confidence in the magistrates, discussion of the corn-supply and the defence of the country, and denuncia-
tions can be made. Lists of confiscated property, inheritances and
heiresses are to be read out. The second assembly of the prytany is for
supplications, while the third and fourth deal with three religious
matters, three concerning heralds and envoys and three secular matters. In the sixth prytany there is a vote on ostracism, and motions
against sycophants and those who break promises to the people.

Several points can be made about the agendas. The first is that the
topics scheduled for regular discussion tend to be matters internal to
the polis, not events of significance from outside. This of course held
true only for the four scheduled assemblies in each prytany; if decisions
needed to be taken because of unexpected events, an assembly could be
summoned to debate a particular matter, in addition to the agenda
requirements.[3] By its nature, the assembly was concerned with current
affairs of interest to the polis – an event or piece of information would
be reported or discussed only if it were directly relevant to a decision
that had to be taken. The reception of heralds from other poleis provided an opportunity for news from outside to enter the city, but the
presentation of such messengers was not guaranteed, being at the
discretion of the Boule.[4]

In 371 the unexpected defeat of Sparta by Thebes dramatically
altered the political situation in Greece, and the circumstances in which
the news of this was disseminated in Athens illustrate some of the
limits of the assembly system. The Thebans took it upon themselves to
send a herald to Athens to report their victory (a step unusual in itself),
and request Athenian aid in their expedition to the Peloponnese. The
herald was received by the Boule on the Akropolis, and his message was

discussed. The Boule proved to be unfavourable to the request for help, so the messenger left without being offered hospitality and without being presented to the assembly.[5] The news was not sought out by the Athenians to be announced in public; on the contrary, the news arrived through a Theban initiative, and was witheld from the assembly. This is not to say that the news of Leuktra did not circulate in Athens by other means, but it demonstrates that the role of the assembly was not to disseminate foreign news.

In general the information that was brought to the assembly was fairly haphazard, even on internal matters. Nor was there a system for the gathering of news, beyond what we see on the agenda. The assembly could tell to the citizens only the news that was brought to it, by citizens or foreigners, and to some extent was at the mercy of its sources. Rumour had to be reported, as with the suspicion of conspiracies alluded to by Athenagoras in the Syracusan assembly in 415, and in special cases opportunities were provided for citizens to come forward (or even non-citizens, as in the Mysteries case), but the information was plainly not always reliable.[6]

The purpose behind the transmission of news by a state authority tends to be complex. In Athens, certainly, the presentation of news simply because it was interesting, though of no present use, was rare. Most obviously, news was given to the people in assembly to allow them to decide the appropriate course of action. But news also has an implicit function in defining the dominant ideology of the state. To be considered newsworthy, events, though unexpected, must be of an expected kind; they must be consonant with the beliefs and expectations of both transmitter and audience.[7] Just as gossip serves to define and enforce social mores, so news from an official source both defines and upholds the ideology of that authority. In the Athenian assembly, this worked in several ways: the type of news that was offered confirmed the authority of the assembly, protected the citizens in threatening situations, and reinforced the principles of democracy.

One of the few situations when the assembly does appear to be simply disseminating news is the announcement of military victories. A defeat generally required a decision of some kind by the assembly, and hence an announcement of defeat allows both motivations, but victory could be simply announced without need for further action. We have seen that generals on campaign kept in touch with the state by dispatch, and Aischines makes a claim for particular favour from the citizens in his Embassy speech, because he brought the news of the victory at Tamynai to Athens in 349/8.[8] Just as it was important for a general to keep in touch with the polis, so it was equally important for the polis to be seen to pass on information received from its agents to the citizens.

The opening of Plato's *Charmides* makes a clear distinction between the official announcement in the assembly, and news heard from a friend or acquaintance. Sokrates has returned from a campaign at Potidaia, and his friends ask him for news:

> Indeed, it was reported here, he said, that the fighting was very fierce, and that many of our acquaintance died in it .... So sit down here and tell us everything in detail, for we haven't yet heard a clear account.[9]

Obviously one would derive different information from private sources, which would tailor an account to one's particular concerns. The assembly alone could not supply all necessary information, but it provided the citizens with a basic outline of events affecting themselves and the city.

A longer account, of events in the assembly after the news arrived about the loss of Elateia in 339, describes in detail the practice that was followed:

> It was evening, and a messenger came to the prytaneis with the news that Elateia had been taken. Some of them straightaway got up from their dinner and drove the people from their stalls in the Agora, and set fire to the booths. Others sent for the generals and summoned the herald; and the city was full of uproar. On the following day, as soon as it was light, the prytaneis called a council meeting in the Bouleuterion, and you [the citizens] went off to the assembly. Before they had completed their business and framed a proposal, all of the citizens were sitting up on the Pnyx. After this, when the Boule had come in, and the prytaneis announced the news they had received, and brought forward the messenger to report it himself, the herald put the question, 'Who wishes to speak?'[10]

There was little obvious need for the news to be delivered at this time, since it had clearly been effectively circulated the previous night. The supplying of accurate information, as opposed to indefinite rumour, was obviously important here, but it is hard to imagine that the basic facts were not known. Here we have the assembly fulfilling another part of its function, that of containing difficult or threatening events within the structured framework of the polis.

The insistence on correct procedure under such circumstances, the formal announcement of the news and the introduction of the messenger to deliver his statement, all make the news of defeat less threatening by the conviction that the proper process is being followed. Even in less extreme circumstances, the element of mediating information through the system of the assembly remains significant. There was a sense in which the purpose of the assembly was to affirm the role of the polis by the act of informing its citizens. Where information was given in a straightforward way, as we see from the agendas, it was on matters important within Athens and which occurred with predictable frequency, such as confiscation of properties or inheritances. The intention given in the *Athenaion Politeia*, 'so that nothing should escape anyone's notice' is very like the principle of *ho boulomenos*, 'anyone who wishes', being able to see a law or decree – the availability of the information is what matters.[11] Hansen sees the assembly as an important centre for the dissemination of news generated within the polis, stating, 'it is reasonable to assume that any citizen affected by the proclamations was expected to approach the competent magistrate after the session', but there is more to this than simply providing a central point where such information could be broadcast.[12] With the announcement of honours, for instance, the motive was not solely to inform, as a significant part of the honour accorded by the state was the announcement itself before the assembled citizens. The fact that an announcement was made was as or more important than the information that it contained; the nature of the assembly as symbolic centre of the polis dictated the range of information that it offered.[13] The assembly was important in the state as the symbol of democracy, and much of what went on there had a symbolic value in what it represented to the people.

The example of the Elateia debate illustrates further that news passed on by the assembly was rarely very new. The prytaneis were required to publish the agenda for an assembly in writing, and four or five days in advance, and this was exhibited usually before the statues of the Eponymous Heroes in the Agora.[14] Word-of-mouth was undoubtedly important for the spread of the news that an assembly was to be held, and our sources demonstrate that most citizens attending an assembly would know in advance the matters to be discussed, and very probably hold an opinion on them too. The debates recorded by Thucydides on the fate of the Mytilenean prisoners in 427 show an assembly that had predecided the issue: when the Mytileneans and their supporters wanted the debate reopened,

> they won their point the more easily because it was clear to the authorities that most of the people wanted an opportunity to reverse their judgement.[15]

In Aristophanes' *Ekklesiazusai* the foolish Blepyros may be unaware of the reason for the assembly that has been held, but his neighbour Chremes clearly expects him to remember the day's main topic:

> Blepyros: But what was on the agenda, to bring out such a crowd so early?
> Chremes: Surely you remember – the prytaneis decided to canvass opinion on how the city can be saved.[16]

while at the start of Aristophanes' *Acharnians* Dikaiopolis has travelled in from the country to the assembly in order to ensure that nothing but peace is discussed. The more important the news, the more likely it was to be known independently of the assembly.

Most of the detailed accounts of assemblies that we have relate to

situations of gravity or danger, when the reason for the assembly was
widely known beforehand, and the people gathered to hear speeches on
a topic they already knew – the debate after Elateia, that over the
sending of the Sicilian Expedition, the Mytilene Debate, the assembly
after Aigospotamoi.[17] Plutarch's *Nikias* and *Alkibiades* state that
Alkibiades encouraged informal discussion of his proposal for the expedition to Sicily before the assembly was held, and that groups of men
sat about in the gymnasia and public places drawing maps and discussing it.[18] Certainly in these cases the demos appear to have formed an
opinion before the debate was held.

Indeed, some aspects of forthcoming business would be difficult to
keep secret: the very presence of a foreign embassy in a city would be a
matter of note, when the ambassadors would stay at the house of a
proxenos for some time before being introduced to the assembly.[19]
Demosthenes often introduces statements in his political speeches with
tags such as 'as you all know', and while one may see rhetorical
technique in this, as in legal speeches, such a claim could not be made
if completely untrue.[20] Even if the assemblies about which we know
most were anomalous, in that they were emergency measures called to
debate a specific event, it does not imply that regular assemblies, in
contrast, provided people with news they had not previously heard, only
that the business transacted was more mundane and internal.

The requirement that matters be debated first by the Boule also
meant that news was not produced for the first time in the assembly.[21]
What was discussed and decided in the assembly then became newsworthy in its own right and was spread by other means: we have many
examples of citizens asking what had been decided. Should this imply
that a consideration of the assembly has no place in a discussion of
news? Information coming to the polis, however it arrived, official or
unofficial, was ultimately brought before the people in the assembly,
whether or not it was known beforehand. It was very often not news to
anyone who was there, having entered the polis or been disseminated
previously, and this was usually necessary if a proposition was to be
discussed. The assembly system, however, provided opportunities for
the mediation and control of that news in significant ways. Furthermore, the nature of assembly debate also conditioned the way the
audience thought about news. I will examine three key areas: what
news was disseminated through the assembly, how it was presented,
and how the audience's expectations conditioned their reactions to the
news.

2. Information and leadership

Xenophon's *Memorabilia* provides a good illustration of some of the
attitudes towards information in the assembly. *Memorabilia* 3.6 con-

sists of Sokrates' advice to Glaukon, whose ambition to become a leading politician in Athens has been thwarted by a poor reception in the assembly. Glaukon's inadequate preparation for his role of adviser to the assembly is exposed, as Sokrates enumerates the topics which he should be competent to discuss, and forces him to admit his ignorance. This seems to represent a Xenophontic/Sokratic ideal rather than the reality depicted by historians and orators; the orator should know all these things, but that does not mean that every speaker in fact did. Nevertheless, those topics which Sokrates singles out as important for the public speaker are interesting; they are economic and military – the state revenue and expenses, the relative strengths of Athens and other states, the defence of the country and requirements for imports of corn. This accords closely with Aristotle's list of the most important topics of deliberative oratory in the *Rhetorika*: resources, war and peace, the defence of the country, the food supply and legislation.[22] Most of these topics are internal to the state, and the expectation is that this kind of information could be gathered within the polis, and did not require special sources. On the question of making the state richer, for instance, both sources suggest that an orator should be able to list the income and the expenditure of the state, which Glaukon has been unable to do simply for lack of preparation.[23] Similarly Sokrates suggests that he would be able to find out about the income from the silver mines at Laurion by visiting the area.[24]

Glaukon is criticised by Sokrates not because he is unable to inform the people of what they need to know, but because he lacks the personal preparation which would enable him to speak with authority. He is not endowed with particular resources unavailable to anyone else in Athens, and he is expected to be able to discover the facts from records already in existence. In Aristophanes' *Wasps* Bdelykleon does some quick reckoning of the city's income from the empire and its expenditure on jury pay, suggesting that information of this nature was readily available to any citizen.[25] Glaukon is said to have suffered ridicule in the assembly because of his lack of authority, which would suggest that the audience he was addressing could be expected to be as well-informed as he.

On matters outside the state, it is not clear that the kind of information that Sokrates is recommending was even possible to discover, except in a very vague form. For example, ideas about the military strength of other states are always indefinite. In another passage from the *Memorabilia* Sokrates advises Perikles on the defence of Attika. He advances the idea that the Athenians outnumber the Boiotians, but without any factual discussion; his arguments are entirely abstract.[26] There was no central register of this kind of information in Athens itself, listing numbers of ships, men or resources, and the discussion of Athenian manpower in Demosthenes' *Philippics* reveals some flexibility in listing numbers and expenses.[27] The Spartan habit of living in scattered villages, retained after other states had built their cities, may have been intended to prevent outsiders seeing the total number of Spartiates and gaining an idea of Spartan manpower, but access to this kind of information would depend on chance and guesswork.[28] Thus it suggests that while orators need to have certain information at their disposal, specialised statistical information was not expected.

Was the same true of information about foreign events? In his public speeches Demosthenes appears at various points to have access to privileged information about states outside Attika. In his speech *On the Letter*, for instance, he describes the fear and distrust which Philip inspires in allies and subjects alike. His generals fear him most of all, says Demosthenes,

> and no one in their right mind can disbelieve this. For it is reported by those who have lived with him ....[29]

Yet the way he presents apparently privileged information is noteworthy. Not only does he make little attempt to substantiate any of the information he has about Philip or events elsewhere in Greece, there are occasions when it was clearly possible for him to supply details of the source for his information, but he does not. In the *First Olynthiac* he states that the Thessalians are intending to resist Philip's interventions, and claims a personal source for this information ('I heard from certain individuals'). The individuals are not named, and no support is offered for the credibility of the information.[30] When it came to discussing Macedonia, a modern view would expect that a politician claiming to offer the best advice would have had to supply extra information gathered personally, and such information, if used to promote a certain policy, should have been shown to have some basis in fact.[31] But the kind of substantiation that Demosthenes offers is demonstrated in the *Second Olynthiac*: 'as I heard from a man who had recently been in that place, an individual incapable of lying.'[32]

It is notable that where detail is lacking in the speeches is particularly on matters of external affairs, foreign events and history. Should we suppose that better information or sources were used, but that in preparation for publication this information was excised? The sources themselves suggest that information was difficult to gather. In Sicily in 415 the information the Syracusans could receive from Athens was vague and indefinite, while in the 330s Aischines could afford to make comic capital from his opponent's detailed knowledge of foreign affairs:

> This is the man, Athenians, who first discovered Serrion Teichos and Doriskos, and Ergiske and Myrtiske, and Ganos and Ganias, places whose very names were previously unknown to us.[33]

At all points where recommendations are made to the aspiring orator, the list of subjects on which he is expected to be informed relates mainly to internal affairs. The kind of information required by an orator about other states is very vague.[34] The *Memorabilia* passage on Glaukon shows that if an orator spoke without knowledge of his own city's affairs, he could expect that the audience would recognise his ignorance and react accordingly. But no such indication is given for similar attitudes to knowledge of foreign affairs, and the reason for this is not hard to discern. The democratic system at Athens required that the citizen participated directly in the decision-making process, and that many gained first-hand experience of the running of the city by service in the Boule, and thus it is in keeping with the ethos of the polis to expect a certain level of understanding of internal affairs.

Going abroad, however, was fraught with suspicion, and nowhere more so than in the charged atmosphere of political debate. Demosthenes is wary of revealing contacts outside the polis, and demonstrates unease about some of the areas where he might have had particular knowledge, for example over Thebes. As Theban proxenos he had friends in that polis, but is concerned to play down the closeness of these contacts in case he should be suspected of favouring Thebes: in some cases too much knowledge could make one suspect.[35] Aischines demonstrates that he was vulnerable to accusations about his links with Thebes: 'it was then that the cause was lost, not because of my actions, but through your treachery, Demosthenes, and your public friendship (*proxenia*) with Thebes.'[36] Reluctance to reveal certain facts also appears to affect his discussion of Macedonia: Demosthenes had in fact been to Macedonia on embassies, and had friends there, but the information he offers from this source is knowledge of character rather than of facts. As reported by Aischines, Demosthenes claimed to have accurate knowledge of what Alexander planned to do on his accession, but this accuracy was claimed from understanding of his character, not of his plans: 'and he claimed that this statement was based not on conjecture, but on accurate knowledge.'[37] To indicate specific sources of information in Macedonia, especially non-Athenian ones, would open him to further attack.

We can thus be fairly sure that Demosthenes did not substantiate the facts he offered, where there is no support given to them in the speeches. He is also deliberately vague and avoids giving details of events, either because the audience is presumed to know them already, or because it was unnecessary. The presupposition of public knowledge can be seen, for example, in his reference to the Thracian intrigues of the kings Kotys and Miltokythes as something which everyone knows, which is unlikely in the extreme.[38] It is obviously a convenient rhetorical strategy, but was this unwillingness to go into detail also intended to flatter the assembly-goers? Aischines' attitude towards this varies according to the effect he is trying to achieve – he mocks Demosthenes' precision with the names of the Thracian forts (and Demosthenes accordingly reveals embarrassment about his pedantry), yet he also criticises Demosthenes' actions in claiming a divine source for information from a more earthly authority. On learning from Charidemos' scouts that Philip was dead, he claims, Demosthenes pretended to have heard the information from Zeus and Hera in a dream.[39] In a speech like this it is not hard to see every possible event being twisted to use against the opponent, and consequently one should not imagine that Aischines was calling for Demosthenes to name his sources accurately. But these two examples reveal two interesting ideas.

In the first place, Demosthenes evidently did have some special sources of information about Macedonia, although there is nothing to suggest that the scouts reported to him alone. There does appear to be a distinction made on social grounds between those sources the orators will cite, and those they will not. Aischines quotes from letters from the generals Chares and Proxenos in the Embassy speech, but Demosthenes chose to pretend that his knowledge was divinely inspired, rather than admit that he had heard it from Charidemos' scouts.[40] Similarly the 'man incapable of lying' who provided Demosthenes with his Macedonian information may well have rated no accurate citation because he was not important enough to be considered a serious witness. If he was someone who had recently been in the area, perhaps he was no more than an ordinary soldier. If references to informants of low status have been omitted from the symbouleutic speeches we possess, and from historical accounts too, this may leave a false impression of the amount of control such people had over information.[41]

Secondly, Aischines' attitude over Demosthenes' specialised knowledge of the forts is important. If Aischines could afford to mock Demosthenes for digging up obscure names, does this imply that specialised knowledge was not expected, or actually counter-productive? In other words, how much was an orator supposed to know? There are two poles of opinion on this question, one that sees the orator as morally required to gain all the specialised knowledge he could, and to lead the people by virtue of his better information, and the other seeing the orator as by and large an ordinary man, who led through personality, but allowed the assembly to make its own informed decisions. One aspect of this question has been discussed by Thompson, who argues that the growing complexity of financial affairs at Athens during and after the Peloponnesian War was not matched by the emergence of leaders who gained their influence by reason of expertise in financial matters.[42] Instead, even in the fourth century, political leaders continued to gain their positions by virtue of eloquence and personal qualities, while the management of the state finances was carried out as before by the annual magistrates; thus a political leader was not expected to be a specialist. Our sources in fact praise most highly the statesman who possesses foresight, the ability to foretell what will happen, rather than any practical knowledge.[43]

Starr, in discussing the processing of information within Athens, represents the role of the political executive as very great, and that of the citizens as correspondingly small.[44] He represents the authorities as trying to control the random introduction of rumour into the city, because this could cause panic, and considers the orators as the main link between the authorities and the citizens. This causes him to interpret the orators as part of the political executive, controlling the information for the citizens' own good. He sees the lack of substantiation in Demosthenes' speeches as reflecting what the people wanted – they preferred to believe in the character of a speaker than to be told facts and details. The main distinction that Starr draws is between statesmen and councillors, and the mass of the people, who knew little and cared less about events; information, in his interpretation, was primarily for the use of a political élite.[45]

At this point it is instructive to reconsider Demosthenes' *Philippics*. It has been argued many times that in this period Demosthenes' policies were mistaken from start to finish, and that the Athenians deserve all credit for rejecting his calls for aggression.[46] It is in some ways remarkable that such rhetorical tours-de-force as the *Philippics* should fail, even if they do represent mistaken policy, and Demosthenes' own answer to this, to blame the Athenian unwillingness to fight, is not satisfactory on its own. But the problem in this context lies in the information presented to the assembly in the *Philippics*: was Demosthenes being deliberately deceitful? In encouraging the Athenians to fight he constantly made capital from Philip's supposed infringements of the Peace of 346 – in Thrace, Euboia, Megara and Central Greece. Was there a basis for his accusations? From what we know of Greek affairs during these years, much of what Demosthenes says is exaggerated or distorted, and this emerges in the type of accusation he makes.

In the Crown speech he produces a list of accusations relating to the breaking of the Peace of Philokrates, confused in structure and vague in detail.[47] He says that Philip was *Megarois epicheirôn*, 'making an attempt on Megara', a description designed to stir up feeling but not detailed enough to be valuable, since the account from Plutarch's *Phokion* suggests a case of internal strife, with one side looking to Philip for support.[48] Similarly the accusations about Euboia are vague, and the evidence we possess about Euboian affairs at this time again indicates internal strife rather than invasion by Philip. This kind of approach to his information, menacing but vague, is discernible on other topics too – in order to magnify his own services to the state, he produces a list of those who have sacrificed the interests of their country for Philip's money.[49] The list is rhetorically arranged and the later comments of Polybios, that Demosthenes is casting his net far too widely, at least throw doubt on the truth of all these accusations.[50] This must surely be classed as deceit, if Demosthenes is producing vague but untrue threats to promote his policy.

But how much information on such affairs could Demosthenes himself command? Finley suggests that Demosthenes' speeches on Macedonia in the years 346-339 provide good evidence of 'the central role of personal associates and lieutenants in Greek politics'.[51] Large numbers of information-gatherers are not visible in the sources; one cannot simply say that their presence has been excised, while references to minor informants remain. In places where it benefits Demosthenes' case to be more detailed, he is able to produce decrees and minute accounts of internal Athenian affairs, but he invariably speaks in outline only about external events. The *First Olynthiac* furnishes a very good example of this – Demosthenes says:

> we must suppose that the Paionians and Illyrians will not suffer subjection, being unused to obedience, as they say. And by Zeus I think it's true.[52]

The resumé of Philip's affairs at this point is based not on fact but on supposition and hearsay, and this is the only type of private information that the orator offers.

If Demosthenes gives no sign in his speeches of having better information than anyone else, this is hardly surprising in view of what has been said above. Starr's interpretation of the role of orators in the processing of information must be open to question here, because no one was a permanent member of the Boule, and thus full-time politicians usually had no better access to the information entering the city than any other citizen. It is most likely that the details of what Philip has done are necessarily vague, since Demosthenes was as much at the mercy of rumour as any other Athenian, and that he simply presented these rumours in the way that best suited his purposes. Athenian orators would not normally have privileged information, unless they went as soldiers or state representatives to the states which they discuss: the vagueness of their accounts stems not only from reluctance to reveal facts or knowledge, but the necessity to make the most capital out of the information that they had.

The people, in their turn, did not look to speakers in the assembly to hear accurate new information about foreign affairs, and were prepared to take what they were told here at face value, relying on their estimation of the speaker. This in its turn affected what people thought of information as it entered the city – news from abroad could be disbelieved, and the possession of specific information about external affairs was considered unnecessary, and slightly problematic, in contrast to the emphasis placed on a general understanding of internal polis affairs. It was not simply the fact that accurate information was hard to gather that caused the vagueness of what Demosthenes has to say about Macedonia, but the fact that it could make him suspect: what was said was not considered more important than how it was said.

3. The nature of the discussion

News which entered the city through the assembly was not disseminated in any straightforward way. Demosthenes *Against Polykles* gives an account of a decision taken in the assembly to mobilise Athenian forces against Philip: 'an assembly was held, and many serious matters were reported to you; you voted that the trierarchs should launch their ships.'[53] The speaker recounts the matters that were brought before the demos (the seizure of Tenos, trouble in the Chersonese, problems with the corn supply), not so much listing the agenda for the assembly in question, as recalling the substance of the speeches made in support of the proposal at the time. Thus we see certain facts being stated to the assembly by the speakers (and their supporters, an important formulation, revealing the role of personal networks), about the topic of the motion, on the basis of which the vote was then taken.

This was not news for the information of the citizens, but facts designed to influence the decision of the voters. A speaker who supported a motion, for example to mobilise forces, would obviously seek to suggest that a great threat was at hand, whereas one opposing the motion would deny or belittle the same events. This is what we see in Thucydides' account of the debate in the assembly at Syracuse in 415.[54] Of the two speakers Hermokrates describes the threat of invasion in emotional terms and dwells on the military threat to be met, while Athenagoras is keen to dismiss it, although both were speaking from the same information. The basis on which the vote would be taken was thus the persuasiveness of the various speakers, and the personal opinions of the hearers.

The nature of debate in the assembly becomes problematic when one considers the content of some of the speeches, political and legal, which we possess. In the Crown speech Demosthenes defends his actions as an orator and leader of the state from the Peace of Philokrates up to the present.[55] There is an obvious problem in judging the truth of the claims he makes about these events, given that the Crown and Embassy speeches, by Demosthenes and Aischines, together with the other speeches of Demosthenes, are our only sources for these events. It is clear, however, that the narratives offered by Demosthenes and Aischines for these years are contradictory, for example over the responsibility for the Peace of Philokrates itself. The problem arises from what the speakers reveal about the audience's understanding of events.

Demosthenes claims in the Crown speech that because it has taken six years for the case to come to trial, Aischines is now able to distort the facts and alter dates and decrees, which he would not have been able to do had the case been tried immediately:

> it would not have been possible then; all the statements would have had to be truthful, since events were recent and you still remembered them, and had the facts almost at your fingertips.[56]

This should imply that recent events can be backed up by appeals to decrees and factual material, but in practice even recent events are presented through the medium of memory and oral tradition, rather than by decrees and proofs. References to recent court cases and similar are backed up by appeals to the jury – Demosthenes rejects Aischines' claim that the Lokrians were proceeding against Athens, and challenges Aischines to say who in the audience would substantiate it: 'show me who knows this, point him out.'[57] Similarly, even though Demosthenes has claimed that events of six years ago are distant, he appeals to memory for events: in referring to his trial in 338, he says, 'For you know and remember that I was put on trial every day in that first period.'[58]

Thomas, in her study of oral tradition, documents many instances in the orators where the audience are assumed to know about events 'from their elders' or as common knowledge.[59] There was not, however, one simple version of events. The awareness that a story could be told in different ways and that competing accounts existed dates back to Herodotos, who recounts alternative versions of events with more or less discrimination.[60] Equally we should not expect to find orators appealing to one true account, backed up with facts; instead they made the best use of competing stories. The nature of Greek judicial procedure provides an important parallel here – the aim of a Greek trial was not to establish the truth, but to decide betweeen two competing versions of events, and evidence was accordingly used to provide support for one's account, rather than to establish a true version of events.[61] Although all those attending the assembly or trial might remember and know, or even have participated in events, we do not see the expectation that they would cling to one interpretation; events from only a few years previously, which are explicitly stated to be remembered by the audience, are still offered in accounts which differ according to the demands of the speech.[62] One needs to examine how the influence of rhetoric affected the value placed on factual information.

Rhetoric emerged as an art in the late fifth century. The main contemporary criticism of rhetorical teaching was that it allowed a speaker to argue both sides of a case, right and wrong, an idea which originated with Protagoras.[63] There was an early perception that the use of rhetoric led away from a reliance on fact. As I noted above, there are profound differences between Greek and modern legal practice; what is really remarkable about ancient Athenian legal cases is that decisions were not necessarily based on the interpretation of the legal code established by the court. The litigants cited the laws which they felt to be appropriate, and it was common for them to call laws into doubt or deny their rectitude in order to help their case.[64] Arguments from probability, ethos and pathos were accorded as much credibility as physical evidence; both, in legal terms, were *pisteis*, supporting arguments rather than proof.[65] In the *Rhetorika ad Alexandrum* direct proofs are referred to as 'supplementary', and the main emphasis in the legal context is on proof from probability, and we see this borne out in the existing speeches, with their emphasis on character and ethos.[66] This stems from the idea that while a witness could be bribed to lie, or evidence forged, an argument from probability is always susceptible to critical examination by the dikast.

All this obviously relates to procedure in the lawcourts, but it has important implications for what went on in the assembly. Aristotle describes what the orator needs to know in the *Rhetorika*, and it is clear that some kinds of information were hard to find out, especially on matters outside the polis.[67] But decisions still had to be made, and grounds provided to support an argument, so rhetoric gained a correspondingly greater importance. No doubt this worked both ways: the lack of accessible information led to greater reliance on rhetorical arguments, and the audience became correspondingly more used to abstract arguments being used to decide matters of public fact.

The relationship between rhetoric and fact was not purely oppositional, but more complex. Most significant is the application of rhetoric to fields such as science, which led to a predominant tendency to view scientific debate as a contest like a legal or political agon.[68] Since subjects such as medicine were open to debate, it was necessary for a doctor to be capable of defending his ideas and methods, and indeed there was some overlap between private and public roles; a doctor could also act as public physician or advisor, while a philosopher might find medicine a suitable field for debate. According to Buxton,

> [The Greeks] ... extended the range of issues which might be publicly argued about to include an unprecedentedly wide area: politics, morality, law, ontology, theology, medicine.[69]

In medicine one of the criteria for theories was that they be effective in an agon, and we find a treatment being advanced in the following way: 'This treatment is good and correct, and natural, and as well it has a striking quality (*agônistikon*) to it.'[70] The primacy of debate meant that the testing and criticism of theories took second place, and there was more dogmatism than open-mindedness. Obviously if one's main concern was to uphold a theory against those of one's rivals, the last thing one would do is question it in public.

It is hardly surprising if politics too was considered more as a debate than as a means of reaching the best decision. In fact, these are precisely the grounds on which the assembly attracts criticism from Demosthenes and others: that it is more interested in the form of a speech than its content. Criticism of the assembly, and of rhetors, is clear in Demosthenes' speeches. Of course he was himself a political orator, keen to denigrate his opponents and promote his own image as virtuous leader, so what he says about the other orators is no doubt biased. On general points, however, his depiction of oratorical practice in the assembly is quite damaging. He expresses the fear that because the case about the crown has taken so long to come to court, and the events concerned were so long ago, the case will be seen as no more than a *rhêtorôn agôn*, a contest between speakers, and this idea is repeated in the Embassy speech. He suggests that there was felt to be a danger of the facts of the case being obscured by rhetorical skill, and the best speaker rather than the right man winning the case.[71] The same fear is expressed in the context of the assembly, that the most persuasive speaker will carry the day, whether or not his advice is the best.[72]

Demosthenes represents himself as the only reliable orator, and this is no more than standard practice, but some of the things he has to say about Aischines reflect criticism of orators in general. Aischines is accused of manipulating facts, laws and dates to help his case, and Demosthenes equally goes out of his way to deny that he is doing the same. Elsewhere he breaks out into general abuse of the rhetor who thinks and says different things.[73] On their own, such criticisms might not carry much weight. But not only does Aischines have similar comments to make about orators' abuse of their skills, there is also a strong correspondence with the defects of the assembly as described by Thucydides almost a hundred years before.

In the public orations, the fault that Demosthenes continually attributes to all other speakers is that they study to please their audience, but fail to give good advice.[74] While it was possible for a self-serving politician to attempt to mislead the assembly with a specious or untrue argument, the opposite danger was also present – some speakers could be led to diverge from fact because of the reception they might receive. The threat of unpopularity accruing to the speaker who offered unwelcome information or suggestions was apparently a serious one, affecting the accuracy of the reports that the assembly heard. In 414/3 Nikias suspected his messengers of making the situation in Sicily appear better than it was when they reported to the assembly, and one of the reasons advanced for this is the pressure of expectation at Athens. Orators tend to apologise for offering bad news or prognoses.[75] The attitude of the assembly is documented by Thucydides, in the reception at Athens of the news of the revolt of Mytilene in 428; the people were reluctant to believe the bad news out of wishful thinking.[76] Demosthenes' condemnation, however, is not one-sided; the *Fourth Philippic* contains a criticism of the assembly, that they sit and listen while the news is being discussed, but afterwards go away and forget about it.[77]

Thucydides depicts the debate on Mytilene between Kleon and Diodotos partly in order to comment on procedure in the assembly in his day, in line with his chapter on the decline of politics since Perikles' day. Perikles' successors, he says, 'set themselves to pleasing the people, and surrendered control of affairs', and the Mytilene Debate is one of the passages in which this is illustrated.[78] Kleon's speech makes a direct attack on the attitude of the people towards the politicians – they are speech-goers and would rather listen to accounts of action than act. He points out the harm that persuasion can do when it replaces fact:

> You judge future events, whether something is possible or not, on the basis of clever speeches, and as for past events, you consider what you have seen yourselves less trustworthy than accounts you have heard about them, and form your judgements from the words of skilled orators.

and this recurs in Diodotos' speech too, as a general Thucydidean criticism of the assembly.[79] Diodotos, in contrast to Kleon, upholds the primacy of the word and debate, whereas Kleon has called for action to replace words. For Diodotos, however, the assembly demands deceit from speakers, some of whom do use misrepresentation to persuade the city into 'dishonourable actions'. At the start of the assembly, deceitful speakers were cursed in the opening formulae, demonstrating an awareness of the potential for harm in this way:

> This is why the herald pronounces a curse in each assembly, not on those who are themselves misled, but on the man who makes deceitful speeches to the Boule or people or court.[80]

Most importantly, Diodotos says that if certain orators did not speak, the city would not be persuaded into making so many mistakes.[81] His view, that bad and irresponsible speakers led the city into making serious mistakes, is a serious criticism of the use of persuasion. Thucydides illustrates this idea both here – the suggestion is that the *pithanôtatos* (forceful and persuasive) Kleon has led the people to make the first, mistaken, decision to kill the Mytilenians – and later, in Book 6, when the decision to send the large expedition to Sicily is the result of a miscalculated attempt by Nikias to manipulate the assembly. The decision to condemn the generals after the battle of Arginusai was, by Xenophon's account, the same kind of decision – when the people reconsidered their actions, they said that they had been deceived by the speakers, especially Kallixenos.[82] This is the lack of accountability to which Diodotos is referring – the use of persuasion meant that the people took less responsibility for their decisions. This attitude is revealed in Thucydides' treatment of the failure of the Sicilian Expedition; he depicts the Athenians doing just this, blaming those who had misled them: 'when they realised the truth about the disaster, the people were angry with those of the public speakers who had been most enthusiastic for the venture, as though they had not voted for it themselves.'[83]

The central question about the assembly is the role of the orators in advising the people, and Diodotos presents the general Thucydidean view of the assembly, where the people have a small and superficial understanding of affairs, and rely on the orators to be told what to think.[84] But if one allows that the people did rely on the speakers for their information about political affairs, they were clearly at the mercy of any unscrupulous speaker. Should one therefore see the people constantly led astray by the misused eloquence of the orators? This is a claim that Demosthenes advances against both Aischines – 'as happened formerly, when he brought about the destruction of the unhappy Phokians by making a false report here to you' – and others in *Against Leptines*.[85] It is of course impossible to judge in retrospect the difference between the ideal and actual policies, but Athens' failures can be understood as large and systemic, rather than stemming from an individual's mistaken policies. The strength of the city must argue, despite the orators' claims, that relatively few mistakes were made.[86]

Did what the demos saw and heard in the assembly affect their attitude towards truth? Just as Demosthenes harks back to the good old days of the assembly during the Peloponnesian War, so Thucydides looks back to the time of Perikles, when speakers did not study to please but gave good advice without concern for popular approval.[87] If there never really was such a state of affairs, it suggests that political thinkers saw something lacking in the process of the assembly, which was so easily manipulated by the orators. What comes over most strongly in Thucydides' history is the way in which topics were argued in the assembly, in abstract, not factual terms.[88] It is not only Thucydides who presents this view of deliberative speeches; in Xenophon too, Euryptolemos' speech in the Arginusai debate argues both about the principle involved and the 'actual facts'.[89] Plainly the abstract argument could hold as much sway as the factual. If the Athenians became conditioned to discuss everything, both legal and public matters, in abstract terms, the importance attached to facts became correspondingly devalued. On more recent affairs, the orators rarely refer to events in a neutral way; an indication is usually given of how the event should be remembered, the speaker often providing his own resumé of what happened. In this, too, the memory of the demos was required to be flexible.

4. Secrecy within government

The *Hellenika Oxyrhynchia* relates that in 396 the Athenian Demainetos made a secret agreement with the Boule, and sailed to join Konon, who was in command of the Persian fleet. Demainetos went in a state-owned ship, without the agreement of the demos. When the matter became known there was popular outcry, the Boule attempted to dissociate themselves from the venture, and Demainetos was punished.[90] This story reveals both that it was possible for the Boule to act, or to authorise actions, independently of the assembly, and that this was unacceptable to the demos when it was discovered.

Secrecy on the part of the Boule, or of groups of politicians, was recognised as a threat. Stories abound of individuals, generals or politicians who tried to keep the demos in ignorance of their plans, of the Boule setting up secret agreements, and orators practising secrecy over state matters. There is of course a fundamental problem with secrecy in historical accounts: those of which we know are by definition unsuccessful secrets, and those successfully kept can never be known. Further, accusations of secret dealings are a stock in trade of the orators, and the credibility of such claims must be open to doubt. Nevertheless, the number of secrecy stories is striking: Diodoros tells us that in 477 Themistokles was unwilling to divulge his plan for the fortification of the Piraeus in public, and asked the assembly to refer the decision to the Boule in secret, and abide by their decision, which they duly did; Demosthenes refers to the 'much-discussed secret arrangement' between Philip and Athens about Amphipolis.[91] Aischines plays on the idea when he claims that Demosthenes called a secret session of the Boule in order to undermine Aischines' support of the Amphiktyonic war against Amphissa.[92] Andokides, in *On His Return*, claims that he has communicated to the Boule in secret the services that he is about to render the state, to do with the grain shortage, because the council have more responsibility and are more likely to reach the right decision.[93] It is not at all clear why secrecy should be necessary, nor why the people should be judged incompetent to debate the matter. It was obviously useful for Andokides to be able to hint at great benefits without naming them, and he is surely disingenuous in saying that he only wishes he could reveal his secret.[94]

Secrecy in domestic matters is sometimes stated to be necessary, as we saw in Chapter 3 concerning military affairs. In some cases there was a clear need for the short-term control of information, either by the

Boule, or by some other small group. This was particularly so with conspiracies, such as that documented by Andokides in *On the Mysteries*. When information was brought to the assembly about the profanation of the Mysteries, the meeting was cleared of non-initiates, and the matter discussed in secret.[95] Examples like this are easy to understand – the exclusion of those not initiated is explicable in religious terms, and it illustrates the close links between politics and religion, that the political organs of the state should make judgements of this kind. Other secret meetings of the Boule are explicable in the same way: secret meetings were 'on matters which were bound to be made public sooner or later, and where the advantage to be derived from secrecy was surprise action, usually against offending citizens or a foreign state'.[96] Thus the control of information about a suspected conspiracy was a necessary short-term measure of which all could see the need.

If the purpose of the Boule in keeping some matters secret was to prevent information reaching an enemy, this too could be understood. This is Diodoros' explanation for Themistokles' appeal to the Boule for a secret decision: to prevent news of his plans reaching the Spartans, who would prevent the building of fortifications.[97] To be free with information and unable to keep secrets is seen as an occupational hazard of a democracy; what Thucydides presents as an ideal, Demosthenes isolates as a problem eighty years later. Philip, he says, hears of every Athenian plan as it is made in the assembly, through his spies. Aischines, similarly, refers to the ease of access to information from the assembly at Oreos, because the city is a democracy.[98]

But evidence for the suppression of information of this kind is ambiguous: Demosthenes claims in *Against Aristogeiton* that the Boule is mistress of its own secrets thanks to the *kingklis*, the gate at the entrance to the council chamber, yet elsewhere depicts bystanders listening to debates.[99] In comic depictions the Boule is characterised as holding secrets, and there is a feeling that power is invested there. In Aristophanes' *Ekklesiazusai*, Praxagora asserts that women will make better bouleutai than men, because they won't give away council secrets as men do. More seriously, in Lysias' speech *Against Philon*, the speaker says of Philon that he is no use as a *bouleutês* because he cannot keep a secret.[100]

Making the Boule a centre for the privileged access to information was problematic in a democracy. The Boule had a clear responsibility for receiving and disseminating news and information, but where responsibility for news lies, so does the opportunity for exploitation. For executive decisions to be made by the Boule alone, without the people being informed, was to convert the democracy to an oligarchy. The element in the above examples of the demos deferring to the superior judgement of the Boule is particularly interesting, given the supposed sovereignty of the people's decision. It is true that the idea of the demos as unreliable in decision-making is recurrent in our sources, and that behind this is a perception of information as a problem. As we have seen, the blame for a bad decision made by the assembly was most often laid at the feet of an orator who had 'deceived the people', and penalties for deception were laid down in the introductory formulae of the assembly. The idea was that the people must be accurately informed by the speakers before they could make a reliable decision. But it is clear that the claim of misinformation by the orators was often no more than an excuse for a mistake – the orators were not holders of privileged information, nor did they have private sources to inform them, and certainly there was never very much information for them to withold from the people. This may mean that there was a sense in which information was seen as the province of the Boule and the speakers, with decision-making dictated by other concerns in the assembly.

But Athenians resented the idea of official control and were aware of the possibilities for abuse which it offered. Accordingly, safeguards were built into the system to avoid the possibility of the Boule exerting absolute control over information. Among its powers were the reception of heralds and embassies, and the allotting of the right to address the assembly to such foreigners. This meant that sometimes the Boule could control information entering the city before it reached the assembly, though not always: the news of the disaster at Aigospotamoi, as we have seen, was spread through the city from the Piraeus before it reached the prytaneis.[101] Any messenger or herald bringing news, whether from abroad or of internal matters, was supposed to report to the prytaneis first, and the information was debated among by the bouleutai before being announced to the people. The democratic system prevented any long-term suppression of news: although the Boule was responsible for summoning the assembly and drawing up the agenda for each meeting, the scheduling of four assemblies per prytany and provision of slots for the discussion of specific topics meant that its discretion was limited.

It could be further constrained by speakers in the assembly, who could move that a given item must be included on the agenda of the next meeting. Comedy depicts the frustrated Dikaiopolis unable to force discussion of peace in the assembly, but whether used or not, a system to avoid this situation did exist, as the decree concerning first-fruits at Eleusis from 422 demonstrates. After making provision for the collection and administration of the offerings, the decree carries a rider proposed by Lampon. The rider states that Lampon will draft regulations about the first-fruits of olive oil and take them to the Boule, and the Boule must submit them to the assembly.[102]

It is worth noting that many of the 'secret meeting' stories are dubious, and may well have been more suspected secrecy than actual; the paradox of a 'much-discussed secret agreement' merits consideration. When Aischines accuses Demosthenes of holding a secret meeting of the Boule over Amphissa, his intention is to undermine his opponent by suggesting that this was a dishonest and underhand way to go about matters.[103] The slant of the story is made plain by Aischines' admission that Demosthenes' bill was then voted on and passed in the assembly (though he claims the circumstances were dubious): he is trying to use the idea of secrecy in the Boule to reflect badly on his rival. In the orators there are more references to being overheard than to privacy – secrecy was noteworthy when it was practised. Perhaps perceptions of the Boule in comedy also reflect suspicion rather than reality – after all, we see *bouleutai* giving away secrets, not keeping them. The issue is parodied in Aristophanes' *Knights*, where the Boule receive information that sardines are at a record low price, and rush away to take advantage of this news before anyone else finds out.[104]

In fact the Athenians were aware of the potential for abuse, and did their best to prevent it. Athenians were always keen to contrast the freedom of information in democratic Athens with the repression that existed in oligarchic states, and control over information by the executive came to be seen as the hallmark of anti-democratic states. In the accounts of Athens under oligarchic rule, our sources stress the fear and uncertainty caused because information about the decisions, or even composition, of the government, was so hard to find. This was one of the most frightening aspects of the leaders' autocratic power.[105] In contrast, the powers of the Boule in the democracy were very limited, and their opportunities for the control of information smaller than in other states. It was recognised that some short-term benefits could be gained from the control of information, but there was a general perception that it was inappropriate for the Boule to act in this way in a democracy.

In practice we should look to the story of the reception of the Theban messenger in 371, with its many contradictions, to illustrate the reality. The Boule received the messenger after the battle of Leuktra while in session on the Akropolis.[106] Xenophon's account makes it clear that the herald was received and his message discussed by the *bouleutai*, who were unfavourable to the request, and so the messenger left without being presented at the assembly. The very fact that the story is documented means that the workings of the Boule were known to outsiders: this is another story about the suppression of news which relates the supposedly private events. The fact that the Boule were meeting on the Akropolis suggests that the official messenger was not the first, since the Boule met here only in times of emergency. Even though the Boule had the power to keep the messenger's information from the assembly, this did not mean that they could keep his news from the citizens. Their reponse highlights the role of the executive in an open city: to mediate news, but not to control it.

5. The limitations of the assembly

Even within a democracy, while one may refer to 'the people' attending the assembly and hearing news, those who went to the assembly were not the whole of the state. In the first place, in the radical Athenian democracy, only citizen men over the age of eighteen were permitted to attend, and hence exercise political rights; women, slaves and metics were all excluded.[107] Secondly, not even all those entitled to attend were able to do so, either for economic or practical reasons: until the Pnyx was rebuilt *c.* 340 it could hold only in the region of six thousand citizens, a small proportion of those entitled to attend.[108] This means that while some announcements might be made with the intention of informing the state, the assembly could never be the sole or even the principal way in which information was disseminated. There would always need to be other means of spreading information once the assembly was over.

The separation of various groups in Athenian society from access to the assembly had other effects. Such groups were also barred from bringing information before the assembly in the way that citizen men could. In general only citizens could stand up and make proposals in the assembly; information from other sources had to be reported through them. This is illustrated by the events surrounding the exposure of the profanation of the Mysteries. The matter was first brought to light by one Pythonikos, who announced in the assembly that Alkibiades and others had been profaning the Mysteries, and brought forward a slave to give evidence.[109] When the rewards that had been offered for information were apportioned, Pythonikos claimed that he should receive part of the money because he had first brought the matter before the assembly, even though he was not the original informant, only the means through which the slave's information was heard.[110]

This situation could discourage the supply of information which the state might need, for example on the corn-supply. The need for imported corn in Athens was ever-present, and so discussion of the corn-supply was scheduled in the assembly once every prytany. Demosthenes *Against Polykles* demonstrates how important a consideration it could be in the formation of policy.[111] The information the state needed to know if a steady supply were to be maintained was the availability of corn, its price, whether there had been a harvest failure, or shipwrecks, and whether ships were transporting it elsewhere than Athens. But this highlights one of the anomalies of the system – those who possessed most knowledge about trade and economic affairs were the merchants who carried it on, often metics, and there was to a large extent separation between the world of the respectable citizen and the world of the *emporion*. It was not possible for a metic to address the assembly, and Lysias reveals this type of information starting as harbourside rumour rather than being presented to the Boule for debate.[112] The assembly thus had no control over the gathering of the information – it was up to those who possessed it to offer it.

It is also open to question as to how representative the assembly was of the social profile of the city. The institution of assembly-pay in the 390s made it possible for the poor citizen to attend without losing out, but before this date to spend a day, or half a day, in the assembly may have been an unattractive proposition for the farmer or craftsman.[113] The career of political speaker opened up to the poor only as the fourth century progressed, as men like Aischines and Demades rose to prominence. There are indications that poverty and consequent lack of skill in rhetoric may have been a factor inhibiting participation at all levels. Accusations of poverty could be used to undermine a speaker's credibility: Demosthenes' attacks on the impoverished background of Aischines are intended to attack his right to speak as a citizen at all.[114] Although Demosthenes says that he does not wish to insult poverty, he makes a clear link between poverty, lack of right to citizen status, and treachery. It seems that factors may have conspired to inhibit the poor or low-status speaker.

Clearly under such circumstances one could not hope that the assembly would provide all necessary information in Athens, despite its status as flagship of the democracy. Other channels of information that existed for the citizen, of the kind I have described, were essential to supply the information within which the assembly could operate; accepting this places a greater emphasis on the symbolic, non-informative role of the assembly. At this point comparison with other states becomes useful. Within democratic states, the role of the assembly is presented as broadly similar to that of Athens. The debate in the Syracusan assembly, for instance, between Athenagoras and Hermokrates is presented by Thucydides in the same way as those at Athens, and even if Thucydides is making a point, it is a point about democracy in general, not just Athenian democracy. The difficulty of maintaining secrecy is seen as a feature of the assembly in Oreos, and susceptibility to rumour as a problem in Syracuse. But if democratic assemblies were the same, those in oligarchic states show significant differences. The disjunction between informative and symbolic roles becomes much clearer in a constitution where citizenship (and hence attendance at assemblies) was limited. Where an assembly has little or no decision-making power, the announcements made there are for the direct dissemination of information, and the function as a public centre becomes more obvious. But paradoxically the symbolic role also becomes greater, precisely because power in the state is located elsewhere.

In order to illustrate this, I will focus on two states, Sparta, effectively an oligarchy, and Macedonia, a constitutional monarchy. We have already seen that at Sparta the news that reached the citizens was strictly controlled. So too the assembly, like the *sussition*, was seen as a closed gathering – in comparison to Athens, the emphasis was on exclusivity, attendance being a privilege of a small élite group. Assemblies in an oligarchy naturally offer more opportunities for the suppression of information by the state, because there are few, or no, fixed assemblies scheduled, and no requirement that news reaching the authorities be brought before the people. Even serious matters were not always referred to the assembly in Sparta – on the discovery of the conspiracy of Kinadon in 393, Xenophon tells us, the ephors 'did not consult even the Little Assembly', but acted on their own intiative.[115] There is debate over the exact capability of the Spartan Apella to make decisions: Aristotle claims that the body had the right only to vote assent to proposals made by the Gerousia, not being permitted even to speak against them, but historical sources depict both debate and voting on proposals.[116] Although on occasion there does appear to be an element of democratic power exercised by the Spartiates, we have many examples from Sparta of the Gerousia making decisions on their own, with no reference to the assembly, and on the whole the assembly is required to give its support to the decisions of the ephors and Gerousia.[117]

By far the largest role we see the assembly playing is in the making of war and peace, and the prominence of this is not only due to the historians' preoccupation with military affairs. If a polis is to declare war, there must be seen to be unanimity among the citizens, and the assembly is the arena in which the citizen body can make its assent visible. This idea is exemplified in the declaration of war against Athens in 432. Thucydides relates that the vote taken in the Spartan assembly on whether to declare war on Athens was, unusually, taken by division, rather than by shouting. The ephor Sthenelaïdas is said to have imposed this method in order to make the Spartiates keener for war, by forcing them to show their decision publicly.[118] The purpose is to demonstrate the support for his policy as graphically as possible, making it as much of a test of loyalty as a decision.

If the informative role of the oligarchic assembly is minor, this then allows other roles to emerge more clearly. Just as the democratic assembly is designed to allow information to be mediated by the authorities, so in an oligarchy, with the decision-making element far smaller, the assembly can by the act of informing reinforce the power of the state. Kings and ephors at some stages seem to have used the assembly as an arena in which to compete for influence elsewhere. In 243, as Plutarch recounts, the king Agis was unable to gain the agreement of the Gerousia to his radical proposals for the cancellation of debts and redistribution of land, so the ephor Lysander, his ally, held a meeting of the assembly in order to win the approval of the people.[119] No vote was possible without the involvement of the Gerousia, but Agis' position was greatly strengthened by the popular approval his proposals were seen to have. This feature is even more pronounced in a monarchy such as Macedonia. The assembly in Macedonia was the gathering of the army, and for the most part it was summoned by the king when he wanted to inform the people of some matter.[120] This means that it was used in an apparently straightforward way – the king received all the information as it came, and told what he saw fit, in the version he saw fit, to the people without the possibility of debate. Declarations of war and the making of peace, again, are one of the main purposes for which the Macedonians gathered; the symbolic aspect of this is illustrated by the fact that, while some treaties were made in the name of 'the Macedonians', the Athenian envoys who negotiated with Philip II dealt directly with the king at his court only.[121] The assembly also provided the opportunity for the king to cement his relationship with the people: Philip, for instance, according to Diodoros, encouraged the Macedonians to military valour by exhortations in a series of assemblies after his succession, as did Alexander when he came to the throne.[122]

Discussion of the Macedonian assembly has focussed on the extent of its constitutional role: whether or not the Macedonians in assembly were able to elect the king, and give verdicts in captial trials. Modern opinion tends to interpret the assembly as a body without decision-making power, but one which gave assent (or registered dissent) to the decisions of the king.[123] We should interpret the debate in assembly of the Macedonians as the king testing the popular acceptability of his decisions, judicial or political. This helps to explain the prominence of freedom of speech in the Macedonian system – although the people had no power to alter a decision, the expression of disapproval nevertheless had to be possible if the system was to work. Alexander, for instance, in bringing Philotas before the Macedonians on a charge of conspiracy, was informing them of the charge and punishment, but at the same time testing whether his own prestige was great enough to allow him to have Philip's most trusted general Parmenio and his sons executed. Having received the assent of the assembled army to Philotas' death, Alexander felt able to have Parmenio killed without trial.[124]

The role of the assembly was thus primarily to inform the people, of decisions and condemnations, and to gain their assent, but secondly it was an assertion of authority. On campaign in Persia and India Alexander's decisions to turn back at the Hyphasis, and to discharge the Macedonian veterans at Opis were announced in this way; the assembled soldiers were able to show their displeasure, as happened at Opis, but had no opportunity to influence the decision except by seditious action.[125] The assembly allowed the king to present news with his own interpretation, and in an autocracy this is the only version possible. The king has sole power to summon the people to an assembly: there is no other forum in which debate on the king and the state can legitimately take place. Only rival assemblies, summoned by pretenders, can tell a different story.

*

It should not be surprising if the fundamental elements of the political assembly are the same, whatever the constitution. All announcement of news serves the authority by which it is disseminated, by upholding and confirming a particular ideology, and no assembly was an exception to this. One should not see the political assembly in a democracy as the most important source of information, just because it was the most visible and obvious place where news was announced. The assembly may have introduced information to the citizens, but in a fashion which shaped that information for the speaker's, or the government's, own ends. Some types of information were provided more accurately than others, and a range of motivation underlay the announcements; there existed possibilities for the state to withold information as well as disseminate it, possibilities of which democratic states remained uncomfortably aware. All of this suggests that the political assembly could not have the principal role in the dissemination of news, except in those constitutions in which it did not act as a decision-making body. One should consider instead what alternative methods a polis might use to announce news to its citizens.

News and Writing

Sir Adam introduced the ancient Greeks and Romans. JOHNSON: 'Sir, the mass of both of them were barbarians. The mass of every people must be barbarous where there is no printing, and consequently knowledge is not generally diffused. Knowledge is diffused among our people by the newspapers.'

Boswell's *Life of Johnson*, 31 March 1772

Discussion of the assembly has focussed on one way in which the Greek polis informed its citizens, that is, through oral means. But it raises questions about writing in the polis and the dissemination of information. Greek poleis, Athens especially, recorded civic decisions in the form of decrees, treaties, honours and laws in writing with increasing frequency from the fifth century on. How important a place should we give writing in the transmission of news?

In Dr Johnson's comment above an explicit connection is made between the dissemination of knowledge and the existence of mass communication through the printed word. The idea of such a connection obviously arises in part from the circumstances of Johnson's own time, when new printing technology meant that the written word could be more accessible than ever before. But did a lack of written communication hamper the dissemination of knowledge among the ancient Greeks? How did the Greeks use writing to disseminate news? Why do we have quantities of inscriptions on stone from some Greek states and practically none from others? The assumption that poleis produced public written texts primarily in order to disseminate information to their citizens requires examination.

Any potential role of writing in the polis is clearly affected by the extent of literacy. How many people could read? Much has been written on this topic in recent years, culminating in the synthetic works of William Harris, Rosalind Thomas and Mary Beard.[1] The focus of recent discussion has been a refinement of categories beyond the division into simple 'oral' and 'literate', and a concentration on the purposes of literacy. The consensus is that literacy at the top of the social scale need not imply much reading or writing ability among the lower strata of a society, and while many male Greek citizens achieved a level of 'functional literacy', the ability to read and write extensively was far more

limited. Boring concludes for Sparta that there was a large divide
between 'the many officials, generals and business men' who regularly
used writing, and the remainder of the citizens, who rarely needed to
write, although he does not indicate how large he thinks either of these
groups were.[2] Harris argues for a relatively low level of full literacy
(between five and ten per cent of the whole population of Attika), and
uses the institution of ostracism as his benchmark for 'functional
literacy', giving a figure 'comfortably above 6,000'. Thomas argues that
looking for statistical data on rates of literacy is ultimately mistaken,
and a better conclusion is that there were various different levels of
literacy, with the reading of complete poetic texts confined to a few, but
'in cities like Athens where there was a profusion of democratic documents, most citizens had some basic ability'.[3]

We can accept that the ability to read familiar texts was common
among men in Athens, and noteworthy when not achieved elsewhere.
A certain level of literacy was necessary for participation in political
affairs, as *bouleutes*, *demarch* or *epistates*, and this was a need which
strengthened through the fifth and fourth centuries. The use of written
documents became more widespread in the fourth century: the Metröon
had come into use as the public archive at Athens by the end of the fifth
century, and housed copies of decrees and laws passed by the state.
Written evidence replaced oral statements as standard in trials at the
beginning of the fourth century, and was required by law in certain
cases.[4]

Nevertheless, one should not lose sight of the fact that writing was
widely used for purposes other than civic ones. The earliest uses of
writing were private – for dedications, grave monuments, curses and
graffiti – while early public writing recorded laws. Writing was associated with verse and magic for a long time before it came to be associated
with decrees. The assumption that there is a close connection between
literacy and political participation is based too exclusively on the fifth-
and fourth-century evidence. The existence of nonsense-inscriptions
further indicates the appeal of the appearance of writing, and appearance was also significant in the democratic polis: as Thomas notes, 'the
effect [of the stoichedon style] ... is highly ornamental, impressive, and
monumental'.[5] The use of writing to convey information was only one of
its diverse purposes.

Greek poleis employed writing for a variety of purposes: inscription
of laws or decrees, lists, records, ostracism and letters. Writing on
stone, pottery and lead naturally predominates among the remains, but
we have references to other media such as papyrus, wax and wood.[6] A
first principle to bear in mind is that Greek ideas about writing were
not necessarily the same as those today; one must be wary of importing
modern expectations. The attitude towards record-keeping provides a
good illustration of this. Athens, and other states such as Syracuse,

kept some records to establish which citizens were liable for military service, or to pay liturgies or the metic tax. In Athens all citizens were registered with their deme on reaching the age of eighteen, and inscribed on the *lêxiarchikon grammateion* (deme register), although there was no central register of citizens.[7] But the process for establishing one's right to citizenship did not involve simple consultation of the records – the speeches of orators in fact show dependence on personal acquaintance for establishing one's identity as a citizen. In Demosthenes' speech *Against Euboulides* Euxitheos' right to citizenship has been questioned, and because the register has been destroyed, he calls relatives to testify to the citizen descent of his parents, and to his own status, even though he had been enrolled in his deme. The case of Mantitheos against his brother Boiotos reveals the confusion that could arise even when records did exist: two half-brothers were enrolled in their deme under the same name.[8] It is suggested in Plato's *Laws* that every deme should keep a register of its members on a whitened wall, but even in this system, names are to be erased when the individual dies, so no permanent record is intended.[9]

The existence of records did not mean that they comprised a body of information open for consultation; the Athenian cavalry archives are a well-known case in point.[10] Records were kept on lead strips of each cavalryman's horse, with its description and price, yet none of the strips had ever been unrolled and consulted. Clearly although an archive had been created, it either existed alongside an oral system of record-keeping, or was collected out of the sense that such information ought to be written down, even if there was little need to consult it. It is also necessary to remember that there was a practical limit to the amount of statistical data that could be compiled about any community. The records of which we know tend to be of small groups collected for a specific purpose, like taxation. The idea of a wholesale census is less easy to find. In the *Memorabilia* Xenophon's Sokrates discusses the number of Boiotian citizens as a criterion for deciding whether or not to go to war, but it is discussed at an abstract level, not as a figure that can be definitely established.[11] It is certainly true that a census can reveal weakness to outsiders as well as strength – compare the Spartan desire to hide the small size of their citizen body with the Athenian joy in reckoning up the resources of their imperial city.[12] What is disseminated tends to be what is advantageous to the city, and this is as true of records as it is of any other information.

1. Inscriptions: motivation

I wish to turn first of all to public inscriptions on stone.[13] Of all public writing, inscriptions are the easiest to isolate, and the group most directly concerned with news. Riepl's *Das Nachrichtenwesen des Alter-*

tums has no discussion of the role of inscriptions in the transmission of news.[14] Riepl examines a range of means of communication – letters, messengers, fire signals and senatorial *acta* – but his definition of news is such that a means of communication as static and cumbersome as the establishment of inscriptions on stone was not perceived as relevant to his discussion. But there is much to be learnt about Greek attitudes towards both news and information, from a study of epigraphic and other written sources. The context in which I shall consider this is obviously the polis – first, how far news and information which were generated within a state were transmitted to the citizens of that state by written means, and secondly, whether inscriptional sources were instrumental in communicating news between states. Naturally this will embrace public writing on material other than stone as well.

That the Greeks, or some of the Greeks, in particular the Athenians, attached importance to writing down acts of government cannot be doubted. They were certainly very free with writing and made no attempt to restrict its use.[15] The motive for the publication of many of the Athenian decrees, honorary decrees and treaties, titles to land or financial regulations, is something which we can understand relatively easily from a modern standpoint – they are things we would wish to record ourselves. But the purpose behind others, such as the inscription of ongoing building accounts or decisions to send troops to Melos, is less immediately obvious to a twentieth-century perspective.[16] The sheer volume of recorded inscriptions from Athens does show a definite desire to commemorate in stone. But was the desire primarily one to inform? And if the motive was to inform, who were the intended recipients of the information?

It is necessary to emphasise that at Athens, no one who mattered in terms of the state was formally excluded from the decision-making process: the people whom we may suppose to be informed by inscriptions were those able to attend assemblies and participate in government. De facto exclusion is a different matter: the size of the Pnyx limited attendance to six thousand, and until the introduction of assembly pay in the 390s a citizen needed sufficient resources to allow the leisure to attend.[17] But there is nevertheless an assumption that all citizens will know what has been decided, or will have heard by word of mouth. For example, a law of Thasos concerning wine states that ignorance of the law will not be accepted as a defence.[18] Those who were not directly concerned with the making of laws and decrees, women and slaves, were also those whose literacy is most open to doubt. Where we do see women and slaves hearing about the assembly, it is always by oral means – Theophrastos' *Agroikos* discussing the assembly with his slaves instead of his family, or Lysistrata in Aristophanes' *Lysistrata* asking her husband what decisions have been made.[19] It would thus be wrong to suppose an intention to inform those excluded from the processes of government of the decisions made. So it is necessary to account for the use of inscriptions at Athens by more than a desire to inform people who needed to know about the decrees that had been passed, in the interests of democratic participation.

As a starting point, one can consider the explicit justification given in the decrees themselves. In a decree of the Attic deme Cholargos from 334/3, relating to the organisation of the deme festival of the Thesmophoria, the instructions for the publication of the decree are introduced by the clause: 'so that the regulations passed by the demos of Cholargos should last for all time.'[20] This formula, 'for all time', recurs on a decree of Eleusis granting honours to one Philokomos, and thus the concern for the inscription of the decree on stone is to preserve it forever.[21] This immediately poses the question of why the members of a deme would want permanent preservation of such matters, and another deme decree, from Aixone, provides further illumination. The award of honours to two *choregoi* of Aixone, in 326/5, is to be set up in the theatre, to demonstrate to other potential *choregoi* that the deme honours those to whom it is grateful.[22] Those who produced the decree thus had posterity in mind – engraving a decree on stone produced something lasting and kept the decree in mind.

These reasons for committing decrees to stone are easy to understand: the deme is a small community, and wishes its decisions to be made known to all those concerned, present and future. Decrees produced by demes were set up in a wide range of places, usually wherever was appropriate to the content of the decree – the deme agora or theatre, temples, public places, or according to a decree of Eleusis granting honours to Smikythion of Kephale, 'in whatever place seems best.'[23] Many honorific decrees, as well as religious ones, were displayed in temples, but in a small locality such as the deme, the temple was far more a central place than it was in the city. Thus as well as preserving the record of the decree, publication served to spread the information among the community. Deme decrees, in this sense, do not pose a problem.

Explicit motives of this kind, however, appear only on these late deme decrees, and not on those produced by the city assembly. Where an explanation is offered for the epigraphic productions of the polis, the most usual is that the decree is posted for 'anyone who wishes' to read, proof positive of the openness of the Athenian government. The decree of Teisamenos, quoted by Andokides, provides for the new laws when drawn up by the Nomothetai to be inscribed on the wall (of the Portico) where they were before, for everyone to see; Demosthenes refers to the requirement for new laws to be posted in front of the statue of the Eponymous Heroes in the Agora, for the same reason.[24] Such examples provide for laws to be posted in specific 'public notice' places, and reflect concern for the principle of access to the laws. This principle, however, is not sufficient explanation for all inscriptions, since it applies only to written law, not to decrees *per se*. The idea that written law should be accessible to the citizens is one which goes back to the time of Solon, and the fact that the laws should be seen to be accessible was at least as important as the numbers of people actually reading them.[25] But the principle of accessibility does not apply so clearly to decrees: most were set up on the Akropolis, some were displayed in temples with limited access, and others were placed out of the mainstream of communication.[26]

The explicit motives of the polis, then, are little help, so we need to consider those implicit in the practice of inscription. Detienne, in a discussion of publicity and early written law, makes a strong connection between the role of the Agora as the centre of oral communication, and the placing of decrees at the political heart of the city.[27] The invention of writing, he argues, allowed for a new kind of publicity within the city, mirroring the oral role of the Agora. But this is an oversimplification, since most decrees at Athens were published on the Akropolis, not in the Agora, and in other states could go to temples some distance removed from the city proper. Sparta, for instance, placed copies of treaties in the cult centre of Amyklai, five miles from the city itself. Some inscriptions were established in the Athenian Agora, but by far the most numerous of those actually set up are the fourth- and third-century prytany decrees, which were set up outside the *bouleuterion*, where they were most relevant.[28] But Detienne does indirectly suggest a possible intention behind the practice of inscribing. He states that there was always a desire to make a decree visible, and that in wartime this need for the publication to be effective could become acute. He gives in evidence first an inscription which directs that its stele should be put in the most conspicuous place, and second the law of Eukrates dating from 337/6, against attempts to establish a tyranny, passed in the aftermath of the battle of Chaironeia, which is to be put up at the meeting-place of the assembly, and at the entrance to the Areopagos.[29]

The inference from these two decrees is unwarranted, because they both reflect unusual situations; the first concerns the dedication of a statue at Kos and Delos by Cretan auxiliaries in honour of Aglaios of Kos, hardly a matter of public importance, and the desire to find a prominent place for a statue is easy to understand. The anti-tyranny law is equally clear in the reason for the prescription that it be placed by the Areopagos, since the Areopagos councillors are named in the law as a potential threat should the democracy ever be overthrown.[30] Obviously publication at this place was for their benefit, and the placing of a second stele in the assembly can also be seen as a specific measure. So to see this as the desire to publish to as large an audience of citizens as possible is inaccurate.

But in a more general sense, a desire to publish decrees at the appropriate place is detectable. The circumstances of the publication of Eukrates' law can be paralleled from elsewhere. The law relating to the testing of Athenian coinage, from 375/4, states that the text is to be published on two stelai, one before the stele of Poseidon in the Piraeus, and one among the tables in the Agora.[31] These are the two places where the public slaves doing the testing are to sit; evidently the aim was to display the regulations about money, including punishments for transgressors, in the places where they would be most relevant. A similar provision is made in the decree of Athens to send aid to Eretria in 357/6, which calls for action against invaders.[32] The restoration of the final section of this decree is somewhat problematic; three public copies of the decree are to be made, one in marble on the Akropolis and two more in the Agora and the harbour, either on stone or on whitened boards.[33] We see in operation two kinds of publicity, the concern of the city to record its decisions in the cult centre, and the desire to make an important decree immediately accessible to those whom it affects. The possibility of publishing on whitened boards also emphasises the difference in timescale for publication, a topic to which I shall return. The concern to place decrees where they were most relevant is seen in a more generalised way with the placing of religious decrees in specific temples, while political decrees went on the Akropolis. The same treatment can be paralleled at Sparta: the Spartan treaty with Tegea *c.* 560 was inscribed on a stele at the border between Sparta and Tegea, a place where the terms, that Tegeans should expel the Messenians from their country and not grant them citizenship, took on a particular significance.[34] So different types of decree could receive different treatment, and some decrees could be inscribed to publicise specific decisions in the relevant places, though not so much to all citizens, as to those who were directly affected by the decree.

The only reason why it is possible to discuss in such detail the places where decrees were to be exhibited is because most inscriptions, Athenian and non-Athenian, contain the information of who is to see to the inscribing of the decree, where it is to be erected and who is to pay for it. This information is obviously extremely useful for the historian, but it illustrates an important Athenian attitude towards recording decisions. The recording of the way in which the decision was made, and the placing of the decree, are given as much importance as the information contained in the decree itself.

The reproduction of a decree onto stone was usually complete, with practical details about the decree itself included, and any riders passed in the assembly inscribed after the main decree. This shows no difference between the record of public acts kept for the Metröon, the record office, and the published public document.[35] We have two very clear illustrations of this attitude; first, the proxeny decree for Oiniades of

Skiathos from 408/7.[36] In the main decree, Oiniades of Palaiskiathos is praised for his euergesia and awarded the Athenian *proxenia*. There follows an amendment proposed by Antichares in which it is noted that Oiniades' designation should be 'Palaiskiathos' in the decree, rather than plain 'Skiathos'. Meiggs and Lewis comment that this was probably introduced by a friend of Oiniades, and that the distinction was one that was important to him, if not to the Athenians.[37] But what is interesting is that in the inscription the correction has been made; Oiniades is designated as 'Palaiskiathos', although the original *probouleuma* must have referred to him simply as 'Skiathos'. The correction was introduced in the inscription of the stele, yet the rider announcing the mistake and correction has been faithfully reproduced.

The second example is the inscription in honour of Neapolis in Thrace, a fragmentary stele containing two decrees: in the earlier decree, passed in 410/9, Neapolis was described as a colony of Thasos.[38] A second honorary decree, added to the stele in 407, provided among other things for this clause to be altered, as the Neapolitai obviously found it offensive. The first decree therefore has an erasure and new words superimposed, as directed in the second decree, and although the instructions in the subsequent decree are redundant, they have still been reproduced.

The reason for what we may interpret as redundancy has to do with the strict reproduction of the forms of government, reproducing exactly what was passed at the assembly. Perhaps the thinking behind this complete reproduction was that to allow the editing of a decree, especially by a stone-mason, might be dangerous – only by reproducing the complete document could fidelity to the original decision be assured. It is significant that the decree mirrors exactly the process of legislation: the *probouleuma* is inscribed first, and amendments made during the debate at the assembly are appended, not replacing those parts of the *probouleuma* which they countermand, and finally the instructions for publication are added. The decree in this form is a testament that the correct democratic process was used; despite the process of writing it up from a record, the people's decision has not been altered.

The two examples above are individual ones, but this attitude pervades inscriptions in the standard decree formulae. Whenever an award of *deipnon* (dinner) or *xenia* (hospitality) in the *prytaneion* was made to ambassadors or the like, the grant is always recorded as having been made 'for tomorrow'.[39] By the time a stele could be cut and erected, 'tomorrow' was inevitably in the past, yet the formula preserves the present context. Self-reference in inscriptions is also common. A monument-base from Athens is preserved, with a dedication and decrees of the Syllogeis in honour of two of their members.[40] The final clauses of the decrees state that they should be inscribed on the monument when it is set up, and it is clear that this was carried out. A decree was seen as something which happened in the present, and its message was about process as much as about decision.

2. Inscriptions: text and symbol

The reason why the alteration of an inscribed decree was taken so seriously must arise from the attitude that the inscription on stone was in many cases the validation of the document – the stele *was* the agreement in some senses – and so the act of setting up a stele and the provision for a stele to be erected was an important fact in itself. This may be seen in the inscription of a decree of the Epirote Confederacy from Magnesia on the Maiander, which is one of those concerning the establishment of a festival of Artemis Leukophryene; the Magnesians, following a divine epiphany, sent heralds to all the Greek states, inviting them to send *theôroi* to their festival. The Magnesians reproduced all the answers to their letters (where favourable) showing that the states would send *theôroi* to the festival, treating it as equivalent in status to the Pythian festival. The preamble of the Epirote decree, recording proposer and circumstances, has been omitted when the decree was reproduced, but the directions for the placing of a stele at Dodona, the federal sanctuary, have been retained, presumably because the erection of a stele here was itself a significant action.[41]

We should note further that inscriptions which became invalid, or which were revoked, were destroyed, not kept as a historical record of what had been done. This practice is familiar from the Athenian treatment of debts: if a record was kept of a debt owed to an individual or to the state, the record represented the debt, and was destroyed when the money was paid.[42] Diodoros tells us that when Alkibiades returned to Athens in 407 the stele recording his condemnation and the curses against him was taken down and cast into the sea.[43] During the rule of the Thirty at Athens, the oligarchs made a point of destroying many stelai recording decisions of the democracy; on the restoration of democracy, some of these decrees were reinscribed.[44] This may also be the thinking behind the story of Plutarch about the Megarian Decree: when Perikles refused to repeal the decree in the face of a Spartan ultimatum, on the grounds that a law prevented this, Polyalkes suggested that the tablet on which the decree was written could be turned to face the wall. To make the decree invisible is to render it ineffective.[45]

A stele thus embodied a range of information, which was not solely factual. But given these other considerations, what conclusions can we draw about the value as information of the decree published on stone? By far the greatest number of preserved public decrees are honorary, containing notice of grants of *proxenia*, citizenship or other awards. A foreign policy decision, or the impeachment of a magistrate, were far more newsworthy than a grant of citizenship to an individual, and were certainly of interest to a wider audience, yet far fewer of these types of decree have come down to us. One of the differences may perhaps lie in the permanence of the status change, at least as far as citizenship went, but this was not the only reason.

The reason for the proliferation of honorary decrees is obviously that part of the honour was to make the grant known: honouring was a public act. The honorary aspect of the publication is apparent in the form used for the award of *proxenia* – the recipient is written up (*anagraphesthai*) as a *proxenos*; the honour is not only in being a *proxenos*, but in being seen to be one. When in 403/2 Athens granted an award of *proxenia* to Poses of Samos in recognition of his loyalty, it was inscribed at Athens, and at the same time the *grammateus* was ordered to give Poses a document (*biblion*) with the text of the decree from the record-office.[46] This enabled him to take it back to Samos and have it inscribed there, since without the publicity of writing, the honour was invalid. Many decrees provide for the expense of the stele to be met by the honorand, and some betray signs of having been erected on the individual's own initiative, without the involvement of the Boule. Decrees of this kind tend to be abbreviated, and to lack stele directions.[47]

But to publish a decree, on the Akropolis or elsewhere, was quite clearly not the same thing as an announcement. The announcement of an award in the theatre or the assembly was not regular practice with all grants, but was an extra form of honour.[48] If an honour was not an honour unless it was public, the more public it could be made, the greater honour it was. The speech of Aischines *Against Ktesiphon* emphasises the fact that announcements in the theatre were made 'before all the Greeks', and were thus reaching the widest possible audience in the polis.[49] It follows from this that publication on a stele alone was not seen as reaching a total public audience.

So how far was there reliance on the written word for news? To return to my initial point, the decrees which appear on stone on the Akropolis had already been discussed and voted on as oral formulations in the assembly, and there was no question of publishing the 'minutes' of the assembly for those who had not attended. News from within the city did not need to be disseminated in this way. News from outside could also be broadcast verbally. If one considers Demosthenes' account of the news of the capture of Elateia arriving in Athens, it is clear that at every stage the news was passed on by word of mouth.[50] In circumstances like these, written announcements played no part, and even in situations where they were used, as for army call up lists or notices of forthcoming assemblies, there was still reliance on word of mouth to take news of impending assemblies to country demes, or of army-lists to those involved.[51]

It would be valuable in this context if one were able to produce an instance in which a stele was consulted for information about a treaty or policy decision, but our sources are problematic. The consultation of written documents for current, as distinct from historical, information is present only in the speeches of the orators, and their preoccupations are entirely internal to the polis, and mainly legal. Thomas discusses the role played by stelai and written documents in Athenian life, but because she is drawing on forensic speeches, many of her examples concern access to written laws.[52] We do find occasions on which stelai containing treaties are quoted; both Isokrates and Andokides refer to stelai when making points, but these are historical rather than contemporary. Andokides, in *On the Peace with Sparta* in 391, contrasts the current peace terms with those of the Peace of Nikias, which were 'written on the stele'.[53] The thinking behind this is not so much inscription as news as inscription as reference; everyone knows, but needs to be reminded.

Thomas notes further that the type of inscription most frequently consulted in legal cases were public lists of names, of traitors, debtors, benefactors or newly enfranchised citizens.[54] A list of names is one of the easiest things to read, and hence it is not surprising to find their use so widespread, but can this be counted as news? The same principle seems to hold in this case as with honorific decrees – just as one is 'written up' as a *proxenos*, so one is written up as a debtor or a citizen, and it is the writing that provides validity. The formula *en tô(i) grammateiô(i) gegrammenos* (written on the tablet) recurs, to describe those who are recorded as debtors; having your name on the list of traitors or debtors means that you *are* a traitor or debtor. It emerges from the orators that there could be a large amount of doubt associated with such lists, as men tried to erase or add their names to their own advantage: Lysias says, 'there are those who manage, by bribing the proposer, to have their names added to the stele as benefactors', while Aristotle refers in the *Rhetorika* to a case in which one Leodamas was accused of having erased his name from the stele of traitors on the Akropolis during the rule of the Thirty.[55] There may be a greater intention to be informative here, but the real factor is still the honour or the disgrace associated with the act of inscription.

The mention of lists brings us to the point which I raised briefly earlier on, the possibility of written information on materials other than stone. Public writing at Athens was of two distinct kinds – the stele (stone) and the sanis (wooden tablet). The sanis was a wooden board whitened with gypsum, on which notices were written, and which was exhibited in the Agora, usually in front of the statues of the Eponymous Heroes. I referred in my discussion of the inscription on aid to Eretria in 357/6 to the possibility of a decree being put up on whitened boards as a means of fast publication; the norm for inscription on stone was ten days.[56] At first sight this could appear an easy solution to our question, a method of disseminating news much more quickly, displayed in a public place, as opposed to the slow stele. The types of information displayed in this way included lists of magistrates or debtors, those called for army duty, proposed changes to laws, and notices of forthcoming assemblies. We have evidence from comedy for news about army lists being passed on from a notice, and Demosthenes depicts citizens examining the text of new laws on boards.[57]

It is tempting to see this as the equivalent to a newspaper, where information could be published immediately and reach all citizens, in complete contrast to the use of a stele, and drawing on something of the same idea as the display of newspapers on boards in East European countries. There are, however, flaws to be found in this on both sides of the comparison. The newspaper, even in modern terms, is not a homogeneous category. Some, like daily papers, are ephemeral and contain only what is new and/or newsworthy. Others, in contrast, are closer to the idea of a stele, such as a university gazette, which reports decisions and events of which a substantial proportion of its readers will already be aware, having voted on them. The gazette is intended to be kept as a record of the acts of the university, and the reports of degrees conferred is very close indeed to the honorific stele (one is 'written up' as the holder of a degree, and even though the report does not actually confer the degree, to be excluded from the list would be a serious matter).

Equally, the distinction between a board and a stele is too sharp – there is mixing of categories on each side. Publication on stone was withheld for some decrees, because it would have been unfitting, for example over the arrest of citizens.[58] But a formulation of temporary/whitened board and permanent/stele is too simple; some documents on boards, such as leases, were intended to be temporary, while others, like the list of public debtors kept on the Akropolis, were at least semi-permanent. In Demosthenes *Against Theokrines* the speaker claims to have found the name of his opponent's grandfather on the list (on a tablet) of state-debtors on the Akropolis; conversely, another speaker indicates a list on a stele of those owing equipment to the state.[59] A stele was always taken down if superseded, and some were inscribed in the knowledge that they would not last. The building accounts at Epidauros were inscribed on stone, although some represented not completed work, but work in progress. Burford says: 'What we have is a selection of information, chosen at random (or so it seems) for preservation on stone, from the much fuller records which were posted up at the time, on wooden notice boards most likely, so that everyone concerned in the work should know exactly what was expected of him.'[60] The methods of displaying documents may even have depended to a great extent on the ideas of individuals in the assembly; certainly there is no indication of a standard practice for the publication of all decrees.[61]

On some occasions the use of whitened boards shows that quick action was needed in the passage of some piece of information; when Athens voted help for Eretria against an invasion, the provisions were ordered to be reproduced in the relevant places, the harbour, and possibly the Agora, as well as on a stele on the Akropolis. It has been suggested that a copy in the harbour was to be written on a whitened board, as a means of quicker publication, but the directions are uncertain.[62] But one cannot see the boards in the Agora, or those put up in emergencies as 'newspapers', because it was relatively infrequent to do this, and because their content was not so much news as permanent regulations.

3. Inscriptions and oligarchies

A consideration of why the Athenians produced so many inscriptions naturally provokes the complementary question of why other poleis did not. As I noted earlier, Sparta is the non-inscribing polis *par excellence*, but others, like Corinth, produced very few public inscriptions, while those poleis that did, tended to follow Athenian practice and procedure.[63] The explanation most commonly advanced is that of secrecy, and difference between political systems. It is generally accepted that the large number of inscriptions from Athens, especially after 462, can be ascribed to the rise of the radical democracy, and similarly that the paucity of public inscriptions from Sparta and Corinth in classical times is the result of mainly oligarchic government.[64] This argument, however, is not straightforward. Although some have asserted that tyrants feared the openness associated with writing and publicity, there are also instances of tyrants utilising writing, such as the story of Pseudo-Plato that Hipparchos set up herms on roads throughout Attika, each with the inscription 'This is a monument of Hipparchos' and an improving admonition.[65]

To ascribe lack of public decrees to the traditional secrecy of the Spartan government is somewhat problematic. If we are to allow that the Spartan desire for secrecy prevented their producing inscriptions, against whom were they trying to guard? Not foreigners, certainly, since these were allowed at Sparta only under controlled circumstances, and there was in any case little of value that could be learnt from a slow means of communication like inscription. Against the helots? The secrecy perceived in Spartan society was traditionally believed to be a defence against helot revolts.[66] But whereas there might be some benefit in their reading lists of state officers or the like, it cannot really account for the lack of public decrees or honours, and relies on an assumption of widespread helot literacy. It is necessary to look further at Spartan society and ideas before citing secrecy as the sole reason.

Rather than taking the effects of an oligarchic or tyrannical system for granted, it is probably more valuable to consider the way in which the political system affected the citizens. In the first place, it is possible that the number and sophistication of public decrees at Athens has led to unrealistic expectations about publication in other states. Many poleis used writing from an early date to record laws of treaties, but the large-scale recording of public decisions is peculiar to Athens. Other states, particularly those under Athenian domination, adopted the Athenian style of inscription in the fifth and fourth centuries even when it was not entirely appropriate to their political systems, suggesting that there were few other models available.[67] If Athens was the exception and not the rule, it should not be too surprising if other states made far less use of publication.

One might expect that in a state where power was concentrated in the hands of a sole ruler or an oligarchy, there would be more need to disseminate decisions and regulations through written media, than in a democracy where many citizens took part in government.[68] The number of Spartiates, of those with political rights, was much smaller than the number of citizens at Athens, and the requirement for Homoioi to live and eat in their common mess meant that the ruling class was extremely compact. The need for written dissemination of state decisions was thus very small, particularly as the main decisions were taken by the ephors and kings, with the assembly playing a confirmatory role, as opposed to debating and deciding. The preservation of older forms in government, as for example voting by acclaim, not by count of hands, indicates a desire to keep government simple. This is in some ways similar to Athens, but obviously the results were not the same. If forms of government were simpler, this may have meant less need for writing in the political sphere – one aim of the Athenian system was accountability, as written records were kept of the proposers of decrees, and responsibility could thus be fixed on one person. If there was less intervention in the assembly at Sparta, then there was less need for this, as political responsibility always rested with the same few men.

Let us consider, then, the extant public inscriptions from Sparta. It is clear that the temple of Athena Chalkioikos on the Akropolis served as a repository for some inscriptions (although very little survives from there), and that while internal public decrees may not regularly have been put on stone, other matters were. There are eleven extant inscribed public decrees passed by Sparta: from the fifth century there is a fragmentary treaty with the Aitolians and Erxadieans, and two lists of contributions to the war fund, perhaps for the Peloponnesian War. From the second and first centuries there are six honorary decrees, and two further first century decrees.[69] The treaty with the Aitolians was found not at Sparta, but at Delos; there is no sign that there was a similar copy at Sparta. Nevertheless we know that some international treaties were inscribed on stelai at Sparta, because Thucydides records the terms of the treaties made between Sparta and Athens in 421, in which it is prescribed that a stele with the terms be set up at Amyklai.[70] It seems likely that Sparta was not in the habit of setting up a stele for a treaty unless the terms specified it; a Spartan decree relating to certain temples at Delos was found on Delos, but there is no indication that such documents were also set up in the city.[71] Individual Spartans might keep written copies of treaties, as demonstrated by the story of Plutarch that Agesilaos once needed to consult a copy of an important treaty and went to Lysander's house to find it, but equally the story implies that there was no public archive.[72] So what reasons prompted the production of these other inscriptions?

The lists of war-contributions are interesting in this context – one fragment was found near the temple of Athena Chalkioikos, and thus the list was considered worthy of public display. Any number of reasons can be offered for this: honorary purposes, to please those who had contributed, religious motives, as with Athena's lists of tribute, or propaganda value, for Spartans and foreigners alike to see the support that the city had for the Peloponnesian War. But if one contrasts this with the lack of normal honorary decrees (the most common kind of inscription in Attika), it seems that such motives did not apply in every case. The other types of written material which survive from Sparta are illuminating. Many dedicatory objects have been found, some gravestones, and stelai with inscribed victory lists. The existence of other such lists is attested in literary sources – Sosibios refers to a list of victors at the Karneian Games drawn up by Hellanikos, though there is no indication that this was displayed as an inscription.[73] The Spartan prohibition on inscribed tombstones, reserving the privilege for soldiers killed in battle and women in childbirth, suggests that commemoration in writing had a particular significance at Sparta and was not used lightly.[74] Only those judged worthy were accorded the honour, and it was earned through endeavour for the state, on the battlefield, at the Games or in producing new citizens. This is a further possible reason for a lack of inscribed public documents – that writing was used only in cases where commemoration was felt to be especially important.

This resonance which writing had for the Spartans had other effects too. The absence of written law was coupled with a greater emphasis on virtues such as respect and obedience to one's elders. Instead of 'anyone who wishes' (*ho boulomenos*) being able to consult the law and find out his rights, as at Athens, Spartans were more used to doing what they were told (or at least this is the contrast perceived by the Athenians).[75] This meant that if there were a need to control information for fear of the helots, for instance of campaign plans, this was the more easily achieved. Where information was controlled, it was through verbal dissemination and in the short term, and there was little opportunity for the long-term control needed if writing were to be brought into play. Thus a desire for secrecy was not at the root of the absence of many public decrees at Sparta; there was a complex of factors operating, results of the Spartan attitude towards information and writing, and this meant that only some specific types of inscription were set up.

4. Inscriptions at Panhellenic shrines

Some of the same considerations apply to relations between Greek poleis, and the question at issue is the same: what was the role of inscribed information in the international sphere? Many inscriptions have been found outside the states of their origin at international religious centres, and most of these are treaties or agreements between states. The motivation to inform, the inscription as news, is far stronger in this group. Nevertheless, the principle that the inscription on a stele was part of the process of decision has a particular application to international treaties, because the idea of the stele as the physical embodiment of the agreement operates here most clearly. Some treaties, as well as containing directions for the inscription of the document, refer to alterations to the terms of the agreement in terms of the physical alteration of the stele. A monetary pact between Mytilene and Phokaia from the early fourth century allows that 'whatever the cities together engrave on the stele, or erase from it, this shall be authoritative'.[76] Thus it is the act of inscribing that makes the terms effective. Similarly the Athenian financial law discussed above states that any stele bearing the text of laws or decrees which are contrary to the provisions of the new law should be torn down; the removal of a stele was the gesture which repealed a law.[77] In relations between states, the destruction of a stele could symbolise the dissolution of a treaty: the alliance between Athens and Thessaly from 361/0 provides for the stele recording Athens' previous treaty with Alexander of Pherai to be removed from the Akropolis, because the alliance is at an end. The regulations concerning Athenian relations with Ioulis, from 362, refer to the casting down of a stele as an action representing rebellion.[78] Thus at least part of the motive which led states to inscribe copies of their treaties was to create a physical representation of the agreement.

Treaties often instruct that multiple copies of the stele should be placed in particular sanctuaries of the cities involved, and in a major international sanctuary too. Many of the inscriptions recovered from sites such as Olympia and Delphi are treaties, and cities in Ionia and Crete placed their treaties either in panhellenic centres like Delos, or in the largest local cult centre. Obviously the religious motive for such placing should never be overlooked, that is, the setting up of inscriptions which reflect to the greater glory of the god. We know a great deal about the festival of Artemis Leukophryene at Magnesia on the Maiander because the state inscribed the replies to their letters from other Greek states in the shrine, recording the responses because they honoured the god. A similar motive seems to have governed Athens' inscription of the tribute lists on the Akropolis – copies of assessments were kept for legal purposes, but the inscriptions recorded the sixtieth of the tribute that was Athena's money.[79] Building accounts may also be interpreted in this way; the amount of money and work that has gone into the temple is recorded. We find building accounts on many major works, as at Halikarnassos, Epidauros and the Athenian Akropolis.

The publication of a decree at a sanctuary certainly added the sanction of a god to the treaty, and the more important the agreement, the larger the number of deities to watch over it. The Peace of Nikias between Athens and Sparta in 421, for instance, was to be established at Olympia, the Pythian sanctuary and the Isthmus, as well as Amyklai and the Akropolis.[80] The erection of stelai by the Spartans at Amyklai, as opposed to the centre of political life in Sparta, indicates a religious motive for the publication and not an informative one.

But the motivation for publicity of this kind was not entirely religious; we can detect an effort to reach a wider audience by publishing at an international centre. The example of the establishment of stelai at temples not open to visitors is obviously significant here, but it is important to remember that panhellenic sanctuaries, and major city shrines too, attracted large numbers of visitors at certain times. Tourism was not the motive it was to become in Roman times, but the sites themselves, the panhellenic games at the four major sites, and festivals like the Panathenaia or the Hyakinthia at Sparta, attracted *theôroi* and spectators from all over the Greek world. Some festivals were biased towards certain power-axes (the Panathenaia was for a long time the gathering of Athens' allies), but there can be no doubt that such places provided one of the greatest motivations for travel and international contact. In this context, can stelai be interpreted as news-bearing?

This brings us back to the essential quality of stelai – they are a 'passive' means of communication, requiring the reader to come to them, and particularly at a distant sanctuary, they are slow to set up.[81] Even within Athens, when there was a desire for speedy publication, the secretary was instructed to see to the setting up of the stele in ten days. It is not, as I said, that a citizen would find out about a treaty made by his or her city from an inscription at Olympia, nor even that a member of another state would read it and carry the news home – a *proxenos* or sympathiser could have done so weeks before. But it would provide the opportunity to learn the details of a peace or alliance, and to find out about events in more depth. Martin comments on the establishment of treaties:

Les lieux choisis attestent qu'on tendait à faire connaître les engagements pris au delà du cercle des Etats intéressés, à en nantir l'opinion panhellénique .... Informée des conventions souscrites par les Etats grecs, l'opinion, pensait-on, serait à même de réagir si elle en apprenait la violation.[82]

The desire to inform the world at large, so as to gain a guarantee against violation of the terms, is of the same kind as the desire to gain a religious sanction. There are indications that the threat of universal public disapproval was taken seriously, and that poleis were unwilling to risk condemnation in this way. Thucydides shows this as a factor in the debates about war in 431: the Corinthians threaten to leave the Spartan alliance and say, 'we would be committing no offence, either in the face of the oaths we swore to the gods, or in the estimation of mankind.'[83] Nor should the propaganda aspect of an inscription ever be neglected. States on occasion used the international festivals to make a point (as when Sparta received the complaints of Mytilene against Athens very publicly at the Olympic Games in 428), and treaties could also be a part of this, an announcement of new loyalties, or a show of strength.[84] While the religious motivation behind inscription should not be underplayed, it is certainly true that some motive to inform was present too.

There were thus many different reasons for stelai to be erected. To write something down was more than a means of recording it; it was an act that had meaning in itself. While written media in general did not play a decisive part in the direct transmission of news (that is, not many people would gain their primary knowledge of an international treaty or a political decision by their government solely from an inscription), they coexisted with oral dissemination, both inside and outside the city, as an alternative system. Clearly while inscription was a means of disseminating information, it could not be completely divorced from oral means in any context, as will be seen with other written forms such as letters.

5. Letters

On the civic scale, then, writing was a powerful tool in the transmission of information, and its use embodied a multiplicity of meanings. The same is also true of written news on a smaller scale, whether between the state and its representatives, or between individuals. Personal communication through writing, letters, never became common in classical Greece; early writing in Greece was used for religious purposes, for dedications to the gods, for naming objects and for law. Aristotle, in a discussion of education, defines four ways in which writing is useful – business, household administration, learning, and political activity – and from this it can be seen that writing for the exchange of personal news was not an obvious thing to list.[85] Not until Hellenistic times did individuals use writing to communicate over distances as a matter of course. This is not to say that personal letters were otherwise unknown – there are examples of communication by letter between wealthy and less wealthy individuals – but they remained uncommon outside certain well-defined contexts. Perhaps this is suggested too by the Greek mercenaries who left their names as graffiti in Egypt: writing was used to put a name on a monument, but not to communicate with loved ones at home.[86]

The letter exemplifies quite clearly the ambiguous status of writing within Greece as a whole. A letter, when used, was not sharply distinguished from an oral message. A letter was generally delivered by a personal messenger who would expand orally on the text, or carry additional information. In the case of long messages the letter sometimes functioned as a mnemonic aid, supporting rather than replacing an oral message. In some ways a letter could be perceived as less, rather than more secure than a spoken message – a letter might fail to reach its destination, or be lost or stolen, while a messenger going personally was more reliable. Iphigeneia in *Iphigeneia in Tauris* expresses this idea when she suggests that Pylades might be shipwrecked and lose the letter he is carrying, while Plutarch *Dion* contains the diverting story of how a letter to Dionysios II went astray when a wolf stole the messenger's bag, which had a piece of sacrificial meat tied to it.[87]

For the Greeks, the letter had a definite connotation, that of secrecy. This idea is not new: Hartog coments on the attitude of Herodotos to letters 'the letter was a means of transmitting intelligence or instructions, a secret means of communication', and Longo analyses the letter in Thucydides in his article 'Scrivere in Tucidide: comunicazione e ideologica'.[88] Antiphon puts forward the argument in *On the Murder of Herodes* that letters were used either to conceal a message from the bearer, or to convey a message too long to be easily remembered.[89] This is crucial to his argument, as the speaker is attempting to discredit a letter implicating him in the murder, but one can still find support for his claims in other speeches. In a world where literacy is limited, a letter is a secure method of hiding information. Aineias Tacticus devotes a chapter of his *Poliorketika* to the sending of secret messages, and the methods he considers are all either written or encoded. He suggests places for hiding a written message, with or without the knowledge of the bearer (sandal, earring, shoulder, breastplate), and means of handing them over (arrow, capture by enemy), as well as more esoteric methods like marking letters in an innocuous document, or winding string through holes in a piece of wood.[90] It is interesting that the Spartan *skytale* was thought to be a means of enciphered writing, when the Spartans were by their own and others' admission the most unliterate of peoples.[91] In addition to the traditional idea of Spartan deceitfulness, one can see at work the conviction that a written method of sending information must involve secrecy.

As well as stories of plots being hatched by letter, there are also accounts of plots discovered because of letters. The Spartan king Pausanias, for instance, was discovered to be intriguing with Persia in the late 470s when his messenger betrayed him and showed one of his letters to the ephors. Aineias Tacticus recounts a story of a plot discovered when the conspirators betrayed themselves in letters.[92] He also collects three instances in which an individual was informed about a plot in a letter but failed to read it, and so died, in the case of Astyanax tyrant of Lampsakos, with the letter still in hand. One could also add the story of Arrian that Alexander, while undergoing treatment by his doctor Philip, was handed a note by Parmenio claiming that Philip intended to poison him.[93] Stories of this kind highlight what it is about letters that make them suspect: they are an easy way of lying, they can deceive even the bearer, and they can be forged. The likelihood of a written document being forged was felt to be considerable: a letter without a seal is no guarantee. Forged or false letters, or accusations about them, are common among the orators, both in civil and public affairs. Aischines accuses Demosthenes of using forged letters, and Demosthenes in turn quotes a decree condemning any ambassador who sends false information in a letter.[94]

Longo attempts to demonstrate that for Thucydides writing had a particular connotation of truth and accuracy.[95] He asserts that Thucydides denotes letters as both important and effective, as compared to oral communication, citing as examples Nikias' letter to the Athenian assembly in 414, and the letters sent between Themistokles, Pausanias and the Persian King.[96] He detects the same attitude in Herodotos, but turns to tragedy for an illustration of an earlier attitude in which writing was considered something magical, connected with death.[97] Unfortunately, turning to tragedy, Longo finds that the *Hippolytos* and *Iphigeneia in Aulis* fit his scheme, but the letter in the *Iphigeneia in Tauris* does not, and he is forced to consider this as an exception, an indication of changing opinions in the time of Euripides. I think a different interpretation is more accurate: the evidence strongly indicates that from tragedy through to Thucydides, letters are concerned with deceit.

The connection of the written word in tragedy with deceit is indisputable. To an extent this kind of link is symptomatic of the heroic tenor of tragedy – it is set in the heroic age, and thus writing is an anachronistic idea.[98] The connection with betrayal and death begins with the Homeric reference to the *sêmata lugra* (baneful signs) by which Bellerophon carried his own death-warrant, and this is an idea which recurs in historical writing – Pausanias included instructions in his letters to the Persian King that the bearer should be put to death, while Lysander carried a letter from Pharnabazos to Sparta, thinking that it would exculpate him from accusations of disobedience, when in fact Pharnabazos had deceived him, and given him a letter containing a denunciation of his actions.[99]

Letters occur in several plays as important props, most notably in those of Euripides, and the written word is inevitably contrasted as deceitful with the truthful spoken word. In the *Supplices*, the Argive king says, 'these words are not written on tablets, nor sealed in the folds of books; you hear clear words from a tongue that speaks freely,' making clear the association of secrecy with the sealing of parchment.[100]

In the *Hippolytos*, it is Phaidra's letter which carries her accusation of Hippolytos to Theseus, although it is a lie; Hippolytos is unable to speak and so cannot defend himself against the charge.[101] It takes the intervention of a god to explain Theseus' error in believing the letter. The letter is untrue, but more powerful in deception than the spoken word. In the *Iphigeneia in Tauris*, too, the letter is important as a prop, providing the motivation for the scene in which Iphigeneia and Orestes recognise each other. Yet it is not actually the letter which effects the recognition; Iphigeneia cannot read, and states that the letter itself is not a secure means of communication, as Pylades may be shipwrecked and lose it. She tells him the content of the letter orally, so that 'if this letter is lost at sea, and you survive, you will preserve my words as well'.[102] She adds a spoken message, from one person directly to another, and it is this which achieves the recognition. It is of course possible to argue that this is a necessary consequence of the drama – recognition must be effected through oral communication. But it is noteworthy that no attempt is made to read the letter aloud – it remains unread and inactive. The same is true in general of messenger-scenes; we do not see the convention common in English tragedy of messengers carrying letters which they then read out.

What is noteworthy about all these letters is that they are mainly props, like the urn in Sophokles' *Elektra*; although they are physical letters, they do not perform in the play as written means of communication or of information. The only play in which we do see an active informative letter is Euripides' *Iphigeneia in Aulis*. Agamemnon sends a false letter, asking Klytaimnestra to bring Iphigeneia to Aulis in order for her to be married to Achilles, and this is the written communication that is successful, while Agamemnon's truthful letter reversing his decision remains unsent and inactive.[103] Secrecy and disinformation are a function of letters, and this cannot be isolated as a purely Homeric attitude. Oracles and speeches in tragedy may be open to misinterpretation, but letters are outright lies.

This interpretation renders it unnecessary to place the letters in Herodotos or Thucydides within a model of changing attitudes. Those we see in Herodotos are concerned to a remarkable extent with messages whose content needs to be hidden. We encounter the slip of paper sent by Harpagus to Cyrus concealed in the belly of a hare, suggesting rebellion against the Medes, the message tattooed by Histiaios on the head of a slave inciting his son-in-law Aristagoras to rebel, and the letter sent by the exiled Demaratos to the Spartans written under the wax of a writing tablet.[104] Some have tried to establish this 'cunning use' of writing as a specifically barbarian characteristic, but this requires special definitions – Histiaios has to be considered as a tyrant rather than a Greek, and Demaratos to have adopted the customs of the Persian court.[105] Deceit is further carried out through writing by Cyrus (forging Astyages' orders in his plan to incite the Persians to rebellion), and Bagaios (using written orders to turn Oroites' bodyguard against him). Perhaps the only straightforward exchange is between Polykrates of Samos and Amasis, king of Egypt.[106] Similarly in Thucydides one finds the intrigues of Themistokles with the Persian king (involving a deceitful letter), of Pausanias (one deceitful letter and one condemning its bearer to death, by which Pausanias is betrayed), and of Astyochus and Alkibiades in 411 (betrayals and untrue letters).[107] The theme is one which lasted from the fifth century into the fourth: in Xenophon one finds the lies and accusations in the letters at the Arginusai trial, and the same stories follow the Macedonian kings. Polyainos records Philip of Macedon using a forged letter in 338 to trick Chares and Proxenos into removing their guard on the pass at Amphissa, and Kassander bringing about the condemnation of Nikanor in 317 in the same way.[108]

If one accepts this connotation of the letter, it raises problems for the interpretation of the role of letters in the polis. It will certainly go a long way towards explaining the lack of institutionalised postal systems, but it raises the question of why, and in what areas, the polis would make use of written communication. I will examine two fields: letters sent from outside the state, from foreign rulers, and those originating from citizens, generals' and ambassadors' reports.

By far the majority of public letters of which we know come from foreign rulers to Greek poleis – from the Persian, Thracian and Macedonian kings. A letter from Philip of Macedon to the Athenians is preserved among the speeches of Demosthenes, and letters from both Macedonian and Thracian rulers are quoted by Demosthenes and Aischines.[109] It became the practice for Greek states to inscribe the communications they received from foreign rulers, preserving letters such as those of Alexander to the Chians in 332, of Philip Arrhidaios to Eresos *c.* 323/2, and of Antigonus to, variously, Skepsis, Eresos and Teos.[110] There is initially a contrast to be drawn between the functions of the letter as a public document in a democracy and a monarchy. In a democratic state, however limited, it was the state or the people who made treaties, and the system allowed for any citizen to be appointed to act as the representative of the state, in negotiating or swearing oaths. Monarchies, on the other hand, required that all orders and decisions come from the King, who would rely on letters to express his wishes when he could not be present in person. This is why we see, for example, Philip sending letters to Athens while the Athenians send envoys to Pella in return.[111]

The Persian King communicated both with foreign states and with his own subordinates by letter, a necessity in so large an empire. When Artaxerxes, for instance, was involved in the Common Peace agreements in 375 and 366, he sent a document for the Greeks to discuss and accept, rather than negotiating through envoys.[112] One can perhaps see a particularly careful approach in the Persian employment of an individual, Alexander of Macedon, to negotiate in person with the Athenians in 479, if this was a departure from their usual method.[113] The letter of a monarch, moreover, was made authoritative by the use of the seal. It is clear that it was not the writing itself that commanded respect, but the seal and its connection with autocratic power. The seal could quite simply embody authority, as when it was handed over by a ruler to his successor on the deathbed.[114] The relation between letter and seal is well illustrated by both Xenophon, describing Tiribazos' presentation of the Common Peace document to the Greek ambassadors in 387/6:

> Tiribazos showed them the King's seal, and read them the terms in the document

and by Thucydides' account of communications between Xerxes and Pausanias:

> Xerxes gave his reply in a letter to Artabazos, and told him to send it to Pausanias at Byzantium with all speed, and to show him the seal ....[115]

Letters from foreign rulers could be exploited for military purposes: the interception of letters, which were then read for information, was not uncommon. Thucydides records that in 425 a Persian envoy was captured on his way to Sparta, and his dispatches were translated from 'Assyrian characters' and read by the Athenians. In the letter of c. 341 attributed to Philip, the king complains that his herald Nikias was captured and imprisoned by the Athenians, and his letters read out in public. Similarly, within Greece, in 406, the letter of Hippokrates at Kyzikos to his leaders in Sparta was captured and taken to Athens.[116] The fact that the interception of letters was practised is revealing about the kind of information states might want. All these instances concern military affairs, and attempt to find out variously what stage the negotiations between Sparta and Persia had reached, what the situation of the Spartan army at Kyzikos was, and how Philip's campaign in the North was progressing. It is not plans, but current events, which need to be discovered. The story attached to the last incident, that Philip's letter to his wife Olympias, captured along with the official letters, was returned to him unopened, shows a distinction in the nature of the information being sought.[117] Modern intelligence gatherers might well value an unofficial communication more highly than an official one.

But the very fact that letters might be intercepted reveals one of their problematic aspects. It was relatively uncommon in the Greek world to have a captured envoy tortured for information. Thucydides offers an interesting example: when the Athenians captured Aristeus the Corinthian in 430 in Thrace they brought him to Athens, but, fearing that he might escape and damage their cause further, they put him to death immediately without a trial.[118] This was in spite of the fact that he had been responsible for the revolt at Potidaia, as well as being currently an envoy to the Persian King. Any useful information he might have had to reveal was offset by the threat of keeping an enemy in the city. Even when envoys were captured and executed for political reasons, the Greeks seem to have disregarded the possible use of captives as informants.[119] This must derive in part from the position of heralds in the code of Greek warfare – their persons were inviolable, since they were the only official means of contact between warring states. It is possible that the occasional emphasis on the interception of letters is meant to sidestep the issue of torture, but violence towards a herald was always unacceptable. A written communication was more likely to give away secrets than a messenger travelling with an oral message only.

Paradoxically, then, letters are both private and secret, offering opportunities for forgery and deception, and at the same time too public, holding the possibility of being intercepted. When such letters entered the polis, these two issues were sources of unease, arising partly from the threat of secrecy, and partly from problems of interpretation. Aischines, speaking in 330, attempts to stir up his audience with the fear that the democracy is being taken away from them, because the Boule and the demos are being bypassed, and 'letters from the most influential men in Europe and Asia' are being received by private citizens.[120] It is the neglect of democratic practice which Aischines portrays as so threatening – communication should be public and open, not private, or else it begins to hint at plots and secrecy. Letters allow the possibility of private information, which can be kept from the polis at large. A letter on its own, similarly, can be manipulated or distorted, in a way that a messenger cannot: consider Demosthenes' accusations over the fraudulent use of documents in court.[121] A letter cannot be interrogated or probed, and it cannot control the way its information is interpreted.

How far are these same concerns detectable in the polis' own use of letters? Letters were produced by citizens in the service of the polis –

generals and ambassadors sometimes sent written reports to the home authorities, and these could be read in the assembly, produced as evidence in court, or occasionally be intercepted by an enemy. These letters are a difficult group to interpret. If we can see them being treated as authoritative written documents and records, and accepted as accurate, this must call into question the conclusions above, or at least might make us look for a development of attitudes through the fourth century.

We have already seen that a general on campaign was mainly self-reliant in terms of decisions, but this would not prevent his sending reports, verbal or written, back to the council or generals at home. By the time of Demosthenes, evidence certainly indicates both the existence and the preservation of reports from generals abroad. The most detailed accounts appear in Demosthenes *Against Aristokrates*, which reviews the career of Charidemos, and in Aischines' speech *On The Embassy*, which refers in detail to the Athenian campaign against Philip. Demosthenes brings as evidence letters from Athenian governors in the north, from generals on campaign and from Charidemos himself.[122] Aischines too refers to a letter from the general Proxenos, in which he informed the Athenians of the Phokian refusal to hand over the forts controlling Thermopylai, and Aischines gives a date for this event which, he says, is drawn from the public archives.[123]

The appearance of these documents accords with the usual practice among the orators of seeking out texts relevant to their case and reproducing them for citation in court, but does it necessarily imply that all such letters were stored in the public records, and that there were many such? Should we imagine that generals remained in constant written communication with their state, sending back regular reports which were sometimes used as the basis for formulating decrees, and then filed? Hornblower suggests that the use of letters in this way may in fact have been far more widespread than the historical sources show, with all generals on foreign service sending regular written reports to the Boule, which were then preserved as part of the public records in the Metröon.[124] That some of these were not official documents is clear – Charidemos' letter, of which Demosthenes makes so much, was sent to a personal friend, as he was not in Athenian employment at the time.[125] But others, notably those from the Chersonese, clearly were official. One can document the use of reports from generals in the formulation of some decrees. Some inscriptions recording honours paid to benefactors of the city carry detailed information about their deeds that may be drawn from an original report. *IG* ii² 553, for instance, granting citizenship and honours to one Neaios (*c.* 307), states that the generals have written, both on this occasion and before, about Neaios.[126] Where public inscriptions include the source of the information which has given rise to the decree, these can reflect the nature of the report, as in a decision to renew a treaty with Mytilene in 347/6:

> Concerning the reports of the ambassadors of the Mytileneans, and the treasurer of the *Paralos*, and the dispatch from Phaidros the general, it should be decided by the people. ...[127]

The inscriptions do not demonstrate any standard practice, but show that generals could write in a detailed enough manner to allow the city to draw on the information.

Nevertheless, the case for regular dispatches is not as strong as this might suggest. Our sources do not often differentiate between oral and written reports, in accordance with regular attitudes towards letters, and consequently in many cases where reports are mentioned, we cannot be sure whether they were written or not. Fourth-century cases reveal that not all incidents had an appropriate written report which could be produced if necessary. When Demosthenes wished to provide evidence about events at Perinthos and Alopekonnesos in 353, it was recounted by the trierarchs involved; he was not able to produce a letter as he did for the other events he describes.[128] Furthermore, some of the generals' letters in our sources are problematic in exactly the same way as the letters which I have discussed above, for instance those in Xenophon's narrative about the Arginusai trial. There remains a sense that letters can be used to hide the truth, or intercepted. What, then, is the status of the official report?

Three examples will provide some illumination. These are the supposed letter sent to the Athenians by Kleon in 424 (to report victory at Pylos); the letter of Nikias to the Athenian assembly in 414, requesting either serious reinforcement or withdrawal; and the letters sent by the generals after the battle of Arginusai. All of these fifth-century letters represent types which have clear exemplars in the fourth.

The letter of Kleon appears in scholia on the use of the word *chairein*, greetings, in letters: Kleon is said to have been the first to employ the form, in his letter to the Boule and demos reporting his victory at Pylos.[129] Although there is some doubt about the historicity of the letter, in many ways it is immaterial whether it existed or not. The story demonstrates that it was considered normal for a general to send a letter reporting an engagement. The letter of Chares cited by Aischines in the Embassy speech provides the best indication of the content of such communications: Chares reported that Kersobleptes had been deprived of his rule, and that Philip had captured Hieron Oros on 24th Elaphebolion.[130] There is continuity here between the oral and written message: the use of the letter mirrors the preoccupations of the polis as seen in the last chapter, namely the need to report matters officially. There are enough examples of news being sent by verbal means to show that a letter was not necessarily standard practice (Aischines himself is an obvious counter-example), but equally this is the least problematic arena in which letters and reports figure.

The account in Thucydides of Nikias' letter in 414 is useful, as the episode illustrates some interesting contradictions. Nikias saw that the expedition in Sicily must be either reinforced or recalled if it was to survive. He was afraid that his messengers would not report the situation accurately in the Athenian assembly, so he wrote a letter, thinking that this would avoid distortion of the truth. The letter, when it arrived in Athens, was read out to the assembly.[131] Thucydides makes it clear that the circumstances were unusual: the message Nikias wished to send was one of particular urgency, since it was imperative that the government pay attention to his requests. He wrote a letter, as opposed to sending a verbal message only, because a verbal message, he felt, would be open to distortion. Even so, the letter was not read out in isolation: Thucydides tells us that Nikias' messengers delivered an oral message too, and answered questions from the Boule. It is possible to see this as an irregular communication: although Nikias claims that other letters had been sent, and that the Athenians 'know what has been done by us in the past', we should probably see the former letters as reporting engagements or events, and this, cited at length, as a more complex communication. A similar attempt to impress information on the authorities was made by Demosthenes, though unsuccessfully – in the course of the embassy to Philip in 346, he claimed that he tried to send a private letter to Athens, reporting the deeds and situation of the ambassadors, because he distrusted the motives of his fellow-envoys. This letter was suppressed by the other members of the delegation.[132] Demosthenes' letter was not the normal report, but an attempt to undermine the other ambassadors, and set up a competing version of events in the public arena. As a direct and personal communication, the letter could be very effective; the action of Demosthenes' fellow envoys reveals the danger that was also inherent in written communication.

My third example, the Arginusai trial in 406, centred on letters received from the generals, which are particularly difficult to interpret. According to Xenophon, Theramenes attacked the generals at Arginusai for failing to rescue the shipwrecked, producing a letter sent 'to the Boule and the people', which contained a report of the battle and its aftermath.[133] But the account of Xenophon is notoriously unsatisfactory, and Andrewes, drawing on the account of Diodoros, has argued convincingly for the existence of two letters.[134] According to his interpretation, the original letter to the Boule and demos was a report of the battle, such as were normally sent after an important engagement, but the generals agreed to suppress the responsibility of Theramenes and Thrasyboulos for rescuing the shipwrecked, blaming the disaster only on the storm. The second letter was sent in response to the accusation, and contained a detailed defence against the charges. The use of a letter for the suppression of information is surely significant; in the trial, oral accounts by survivors were used to disprove the second letter.

Deceitful letters from commanders are not hard to exemplify: Charidemos, for instance, wrote a letter to the Athenians offering to take the Chersonese for Athens, but, according to Demosthenes, this was simply intended to deceive the Athenians into sending troops to enable him to escape to Kotys, king of Thrace, and he never had any intention of fighting on Athens' behalf.[135] Demosthenes' attempt to prove that the letter was untrue offers a parallel and rival discourse in the form of letters from the Athenian governors at Crithote and in the Chersonese.[136] On the embassy to Philip in 346, Demosthenes also claims that the letter of Philip which the envoys brought home was written for Philip by Aischines, in order to deceive the Athenians as to Philip's intentions. Lysikles, in a fragment of Lykourgos dating from after Chaironeia, is accused of sending false letters to the Boule, and Aristogeiton is more obscurely said to be causing disturbance and political unrest in Athens by means of false letters.[137]

Thus although institutionalised to some extent, letters remained a problem. Where they fitted with the ideals of the polis easily, they were employed, but the letter could not be completely divorced from its deceitful connotations. It might, to take Nikias as an example, give the opportunity for the undistorted transmission of views, but equally it posed the problem of divining the truth of the views expressed: Demosthenes attempted to use a letter at least to influence public opinion, if not to lie. The letter was too easy a vehicle of deceit, offering too little scope for accountability, and it gave far too great an opportunity to the recipient for the control and exploitation of the information it contained.

This is the crux of the matter, because the final section has shown that letters were in fact one of the major ways in which news entered the polis, especially news being passed on by commanders, or those acting on the city's behalf. They were read out at the assembly, and certainly for news of what the city was doing, were of primary importance, both in Athens and elsewhere. Yet this is the paradox at the heart of the polis' treatment of written news. Rome, Persia, even the Great Khan of China, all utilised writing in systems of information gathering and dispersal, creating wide-ranging official postal and dispatch systems.[138] To the Greeks, the letter was never trustworthy enough for this to be valid, so they never exploited the potential of writing for a news-carrying system. The growth of the use of writing in dispatches and public life was matched by an underlying perception of its difficulties. Because the Greeks saw written information as potentially distorted or untrue, they never sought to replace oral communication with written dissemination.

*

This chapter has shown that while Dr Johnson may have been wrong to suppose that information could not be circulated in a society without printing, it would be equally wrong to portray news and writing in as direct a relationship in ancient Greece as they are today. But if information was not the primary reason for the publication of texts within a polis, written public texts were communicative in many different ways. Inscriptions were as much symbolic as informative; the practice of writing gained a central place in political life as much for its implicit messages as its explicit text. The use of writing and record-keeping with the polis grew from the end of the fifth century, though the oral and written remained interdependent. The polis, however, never adapted itself totally to writing and publication, because the ideology of writing was at odds with its conception of public life. Suspicion kept pace with development, and even letters from state officials could not be entertained without concern for the accuracy and accessibility of their contents. Ideas of obedience to the government at Sparta, and of democracy at Athens, called for the oral dissemination of news.

It is only in the international sphere that we see some difference: establishing copies of treaties at international shrines, though not undertaken for the purpose of spreading news, nevertheless contributed to the circulation of information from one polis to another. Indeed the inscriptions, though produced at least partly from motives of propaganda, were one of the reasons for the role of panhellenic festivals as centres of news.

Conclusion

This book has made clear that the dissemination of news in the Greek polis cannot be understood simply by reference to the herald or runner. The figure of Phidippides may dominate the modern idea of Greek news-carrying, but he represents only one aspect, albeit the most picturesque, of Greek systems for the dissemination of news. Organised systems of news, in which one can include the assembly, the herald and the official dispatch, were created in the Greek polis, but unofficial sources of news were equally significant, whether travellers, traders and partisans, or gossip and rumour. Instead of creating systems for gathering and disseminating news, poleis relied on individuals to provide them with the news they needed, and on their citizens to find their own sources of news.

Among the preconceptions that I have been trying to dispel, the most widespread, and the most deceptive, is that based on twentieth-century ideas about the benefits of technological progress. Applying such ideas to ancient Greece inevitably produces a distorted view. Historians of the ancient world, and modern media theorists, have used developments in the technology of communication, such as the invention of writing tablets, or papyrus, or improvements in roads, to mark changes of practice and mentality.[1] The assumption is that each innovation was eagerly awaited, and was put to immediate use to improve communication. While there may be value in this theory for Imperial Rome, it is not true either of Greece or of the Rome of the archaic and republican periods. We should not construct ancient societies as 'deprived' of mass media, struggling to achieve proper communications despite sad limitations on their ability to do so; such a view vastly underrates the sophistication of the Greek concept of news, by concentrating too exclusively on the physical and institutional aspects of news dissemination.

News for news' sake, the idea that hearing about events was valuable as an end in itself, was absent from communication between ancient poleis. Individual citizens exhibited a great appetite for news, but the regular and official passage of news between poleis was entirely absent. This factor alone, however, will not account for the lack of organised systems for gathering and disseminating news, beyond the herald, the scout and the runner; other factors within Greek society were far more important.

The first of these is ideology. The most effective systems of communication with which the Greeks were familiar were those developed by the empires of Persia and, to a lesser extent, Macedonia. Effective reporting and dissemination was seen as the hallmark of monarchic society, and it was recognised that as communication became more efficient, so the possibility of control from the centre became greater. The Greeks had a clear conception of themselves as free and self-governing, and the creation of systems of intelligence-gathering conflicted with this idea. The invention of novel techniques of communication, such as the written or the telegraphic, was associated with secrecy, and this too made their exploitation difficult. Their complexity, and the fact that the information was not open to all, but could be interpreted only by one individual, meant that their use outside the military arena was unacceptable. The desire to retain traditional and ritual elements also militated against straightforward transition from the oral to the written.

The most accurate information was, according to Greek thought, that which was divinely inspired, and this also influenced the treatment of information in the real world. Divine news, even if not entirely credited, remained current as an idea in the historical period, through the existence of oracles, and the attribution of semi-divine status to rumour. By contrasting infallible divine knowledge with that derived from human sources, the Greeks developed a sophisticated attitude to news, recognising that all news is in some way inaccurate. They saw that messengers are easily biased, and stories affected by their narrative context. The effect of rhetoric is significant here; the Greeks realised that how and where news was told, whether in the assembly, the courts, to an enemy general, or to a friend, would affect what was said.

Some limitations on the passage of news were imposed by the nature of Greece, the physical distance between poleis and the relative difficulty of travel, but by far the most important factor was the political separation of the poleis. A comparison with the structures which the Romans imposed on Greece (and elsewhere) provides the clearest illustration of this: the Romans developed a system of roads, established regional centres, imposed a command structure, and instituted central authority with the power to disseminate news. None of this could be achieved without a conception of Greece as unity, and this was an idea which the Greeks themselves did not develop.

Indeed, Greek poleis were far more concerned to emphasise their separation. Contact between citizens of different poleis is presented in our sources mainly through stereotypes. Mobility between poleis was high at all periods, yet it is significant that the response of the poleis was to create systems to integrate these individuals temporarily into the polis. Institutions such as the *proxenia* allowed the traveller or chance messenger to gain some connection with the polis, making clear the element of polis partisanship associated with the bringing of news. In this way, by making the loyalties of the individual clear, the distance between poleis could be maintained. An individual could be loyal to only one polis at a time: the citizen could be defined by his sharing in the communication of information, and his or her relationship towards the information of the polis needed to be made explicit.

*

News was relevant to all areas of Greek life, not only to the military and political, but to the polis as a whole. The role of the polis could be defined in terms of communication with its citizens, and the processes by which this communication was achieved were as important as the information itself; a polis had to be seen to announce or receive items of news. Both inside and outside the polis, in contact with its own citizens and with other states, news was vital to all the interactions of the polis. We see in our sources messages, between poleis and individuals, going astray, being intercepted, disbelieved, misinterpreted or ignored. But this is no reason to believe that the transmission of news was ineffective. It is because of the sophistication of the Greek response to news that we do see a range of possibilities for its exploitation, and a range of reactions to it. Herodas the Syracusan, with whose story I began, does not need to be understood as a spy loyal to Sparta, in order to account for his actions; on the contrary, as a chance messenger with an important message, he is entirely typical of Greek news-transmission.

Notes

Introduction

Epigraph: U. Eco, 'Openness, information, communication', in *The Open Work*, trans. A. Cancogni (London 1989) 46.

1. Xenophon *Hellenika* 3.4.1; see Xenophon *Agesilaos* 1.6.

2. Herodotos 5.35. How and Wells, *A Commentary on Herodotus* (Oxford 1912) observe: 'Herodotos speaks as if this slave were a well-known character like the man in the iron mask, thus arousing the reader's curiosity.'

3. C.G. Starr, *Political Intelligence in Classical Greece* (Leiden 1974) 23. See below, p. 6 and n. 21, on this book. F.E. Adcock and D.J. Mosley, *Diplomacy in Ancient Greece* (London 1975) 176, on the other hand, make the point that Herodas' news was adventitious.

4. J. Hartley, *Understanding News* (London 1982) 5.

5. Ibid. 18.

6. Demosthenes 4.10; the experience of the Western Isles was described to me by a member of the Faculty of Arts at Trinity College, Dublin.

7. M. Stephens, *A History of News from the Drum to the Satellite* (New York 1988) 34-5.

8. Ibid. 59.

9. Stephens, *History of News* 9; Hartley, *Understanding News* 11 emphasises that 'news is not the newsworthy event itself, but rather the "report" or "account" of an event'.

10. On newsworthiness in general see J. Galtung and M. Ruge, 'Structuring and selecting news', in S. Cohen and J. Young (eds), *The Manufacture of News: social problems, deviance and the mass media* (London 1973) 62-72.

11. Architectural display as propaganda is discussed briefly below at p. 42; on Roman propaganda, Z. Yavetz, *Plebs and Princeps* (Oxford 1969), P. Zanker, *The Power of Images in the Age of Augustus* (Michigan 1988), and G. Achard, *La Communication à Rome* (Paris 1991) 288, 292, for further bibliography.

12. Both Thucydides (1.21) and Herodotos (2.18; 3.122) draw a distinction between myth and history, but still treat heroic poetry as dealing with real events. See further C.W. Fornara, *The Nature of History in Ancient Greece and Rome* (Berkeley 1983) 4-12.

13. Demosthenes 4.48-50.

14. Aristotle *Politics* 1326a.

15. Aristophanes *Lysistrata* 808; *Birds* 1549; Pausanias 1.30.4 describes Timon as 'the only man who could find no other way to be happy than by fleeing all other humans'.

16. Thucydides 4.40.

17. Thucydides 3.2; Xenophon *Hellenika* 2.2.3.

18. J.M. Camp, *The Athenian Agora* (London 1986) 99: 'In the days before radio and television, newspapers and the telephone, the monument of the Eponymous Heroes was a crucial element in the dissemination of official information'; J. Ober, *Mass and Élite in Democratic Athens: rhetoric, ideology and the power of the people* (Princeton 1989) 148: 'Much depended on rumor and gossip, which were particularly important in a society that lacked organised news media.'

19. Progressive model: seen most recently in G. Achard, *La Communication à Rome* (Paris 1991); also W. Riepl, *Das Nachrichtenwesen des Altertums mit besonderer Rücksicht auf die Römer* (Leipzig 1913), which is firmly rooted in its period. Riepl's introduction sets ancient news in a context of development in methods of news carrying which had reached its climax at the start of the twentieth century, with an explosion of new inventions: the telegraph, telephone, aeroplane, photograph and radio; Stephens, *A History of News* is not entirely exempt. Notable for her contrasting insight is R. Thomas, *Oral Tradition and Written Record in Classical Athens* (London 1988); also *Orality and Literacy* (Cambridge 1991).

20. Riepl, *Das Nachrichtenwesen* 46-74 (fire-signals in Greece and the East), 75-90 (in Rome), 91-122 (telegraphic systems); J.P. Hershbell, 'The ancient telegraph: war and literacy' in E.A. Havelock and J.P. Hershbell (eds) *Communication Arts in the Ancient World* (New York 1978) 81-92, has bibliography.

21. C.G. Starr, *Political Intelligence in Classical Greece*, Mnemosyne Supplement 31 (Leiden 1974). The introduction claims that the brevity of the work (48 pages) was unavoidable: 'The discussion which is presented in the following pages is not long, but in truth the evidence for political intelligence in Greece is not overabundant.' The military is the field in which most recent work on news has been written, including A. Gerolymatos, *Espionage and Treason: a study of the proxenia in political and military intelligence gathering in Classical Greece* (Amsterdam 1986); L.A. Losada, *The Fifth Column in the Peloponnesian War*, Mnemosyne Supplement 21 (Leiden 1972).

22. Diodoros 15.74.1-2.

23. Stephens, *History of News* 32.

24. Herodotos 1.123.4; see Riepl, *Das Nachrichtenwesen* 303.

1. News Within the Community

Epigraph: A. Trollope, *Framley Parsonage* (Oxford 1980) 123.

1. Aristophanes *Clouds* 1003: *stômullon kata tên agoran tribolektrapel' hoiaper hoi nûn* (chattering in the Agora making rude jokes as [young men] do now).

2. Demosthenes 39.5, 20, 40.6, 20ff.; C. Carey and R.A. Reid, *Demosthenes: selected private speeches* (Cambridge 1985) on 39.22.

3. R.G. Osborne, *Demos: the discovery of classical Attika* (Cambridge 1985) 146-51.

4. E.g. Demosthenes 36.44-5, Lysias 31.20-2, Isaios 3.11-15.

5. V.J. Hunter, 'Gossip and the politics of reputation in classical Athens', *Phoenix* 44 (1990) 299-325 (= Hunter, *Policing Athens: social control in the Attic lawsuits 420-320 BC* (Princeton 1994) ch. 4); against Hunter's view, P. Harding, 'All pigs are animals, but are all animals pigs?', *AHB* 5 (1991) 145-9.

6. Hunter, *Policing Athens* 106-9 on *dokimasia*.

7. Aristophanes *Knights* 1304.

8. Xenophon *Hellenika* 2.3.31; Aristophanes *Frogs* 538-41.

9. Hunter, *Policing Athens* 100-2.

10. Semonides fr. 7.12-14.

11. Aristotle *Politics* 1277b22-3; Aristophanes *Ekklesiazusai* 120, *Thesmophoriazusai* 393. Aischylos *Agamemnon* 483-7 depicts women as more susceptible to rumour than men.

12. Andokides 1.130.

13. Demosthenes 25.56-8.

14. See below p. 22.

15. Lysias 1.15; also Aristophanes *Ekklesiazusai* 528-9 (visiting a friend who is to give birth).

16. D. Cohen, *Law, Sexuality and Society: the enforcement of morals in classical Athens* (Cambridge 1991) 49-51, 161.

17. Plato *Laws* 783E-784E, 794A-B, 795D, 930A, 932B; Aristotle *Politics* 1313a11-15.

18. Isaios 8.19-20, 3.80; for concern for reputation, Euripides *Medea* 214-18, *Alkestis* 315-16.

19. Hesiod *Works and Days* 760-4; Aischines 1.128.

20. Hesiod *Works and Days* 763-4: 'Rumour which many people spread never dies entirely; Rumour also is some kind of divinity.'

21. Aischines 2.145, Demosthenes 19.243-4, 21.80, Lysias 10.23; Virgil *Aeneid* 4.173-94 has exactly the same kind of distancing.

22. Aischines 1.127.

23. Herodotos 9.100.

24. Schol. Aischines 1.128. There is also the story of Aelian *Varia Historia* 9.2 that the news of Taurosthenes' victory at Olympia was reported to his father on Aigina on the same day by a *phasma* (apparition) (see below p. 42 and n. 104). Riepl, *Das Nachrichtenwesen des Altertums* 235-40 comments on the Roman conception of rumour as something to be contrasted to normal news, citing examples where rumour travelled faster than an ordinary messenger. He notes that both the Greeks and Romans failed to develop relay systems in the fashion of the Persians or the Gauls, so that rumour needed to be explained in different ways, and from this derives the idea of divinity.

25. Demosthenes 25.51-2.

26. Aischines 1.48, 121, Demosthenes 18.10, Hyperides 1.14, Demosthenes 54. 15-16.

27. Aischines 1.90, 31, Xenophon *Agesilaos* 5.6-7, S. Brandes, *Kinship, Migration and Community* (New York 1975) 153, for a similar conception of privacy in modern Spain: 'In Becedas, only the woman who lets her neighbour know about her activities is trustworthy. Conversely, a woman who wishes to be trusted will be sure to stay within the public eye.'

28. Demosthenes 42.14; for putting rumours around the Agora, Demosthenes 21.103-4 and 24.15 are examples. Xenophon *Hellenika* 1.7.8 documents Theramenes' very visual show of spurious mourners at the Apatouria at the time of the Arginusai trial in 406.

29. Pindar fr. 75.5 (quoted by Starr, *Political Intelligence* 33).

30. Plutarch *Nikias* 30, Theophrastos *Characters* 8, Demosthenes 18.169.

31. M.I. Finley, *Politics in the Ancient World* (Cambridge 1983) 82, 71-5.

32. Plutarch *Nikias* 12.1, *Alkibiades* 17.3; also Isokrates 7.15, 18.9.

33. Aischines 1.9-12.

34. S.C. Humphreys, *The Family, Women and Death: comparative studies*, (London 1983) 22-32.

35. M. Jameson, 'Private space and the Greek city', in O. Murray and S.R.F. Price (eds), *The Greek City from Homer to Alexander* (Oxford 1990) 171-95, 179-86.

36. Cohen, *Law, Sexuality, and Society* (above n. 16) 74.

37. Lysias 24.19-20.

38. Demosthenes 34.13; Xenophon *Memorabilia* 4.2.1.

39. Aristophanes *Wealth* 377-8 (and also *Ekklesiazusai* 302); *Birds* 1441.

40. Osborne, *Demos* 64-5; Hunter, *Policing Athens* (above n. 5) 97-8.

41. Lysias 23.3; also *IG* ii² 1327 63-4. A modern comparison was suggested by Anton Powell: in the late 1980s Polish men met outside the meat market in the Nottingham Victoria Centre.

42. Lysias 23.6.

43. Polybios 3.20.5: 'There is no point in saying more about such writings as Chaireas and Sosylos produce; for they do not possess the order and authority of history, but resemble the common gossip of the barber's shop.'

44. Barber's shop: Aristophanes *Wealth* 377-8, *Birds* 1441, Eupolis fr. 180, Lysias 32.20, Theophrastos *Characters* 11 (*Bdelurias*), *Anthologia Palatina* 6.307, Theopompos *FGH* 115 283B, Philodemos *De Ira* col. 21 ll.23-6; Perfume-shop: Aristophanes *Knights* 1375, Lysias 24.20, Demosthenes 25.52, 34.13, Pherekrates fr. 32, Theophrastos *Characters* 11, Philodemos *De Ira* col. 21 ll.23-6.

45. Aristophanes *Knights* 1375-80.

46. Demosthenes 54.7-8; Carey and Reid, *Demosthenes* (above n. 2) ad loc.: 'if Pamphilus' shop attracted this [ne'er-do-well] element, there may be a particular point in the mention of his name.'

47. Theophrastos *Characters* 21.

48. Hairstyle as an indicator of sophistication appears in Aristophanes *Clouds* 43-4 and Theophrastos *Characters* 4; the distinction persisted in Roman times, for example in Horace *Satires* 1.3.30-1. Compare also Frank Churchill's visit to London to have his hair cut in Jane Austen's *Emma* (ed. James Kinsley (Oxford 1990) 184).

49. Lysias 24.19-20.

50. Demosthenes 37.39: *to ergastêrion tôn sunestôtôn* (nest of conspirators); 39.2 and 40.9: *ergastêrion sukophantôn* (gang of blackmailers); 32.10: *ergastêrion mochthêrôn anthrôpôn sunestêkotôn* (gang of rascals plotting); see Carey and Reid *Demosthenes* (above n. 2) on 37.39.

51. Isokrates 7.15.

52. Aristotle *Politics* 1271a26-37.

53. Sparta: Plutarch *Lykourgos* 12.4, Xenophon *Lakedaimonion Politeia* 5.5-6; Crete: Ephoros *FGH* 70 F149 (= Strabo 10.4.16), Dosiadas *FGH* 458 F2 (= Athenaeus 143D): 'After dinner they are accustomed first to debate matters of public concern, then afterwards they recall deeds of courage in war, and praise men who have shown virtue, encouraging the young men to bravery and good citizenship.' On laughter as a means of promoting solidarity in the *sussition*, E. David, 'Laughter in Spartan society', in A. Powell (ed.), *Classical Sparta: techniques behind her success* (London 1989) 1-25, 3-7.

54. Plutarch *Moralia* 236F, 697E, *Lykourgos* 12.5.

55. J. Bremmer, 'Adolescents, *symposion*, and pederasty', in O. Murray (ed.), *Sympotica: a symposium on the symposion* (Oxford 1990) 135-48, 136-9; Pindar *Pythian* 1.97, Xenophanes fr. 22, Aristophanes *Peace* 1265-1302.

56. Aristophanes *Clouds* 1357-8, 1362.

57. O. Murray, 'The affair of the Mysteries: democracy and the drinking group', in *Sympotica* (above) 149-61, 150-1; on the role of the *hetaireia* in political life, M.H. Hansen, *The Athenian Assembly in the Age of Demosthenes* (Oxford 1987) 79-81; W.R. Connor, *The New Politicians of Fifth-Century Athens* (Princeton 1975) 25-30.

58. Andokides 1.37-8 (see Murray, 'The affair of the Mysteries' 151), Thucydides 8.54.4, 48.2. Aristophanes *Knights* 475-7 refers to secret meetings of conspirators on the Acropolis by night.

59. Andokides 1.67, Thucydides 8.73.3 (murder of Hyperbolos).

60. Andokides 1.54-6.

61. On philosophers meeting in the shops of craftsmen, *Anthologia Palatina* 6.307, also Diogenes Laertius 2.122, *Socraticorum Epistulae* 13; Eupolis fr. 180.

62. Thucydides 8.40.2; Onasander *Strategikos* 10.24; on desertions of slaves from Athens and Sparta during the Peloponnesian War, Thucydides 7.27 (to Dekeleia), 5.14, 7.26 (to Kythera).

63. Theophrastos *Characters* 4 (*Agroikos*): 'He distrusts his friends and family, but talks freely to his slaves on matters of importance. Indeed, when working in the fields, he describes in detail to his hired workers everything that was discussed in the assembly.'

64. Thucydides 4.80; Plutarch *Lykourgos* 28.1-3; Herodotos 9.10, see Powell, 'Mendacity and Sparta's use of the visual' in Powell (ed.), *Classical Sparta* (above n. 53) 173-92, 180-1.

65. Aristophanes *Frogs* 750-2; K.J. Dover, *Aristophanes Frogs* (Oxford 1993) comments on l.752: 'The passage is an interesting reminder that it is hard to keep secrets in a society where people constantly have slaves in attendance.'

66. J. Seabrook, *The Unprivileged* (1967) 7.

67. Demosthenes 50.48. Much later, Seneca (*Dialogues* 5.3.2) refers to those who strike their slaves for being talkative, or muttering under their breath. This idea is carried to its extreme in the suggestion that tyrants have mute or deaf slaves, in order to keep their affairs secret.

68. V.J. Hunter, *Policing Athens* (above n. 5), 70-89.

69. Andokides 1.12, 17; see below ch. 4 p. 157.

70. This is in contrast to Dorian traditions, which contain many myths about slaves taking power; see P. Vidal-Naquet, 'Slavery and the rule of women in tradition, myth and utopia', in R.L. Gordon (ed.), *Myth, Religion and Society* (Cambridge 1981) 187-200.

71. Aristophanes *Ekklesiazusai* 264-5; *Lysistrata* 507-20 (and see [Demosthenes] 59.110-11 for respectable women seeking information through their husbands); *Ekklesiazusai* 84-7, 132-244, 262-7.

72. Thucydides 2.46, Xenophon *Oikonomikos* 7.5-6.

73. E.C. Keuls, *The Reign of the Phallus: sexual politics in ancient Athens* (New York 1985) 30 and 67-79.

74. D. Cohen, 'Seclusion, separation and the status of women', *G&R* 36 (1989) 3-15; also *Law, Sexuality and Society* 146-59.

75. Aristophanes *Thesmophoriazusai* 446-9, [Aristotle] *Athenaion Politeia* 14.4, Pherekrates fr. 2; *Ekklesiazusai* 302.

76. Cohen, *Law, Sexuality and Society* 159-67 (an excellent discussion).

77. See Vidal-Naquet, 'Slavery and the rule of women' (above n. 70).

78. Aristophanes *Acharnians* 502-5 and scholia; see S. Halliwell, 'Comic satire and freedom of speech in classical Athens', *JHS* 110 (1991) 48-70, 65.

2. News Independent of the Polis

Epigraph: *Acts* 17.21.

1. Plato *Phaedo* 57a-b: 'For no citizen of Phleious has been abroad to Athens recently, nor has any foreigner come to Phleious for a long time, who could give us an accurate account of events, except only that Sokrates had drunk hemlock and died.'

2. Demosthenes 23.182; also 7.41, 50.3, Lysias 20.29.

3. Plato *Charmides* 153A-C.

4. Thucydides 2.6.

5. Xenophon *Hellenika* 2.3.1, 2.4.1.

6. Information on manpower suppressed: Thucydides 5.68 on Spartan numbers at Mantineia.

7. Aristophanes *Acharnians* 751-9.

8. Demosthenes 4.10, 12.17, Aischines 2.288, Theophrastos *Characters* 8.

9. Xenophon *Poroi* 5.1-4 and passim; travel through Greece: 1.6.

10. Lykourgos *Against Leokrates* 18; Aristotle *Politics* 1291b24-5.

11. Thucydides 1.118, 6.88; Xenophon *Hellenika* 4.6.1, 5.2.11, 23, 6.1.2. In Xenophon's work there is probably also an element of other poleis appealing to Spartan power.

12. Plato *Laws* 949E-950A, and in general 949-53; Aineias Tacticus *Poliorketika* 10.8-12.

13. Plutarch *Lykourgos* 27.6-8; also Xenophon *Lak. Pol.* 14.4; Aristotle *Politics* 1327a11-18. Appointments to *proxeniai* were also in the control of the state at Sparta: Herodotos 6.57.2 and D.J. Mosley, 'Spartan kings and proxeny', *Athenaeum* 49 (1971) 433-5.

14. Plutarch *Solon* 6, *Moralia* 236B-C.

15. Herodotos 6.127.

16. Thucydides 8.6.3, 2.13; on this see G. Herman, *Ritualised Friendship and the Greek City* (Cambridge 1987), 143-5.

17. Herman, *Ritualised Friendship* 130-42.

18. Andokides 1.145, Demosthenes 24.202, 49.22, 40.37. The story of the 'sale' of Timokrates' sister to a foreigner (202-3) is undoubtedly exaggerated, and need testify to no more than the relationship of *xenia* between the two men.

19. Aischines 3.250.

20. Demosthenes 18.137, Aischines 3.103-5.

21. Andokides 1.137: 'for when are men in greater danger that on a winter sea voyage? ... Further, since it was wartime, there were warships at sea everywhere, and pirates, by whom many were captured, lost all of their property, and ended their lives in slavery.' For an example of sabotage on a sea voyage, Demosthenes 32.5-6, and N. Purcell, 'Mobility and the *polis*', in O. Murray and S.R.F. Price (eds) *The Greek City from Homer to Alexander* (Oxford 1990), 29-58, 32.

22. Starr, *Political Intelligence* 25: '... common folk proper were probably less likely to undertake the risks of travel abroad than were aristocrats, who could rely on a network of friendships and were escorted by a retinue of servants and guards.'

23. Purcell, 'Mobility and the *polis*' (above n. 21); P. McKechnie, *Outsiders in the Greek Cities in the Fourth Century B.C.* (London 1989).

24. L. Casson, 'Mediterranean communications', in *Cambridge Ancient History* vi, ed² (Cambridge 1994), 512-26.

25. Xenophon *Memorabilia* 3.13.5, Demosthenes 19.155, 163-4, Aischines 2.98-9, also 3.76.

26. Casson, 'Communications' (above n. 24), 512-13; Pausanias 1.44.6-7.

27. E.W. Kase, in E.W. Kase, G.J. Szemler and N.C. Wilkie (eds), *The Great Isthmus Corridor Route: explorations of the Phokis-Doris expedition* i (Iowa 1991) 21-45, describes the road system of the 'Great Corridor Route', which he claims followed the natural corridor across mainland Greece, from the Spercheios Valley to Kirrha. On p. 21 he seems to suggest that the road system was conceived and built as a single project, but his historical section makes clear that the natural route was used even before its various sections had been made into built roads.

28. W.K. Pritchett, *Studies in Ancient Greek Topography* iii (Berkeley 1980) 151-8.

29. R.J. Forbes, *Studies in Ancient Technology* ii (Leiden 1955) 137-8.

30. Plutarch *Moralia* 304E.

31. *IG* ii² 1126, 40-44 (380/79): 'Roads: the Amphiktyons are to repair the [---] and the bridges, each seeing to his own, and they are to take care in the future that they are not damaged, and the Amphiktyonic representatives are to see to the roads, whatever is necessary ....' *IG* ii² 1191 records honours granted by Eleusis to Xenokles, for (among other things) building a bridge.

32. See Lysias 33.1-2, where Herakles is credited with the creation of the Olympic festival in order to encourage friendly relations between the Greek states. Also Pritchett, *Studies* iii (above n. 28) 151, Forbes, *Studies in Ancient Technology* ii 136-7.

33. Herodotos 2.7.1, Thucydides 6.54.7; Spartan kings: Herodotos 6.57.4, and P.A. Cartledge, *Sparta and Laconia* (Cambridge 1979) 187, on the contrast between routes into and within Sparta; roadbuilders (*hodopoioi*) at Athens: [Aristotle] *Athenaion Politeia* 54.1; on the responsibility for roadbuilding, Pritchett, *Studies in Ancient Greek Topography* iii 145-51.

34. Xenis: Polybios 11.11.5, *SIG*³ 636.24, IG V 2 443 l.45, Pritchett 156; Plato *Laws* 760-1.

35. Starr, *Political Intelligence* 23; D. Mosley, *Envoys and Diplomacy in Ancient Greece* (Wiesbaden 1973) 7-8.

36. Xenophon *Hellenika* 3.4.1: 'embarking on the first ship for Greece he brought the news to the Spartans ....' This point is made by C.M. Reed, *Maritime Traders in the Greek World of the Classical and Archaic Periods* (Oxford D.Phil thesis 1981) 134.

37. Starr, *Political Intelligence* 22-4.

38. An exception to this is Purcell, 'Mobility and the *polis*' (above n. 21) 53-4, which concentrates far more on the kind of people who travelled.

39. Starr, *Political Intelligence* 22.

40. Reed, *Maritime Traders* 3.

41. P. McKechnie, *Outsiders* (above n. 23) 185-6.

42. Demosthenes 23.40 (= *IG* i³ 104, 27); Xenophon *Poroi* 1.7.

43. C. Mossé, 'The "World of the Emporium" in the private speeches of Demosthenes', P.D. Garnsey, K. Hopkins and C.R. Whittaker (eds), *Trade in the Ancient Economy* (London 1983) 53-63.

44. The first reaction of characters in comedy and anecdote is to ask what is happening elsewhere: this perhaps suggests continuity across class strata.

45. Aristophanes *Acharnians* 520-2.

46. B.R. MacDonald, 'The import of Attic pottery to Corinth', *JHS* 102 (1982) 113-23, 119-22. *IG* i³ 174 (Walbank, *Athenian Proxenies* 280-4) records honours to Lykon the Achaian, with a possible limitation on trade in the Corinthian Gulf.

47. Even if the goods in the *Acharnians* are suspect because they have been brought by individual enemy citizens, this still implies a lack of contact between citizens, as opposed to neutral traders.

48. Demosthenes 2.17, 59.36.

49. [Demosthenes] 50.56.

50. Aischines 2.15: Aristodemos the actor was sent to Pella as an envoy; Demosthenes 5.6: the actor Neoptolemos an agent of Philip. See Mosley, *Envoys and Diplomacy* 59. At Demosthenes 19.193-5 and Diodoros 16.55 the actor Satyros appears as an intimate of Philip.

51. McKechnie, *Outsiders* 185-6.

52. Ibid. 150-2.

53. S.M. Sherwin-White, *Ancient Cos* (Göttingen 1978) 264: 'Physicians when trained were attracted abroad by the need for employment, by prospects of adventure and patronage and also by the search for knowledge, since ... experience of different human environments accumulated with travel.' Hippokrates *Epidemics*, for instance, uses cases from a wide variety of poleis: Thasos, Larisa, Abdera, Kyzikos and Meliboia are named.

54. McKechnie, *Outsiders* 150-4; on Neaira see below pp. 43-4.

55. Plutarch *Nikias* 30.1, *Moralia* 509A-C; the story in Xenophon *Hellenika* 1.1.15, that Alkibiades seized all small craft in the Hellespont to prevent the Spartan general Mindaros learning of the size of his army, is also dubious; the craft may have belonged to traders, but this did not mean they would be the ones to carry the news.

56. Examples are the Siphnians of Isokrates *Aiginetikos*, and the Plataians at Athens (Lysias 23).

57. M.I. Finley, *Politics in the Ancient World* (Cambridge 1983) 74.

58. Thucydides 6.1; Plutarch *Nikias* 12 (quoted above p. 15). Thucydides' account of the Athenian knowledge of Sicily contradicts Plutarch, in that he claims 'the majority were ignorant of the size of the island, and the large number of its inhabitants'. Dover (*A Historical Commentary on Thucydides* iv (Oxford 1970)) comments that the versions are not irreconcilable, the knowledge even of those who had visited Sicily as part of former expeditions being imprecise and of little use.

59. Demosthenes 21.132, Aischines 2.168-9, Lysias 20.29.

60. Demosthenes 19.158; also 7.41.

61. Apollodoros' speech concerns his trierarchy; Mantitheos was elected taxiarch (40.34) and was in charge of collecting money at Mytilene (36); Ariston states that both he and his father served as trierarch (54.44); Astyphilos is said to have gone abroad as *lochagos* (Isaios 9.14).

62. Demosthenes 40.37.

63. [Demosthenes] 50.51, 56.

64. Thucydides 8.75, *IG* i³ 127 (M-L 94).

65. Plutarch *Moralia* 778A.

66. Thucydides 6.64.2-3.

67. Aineias Tacticus *Poliorketika* 12, reflecting the situation of the besieged city, comments on the undesirability of allowing large numbers of foreign troops, allied or mercenary, into the polis, suggesting that under normal circumstances it was avoided. Polybios 2.7.12 expresses the same idea.

68. See A.J. Woodman, *Rhetoric in Classical Historiography: four studies* (London 1988) 17-23, on the individual's experience of war.

69. Thucydides 6.24.3.

70. W.K. Pritchett, *The Greek State at War* ii (California 1974) 227.

71. [Demosthenes] 50.15-16.

72. Demosthenes 57.18.

73. Plutarch *Nikias* 29.2-3; Thucydides 7.87.

74. [Demosthenes] 53.6; Diodoros 15.68.4, 16.2.2-3, Plutarch *Pelopidas* 26.4; see A. Aymard, 'Philippe de Macédoine ôtage à Thèbes', *REA* 56 (1954) 15-36.

75. The embassy speeches of Demosthenes and Aischines contain many references to the ransoming of prisoners from Philip: Demosthenes 19.166, 169-72, 229-30, Aischines 2.12, 100. McKechnie, *Outsiders* 118-19 discusses the inscriptions in connection with piracy.

76. Demosthenes 53.8.

77. Demosthenes 19.305.

78. A slave, on entry into Athenian society, became divorced from his or her background, and considered only as a slave. This is interesting in view of the prominence given to personal travel among early historians and ethnographers as a method of collecting information.

79. Isaios 2.6; 11.48.

80. Isaios 4.8.

81. The Lydian: Xenophon *Anabasis* 3.1.31; units: 5.2.29-32, 4.2.28, 1.2.6, 9 (although the latter are primarily military distinctions); polis: 5.6. 15-16. Although Xenophon is obviously including the existing population in his plans, the polis is nevertheless intended to gain territory and influence for Greece.

82. Riepl, *Das Nachrichtenwesen des Altertums* 327.

83. See ch. 3 sect. 5.

84. M.I. Finley and H.W. Pleket, *The Olympic Games* (London 1976) 55; Starr, *Political Intelligence* 25.

85. Pausanias 5.6.7: 'It is a law of the Eleians to cast into this gorge any woman they discover attending the Olympic games, or even one who has crossed the river Alpheios, on those days which are forbidden to women.'

86. Aristophanes *Lysistrata* 636-47.

87. Isaios 8.20.

88. D. Whitehead, *The Demes of Attica* (Princeton 1986) 247-8.

89. Plutarch *Alkibiades* 11-12; Plato *Hippias Minor* 363C-364A. Sophists' debates: Diogenes Laertius 9.52, Lysias 33.2, Philostratus *Lives of the Sophists* 1.9.5.

90. Lysias 33; Diodoros 14.109, Dion. Hal. *De Lysia* 29-30. Dionysios' brother Thearides was present as Dionysios' envoy, and lodged luxuriously as a sign of Dionysios' wealth.

91. Eleusis: Herodotos 8.65; for other sources see G.E. Mylonas, *Eleusis and the Eleusinian Mysteries* (Princeton 1961) 247-8. On the social status of those connected with Asklepios in Athens, S.B. Aleshire, *The Athenian Asklepieion: the people, their dedications, and the inventories* (Amsterdam 1989) 52-71; on Asklepios in general, E.J. Edelstein and L. Edelstein, *Asclepius* (Baltimore 1945).

92. *IG* iv² 1, 121-2; the most frequently appearing place-names are, it is true, Peloponnesian – Halieis, Troezen and Epidauros itself – but also mentioned are Athens (4), Thebes (28), Torone (13) and Mytilene (19).

93. Aelian *De Natura Animalium* 9.33; fr. 100.

94. Plutarch *Moralia* 408C.

95. L. Casson, *Travel in the Ancient World* (Oxford 1977) 84-5.

96. Collected in H.W. Parke, *The Oracles of Zeus* (Oxford 1967) Appx 1.

97. Parke, *Oracles of Zeus* Appx. 1 nos. 1-8 (poleis); 17, 18 (occupations); Parke comments (114), 'No doubt at all periods the private enquirer with his apparently trivial wishes and anxieties provided the main core of the consultants at Dodona and at Delphi'. It is also significant that two of the Dodona tablets were written by women, in view of what Price has to say about Delphi: 'Those who came to consult the oracle were always men rather than women, who lacked an official voice in decision-making' (S.R.F. Price, 'Delphi and divination', in P.E. Easterling and J.V. Muir (eds), *Greek Religion and Society* (Cambridge 1985) 128-54, 134). The Dodona tablets, since also they contain some third-person questions, show that women were not debarred from enquiring in person.

98. Xenophon *Anabasis* 3.1.5-7.

99. R.C.T. Parker, 'Greek states and Greek oracles', in P.A. Cartledge and F.D. Harvey (eds), *Crux: essays in Greek history presented to G.E.M. de Ste. Croix* (London 1985) 298-326, 300-2.

100. Epiktetos *Discourses* 1.6.26-7, Dio Chrysostom *Or.* 8.9, Lucian *Peregrinos* 35; Aelian *Varia Historia* 4.9.

101. Aristophanes *Peace* 879; Schol. Pindar *Olympian* 10.55b.

102. Aelian *Varia Historia* 4.9.

103. M.P. Nilsson, *Greek Popular Religion* (New York 1940) 98-101; also P. Cartledge, 'The Greek religious festivals', in P. Easterling and J.V. Muir (eds), *Greek Religion and Society* (Cambridge 1985) 98-127.

104. Aelian *Varia Historia* 9.2. Aelian also offers the alternative account that the news was brought supernaturally by a *phasma* (apparition). See ch. 1, p. 13 and n. 24.

105. Plato *Ion* 530A-B.

106. The temple-builders and craftsmen would remain a small and self-contained group, and one should not see new techniques being disseminated in this way; what would be known was the fact that statues or treasuries had been built, and at whose expense. See C.M. Havelock, 'Art as communication in ancient Greece', in E.A. Havelock and J.P. Hershbell (eds), *Communication Arts in the Ancient World* (New York 1988) 95-118; on temple construction, A. Snodgrass, 'Interaction by design: the Greek city state', in C. Renfrew and J.F. Cherry (eds), *Peer Polity Interaction and Socio-political Change* (Cambridge 1986) 47-58, 54-7.

107. Isokrates *De Pace* 82; see S. Goldhill, 'The Great Dionysia and civic ideology', J.J. Winkler and F.I. Zeitlin (eds), *Nothing to Do with Dionysos?* (Princeton 1990) 97-129, 98-106.

108. Isokrates *Panegyrikos* 45-6; Theophrastos *Characters* 9.5.

109. On Euripides especially, E. Delebecque, *Euripide et la guerre du Peloponnèse* (Paris 1951), and contra, G. Zuntz, 'Contemporary politics in Euripides', *Opuscula Selecta* (Manchester 1972) 54-61; on comedy, A.H. Sommerstein, 'The Decree of Syrakosios', CQ 36 (1986) 101-8, S. Halliwell, 'Comic satire and freedom of speech in classical Athens', *JHS* 111 (1991) 48-70, 65.

110. Aristophanes *Knights* 465-80 (suggesting intrigues with the Argives and Boiotians), 1300-15 (suggesting a plan to attack Carthage).

111. Aristophanes *Acharnians* 502-5; see S. Halliwell, 'Comic satire and freedom of speech'.

112. [Demosthenes] 59.21-4, 33-6; 30, 37 (visits by Stephanos and Phrynion).

113. Ibid. 33.

114. Antiphon *Abuse of Alkibiades* fr. 1; Isokrates 17.4. This last example is clearly in the same tradition as Herodotos 1.29, where Solon is said to have travelled to Egypt both in order to leave Athens with his new laws, and for *theôria*, 'the pleasure of travel'.

115. Antiphon 1.16; 5.20; Lysias 3.32.

116. Aristophanes *Acharnians* 523-9, Andokides 1.15, Lysias 7.4, M-L 85, Thucydides 8.92, Demosthenes 29.3, 25.56, Dinarchos 1.58, 94, Lykourgos *Leokrates* 90. Schol. Ar. *Wasps* 191, on the origin of the phrase 'a quarrel about a donkey's shadow', concerns a journey made by road from Athens to Megara; also Lysias 12.17.

117. Lysias 3.32; Lykourgos *Against Leokrates* 17.

118. Andokides 1.76.

119. Isokrates 5.120; see McKechnie, *Outsiders* (above n. 23) ch. 4.

120. Athenaeus 9.397 c-d, Antiphon fr. B12.

121. Xenophon *Poroi* 5.4, Lysippos fr. 7; Hyperides fr. 70.

122. Demosthenes 25.60.

123. Dinarchos *Against Philokles* 19, also Lysias 13.97: 'so you will be seen by all mortals to have given a just and righteous verdict.'

124. Aischines 3.56.

125. Lysias 28.15; 6.7, 54.

126. Lysias 12.35, 6.54.

127. Lysias 6.6, Andokides *Against Alkibiades* 30.

128. Lysias 6.6-7, Andokides 1.145.

129. Aristophanes *Acharnians*: 100-22 (Persian envoy), 729-835 (Megarian trader), 860-954 (Boiotian trader); *Lysistrata*: 81ff. (Lampito), 86-92 (Corinthian and Boiotian women), 1076ff. (Spartan envoys); *Peace*: 459-506 (chorus of Greeks).

130. In the second part of the *Acharnians* the contrast between Dikaiopolis who is at peace, and the rest of Athens at war, remains to be exploited by bringing on foreign characters. In plays with internal themes the action is entirely Athenian, with references to foreigners only of a proverbial nature.

131. Aristophanes *Acharnians* 738; 307-8.

132. On linguistic attribution of sexual vice to outsiders, see R. Hodot, 'Le vice, c'est les autres', in R. Lonis (ed.), *L'Etranger dans le monde grec* ii (Nancy 1992).

133. Aristophanes *Peace* 236-53; *Wasps* 1157-65 (Spartan shoes); *Acharnians* 519 (Megarian cloaks); *Lysistrata* 36, 702, *Acharnians* 880-94 (Theban eels); *Acharnians* 900-3 (Athenian pottery and whitebait); *Acharnians* 760-3 (Megarian garlic and salt). Identification with food products was also made for Attic demes; see Whitehead, *The Demes of Attica* (above n. 88) 331.

134. Aristophanes *Wasps* 474-6, Plato fr. 124.

135. Aristophanes *Acharnians* 867, *Lysistrata* 983, 988, 1105, 1174.

136. Aristophanes *Lysistrata* 1296-1321.

137. Kratinos fr. 95, Eupolis fr. 179, 138-44, Plato fr. 67-73, Nikochares fr. 10, see E.N. Tigerstedt, *The Legend of Sparta in Classical Antiquity* i (Stockholm 1965) 123; on Boiotia, eels n. 136 above; Kratinos fr. 310.

138. Demosthenes 24.139-41; Diodoros 12.17.

139. Lykourgos *Against Leokrates* 128-9; also Demosthenes 20.107-8.

140. Andokides 3.2; Aischines 1.180-1; Euripides *Supplices* 187, *Andromache* 451-2; Thucydides 5.105, Herodotos 9.54; see A.S. Bradford, 'The duplicitous Spartan', in A. Powell and S. Hodkinson (eds), *The Shadow of Sparta* (London 1994) 59-85.

141. Thucydides 1.70, 84, 4.84. L. Edmunds, *Chance and Intelligence in Thucydides* (Cambridge, Mass. 1975) 89-97 discusses the contrasted stereotypes in the speech of the Corinthians; see also C.B.R. Pelling, 'Thucydides' Archidamus and Herodotus' Artabanus', in *Georgica: Greek studies in honour of G.L. Cawkwell*, BICS Supplement 58, (London 1991) 120-42, 122-3.

142. Lysias *Against Philon* 31.5-6; also Antiphon 5.78, where the speaker defends his father: 'if he likes to spend time abroad in Ainos, this does not mean he is turning his back on the duties he owes to this city, nor that he has become a citizen of another polis ....'

143. Thucydides 4.80, 5.68, Xenophon *Hellenika* 6.5.28, Plutarch *Lykourgos* 1. On the 'mirage Spartiate', F. Ollier, *Le Mirage spartiate: étude sur l'idéalisation de Sparte dans l'antiquité grec* (Paris 1943), E. Rawson, *The Spartan Tradition in European Thought* (Oxford 1969) chs 2 and 3, P.A. Cartledge, *Agesilaos and the Crisis of Sparta* (London 1987) 414-17.

3. Offical Communications

1. Aristotle *Politics* 1326b1-7.

2. Herodotos 7.133-7, 6.60 records that Talthybios had a shrine at Sparta, and received worship as the head of the Talthybiadai, the hereditary class of heralds. The Spartans incurred his anger when they killed the heralds sent by Darius in 491. Hereditary genos of *kêrukes* at Athens: Pollux 8.103, Schol. Aischines 1.21.

3. Roles for heralds in Homer: *Iliad* 2.96-7, 2.278-82, 2.437-44 (marshalling the army), 3.269f. (religious ritual), 7.277, 18.505, 23.567; *Odyssey* 2.37 (assembly), 8.62; Aristotle *Athenaion Politeia* 43.4, 62; Andokides 1.36 (convening the Boule); Aristophanes *Acharnians* 1073-7 (carrying messages). Thomas, *Oral Tradition* 64 n. 162 comments that in some cases the requirement for a herald to make a public proclamation 'may be an archaic survival'.

4. Aristophanes *Ekklesiazusai* 711-13, 834-52.

5. C. Daremberg and E. Saglio, *Dictionnaire des antiquités grecques et romaines* (Paris 1877-1919), s.v. *praeco*; in Aristophanes *Peace* 433ff. Hermes appears in a parody of this role.

6. Thucydides 6.32.

7. Xenophon *Hellenika* 2.4.20-2; see also Theophrastos *Characters* 21 (Petty Pride) 11, a man who takes inordinate pride in the role of proclaiming sacrifices for the prytaneis.

8. Andokides 1.112, *IG* ii² 145, J. Kirchner, *Pros. Att.* 5732. A descendant of Eukles, also named Eukles, is mentioned as *kêrux* at the end of the third century in *IG* ii² 678, 848, 914-15. The post is common in the second-century prytany decrees.

9. See C. Collard, *Euripides Supplices* ii (Groningen 1975) 209, 225.

10. D. Whitehead, *The Demes of Attica* (Princeton 1985) 141-2.

11. Erchia: *SEG* 21.541E; honours *IG* ii² 1176, 1199, *Hesperia* 39 (1970) 47-53.

12. Demosthenes 44.4.

13. Plutarch *Alkibiades* 3, Demosthenes 39.39; also Plutarch *Themistokles* 2.

14. Herodotos 6.58.1.

15. Lysias 3.45; also Aristotle *Athenaion Politeia* 61, and see W.K. Pritchett, *The Greek State at War* ii (Berkeley 1974) 242.

16. Aineias Tacticus *Poliorketika* 27.11-13; the same story is told at Xenophon *Anabasis* 2.2.20 and Polyainos 3.9.4.

17. Messengers from armies: Thucydides 7.8, 8.1, Xenophon *Hellenika*

2.1.24-30, 6.4.16, 7.1.32; Lechaion: Xenophon *Hellenika* 4.5.7; other important events: Thucydides 8.11 (Alkamenes), Xenophon *Hellenika* 1.6.36.

18. Xenophon *Hellenika* 2.1.30; not all these individuals are heralds, but they all fulfil the role of official messenger.

19. Aischines 2.169.

20. Plutarch *Moralia* 347C-D.

21. Xenophon *Hellenika* 7.1.32.

22. Stories about Athens tend to show news reaching the populace in an uncontrolled way: Plutarch *Nikias* 30, Demosthenes 18.169, Xenophon *Hellenika* 2.2.3. The problems associated with this are treated in ch. 4.

23. Xenophon is a particularly good source for accounts of this kind, and he was keen to praise Spartan discipline, as for example the restraint shown in reaction to the disaster of Leuktra in 371 (*Hellenika* 6.4.16): the relatives of the dead were told to refrain from lamentation because there was a festival in progress.

24. The story of Phidippides bringing the news to Athens first became attached to the Marathon story in a fragment of Herakleides Ponticus quoted in Plutarch *Moralia* 347C. It appears to be based on a similar story relating to an Eleian runner.

25. Plutarch *Moralia* 347C: 'But suppose a goatherd or oxherd on a hilltop or vantage point looked down on the contest from afar, and saw that idescribably great victory, and came to the city, himself unwounded and unbloodied, as a messenger ....' See F.J. Frost, 'The dubious origins of the "Marathon" ', *AJAH* 4 (1979) 159-63.

26. Demosthenes 18.169ff. (discussed in detail in ch. 5, pp. 100-2ff.).

27. Thucydides 4.3 (opposition to Demosthenes' plan from the other generals), 30 (Kleon brings peltasts and light troops, as Demosthenes had asked).

28. Thucydides 4.122.

29. Xenophon *Hellenika* 1.6.36-7.

30. Ibid. 4.3.13-14.

31. Diodoros 11.35.

32. Herodotos 8.75-80.

33. Ibid. 8.80.1.

34. Xenophon *Anabasis* 3.2.1; 5.6.22-34.

35. Ibid. 1.4.12: 'the soldiers were aggrieved with the generals, and accused them of having known the plan all along, and hidden it ....'

36. Ibid. 6.1.18.

37. Andokides 3.34.

38. Andokides 2.19. See below p. 115.

39. Lysias 12.69.

40. A. Andrewes, 'The Theramenes Papyrus', *ZPE* 6 (1970) 35-8. The papyrus appears to be a fragment of a contemporary political pamphlet defending Theramenes; the rebuttal of the charge from Lysias suggests that it was widely known.

41. S. Hornblower, *The Greek World* (London 1985) 122.

42. A. Powell, 'Mendacity and Sparta's use of the visual' in A. Powell (ed.), *Classical Sparta: techniques behind her success* (London 1989) 173-92, 178.

43. Thucydides 7.48.

44. Herodotos 8.141. It is interesting to contrast the pretext used by the Spartans at 6.108 to reject an alliance with Plataia: 'We live too far away, and we would be a cold comfort to you. For you could have been enslaved many times over before the news of it reached us.' The argument is clearly specious, but obviously the question was of significance.

45. Herodotos 6.77-8.

46. Thucydides 2.6.1-3.

47. Herodotos 8.98.

48. E.g. Xenophon *Cyropaideia* 8.2.10-11, Herodotos 1.100; on the King's Eye, S.W. Hirsch, *The Friendship of the Barbarians: Xenophon and the Persian Empire* (Hanover and London 1985) 101-39; Riepl, *Das Nachrichtenwesen des Altertums* 282.

49. Herodotos 1.121, 5.35.3.

50. Xenophon *Hellenika* 3.2.12, 5.4.66, and see in general Pritchett, *The Greek State at War* ii (above n. 15) 47-56.

51. L. Casson, 'Mediterranean communications', in *Cambridge Ancient History* vi, ed² (Cambridge 1994) 520-3. The speeds noted in our sources, such as three days to reach Mytilene from Athens, or Sparta from the Hellespont, tend to be those of unusual circumstances. A general relying on home decisions would have to contend not only with sailing time, but also with the passage of instructions through the assembly or government.

52. Pritchett, *The Greek State at War* ii, 61-116 discusses the extent to which fourth-century generals should be seen to act independently of their home government. He concludes that in very few cases did a general become completely independent, as they usually acted in accordance with their instructions and were subsequently answerable for their deeds. But as the case of Chares shows, this does not mean that they relied on instructions from home for every decision while on campaign.

53. Xenophon *Hellenika* 1.1.23.

54. Diodoros 16.22; Jacoby *FGH* 105.4.

55. Thucydides 4.108.6-7.

56. Ibid. 4.132.

57. Ibid. 4.122-3: 'While this was going on, Mende revolted from the Athenians … and Brasidas received them into the Spartan alliance, not thinking that he was doing wrong, although they had gone over to the Spartans when the truce was clearly in force. For he had some complaints against the Athenians of transgressing the terms of the peace.'

58. Thucydides 6.47-50; 7.11.

59. Aischines 2.104; 107.

60. Demosthenes 19.110, 248.

61. Lysias 13.9-10 emphasises by repetition that Theramenes was an envoy *autokratôr* (with full powers to negotiate).

62. Aristotle *Politics* 1313b11-15, 32-7.

63. Inviolability: Pollux 8.139, Herodotos 7.133-4, Euripides *Herakleidai* 271, [Demosthenes] 12.2-4, Pausanias 1.36.3, 3.12.7.

64. Thucydides 2.1; Aischines 2.37, Xenophon *Anabasis* 3.3.5; J. de Romilly, 'Guerre et paix entre cités' in J-P. Vernant (ed.), *Problèmes de la guerre en Grèce ancienne* (Paris 1968) 207-20, 213.

65. On the request for the bodies of the dead, Pritchett, The *Greek State at War* iv (Berkeley 1985) 246-7; D. Lateiner, 'Heralds and corpses in Thucydides', *CW* 71 (1977) 97-106.

66. Herodotos 7.133-4. See L.M. Wéry, 'Le meutre des hérauts de Darius en 491 et l'inviolabilité du héraut', *Ant. Class.* 35 (1966) 468-86.

67. G. Herman, *Ritualised Friendship and the Greek City* (Cambridge 1987) 128-42.

68. Aischines 2.133-4.

69. D. Mosley, *Envoys and Diplomacy in Ancient Greece* (Historia Supplement 22) (Wiesbaden 1973) 24 comments: 'It was left to the Athenian general Proxenos to send envoys, Metagenes and Kallikrates, to find out what was going on and to inform the Athenians that the negotiations had been rendered invalid.'

70. Xenophon *Hellenika* 1.4.4-7.

71. *IG* i³ 71 ll.5-6; see also *IG* i³ 34, ll.26-8. R. Meiggs, *The Athenian Empire* (Oxford 1972) 245, states: 'some such divisions probably go back to the early days of the league. As soon as it was necessary to send out heralds to the allies to announce decisions of the Council at Delos, it would be logical to divide the allies up into districts. The headings that we find in 442 correspond to natural divisions.'

72. *IG* i³ 71 (M-L 69) ll. 41-2 orders that the routes to be travelled by the heralds announcing the reassessment of tribute are to be prescribed by the assessors. The Magnesia inscriptions, collected in O. Kern, *Inschriften von Magnesia am Maeander* (Berlin 1900), fall into distinct groups: Athens group nos. 37, 48, 47, 34; Apollonia group nos. 45, 46, 44, 35, 36; Peloponnese group nos. 38-43.

73. C.G. Starr, *Political Intelligence* 20-2.

74. See J.S. Morrison and R.T. Williams, *Greek Oared Ships* (Cambridge 1976) 245 and n. 17.

75. Thucydides 3.49, 4.16.2. See also 3.72.2 (Corinth conveys Spartan envoys); Mosley, *Envoys and Diplomacy* 75-6.

76. Thucydides 8.74; 6.61. It is significant that in the events of 411 the crew of the *Paralos* were treated as a body, and one that was particularly dangerous to the oligarchy, indicating that the 'Paraloi' were not merely the best sailors, but had a further non-military role.

77. *IG* i² 34 (M-L 46) ll. 26-7.

78. Thucydides 6.46; see S. Hornblower, *Thucydides* (London 1987) 23 on the nature of this story.

79. Thucydides 8.6, *Hellenika Oxyrhynchia* 18.

80. See A.J. Holladay and M.D. Goodman, 'Religious scruples in antiquity' *CQ* 36 (1986) 151-71.

81. Xenophon *Hellenika* 4.7.2-3.

82. Ibid. 6.4.19-20.

83. Ibid. 4.3.2-3.

84. Ibid. 4.8.1-2

85. Aristophanes *Acharnians* 65-7; 89-90.

86. Above n. 72.

87. Plutarch *Timoleon* 23.

88. Demosthenes is accused by Aischines (2.61-2) of having used the delay before the return of envoys to push through the assembly the peace and alliance with Macedonia. Demosthenes in turn tries to suggest (9.15-16) that Philip was also guilty of this kind of exploitation in his campaign before the oaths of the Peace of Philokrates were taken.

89. Riepl, *Das Nachrichtenwesen* 327: 'The Olympian, Pythian, Nemean and Isthmian Games offered virtually the only opportunity to see the fragmented Hellenic world gathered together at one national centre.'

90. Livy 33.32.2.

91. On the Exiles' Decree and 'Freedom of the Greeks', see below; political speeches: Gorgias *Olympikos*, Isokrates *Panegyrikos*, Lysias 33 (*Olympikos*);

Lucian *Herodotus* 3: 'The sophist Hippias, a native of Elis, Prodikos of Keios, Anaximenes the Chian, Polos of Akragas, and countless others read their works at the Games, and as a result became well-known in a short time'; Dio Chrysostom *Or.* 8.9.

92. Lucian *Herodotus* 1-2 says that *hoi aristoi* (the most distinguished men) were gathered from all over Greece.

93. Lucian *Herodotos* 8.

94. Antiphon *Against Alkibiades* 4.29; Plutarch *Themistokles* 17.2; *Philopoimen* 11.

95. Pausanias 6.13.1, Herodotos 6.103.

96. Thucydides 8.9-10.

97. Herodotos 6.126.2.

98. Demosthenes 18.90-2.

99. Demosthenes 18.91.

100. H. Wankel, *Demosthenes: Rede für Ktesiphon über den Kranz* i (Heidelberg 1976) 497-8.

101. Diodoros 18.8.2-6.

102. Livy 33.31-2.

103. Diodoros 18.8.4.

104. Ibid. 8.5.

105. Livy 33.32.3.

106. Both Diodoros (17.109) and Curtius (10.2.4-8) associate the promulgation of the Exiles' Decree with events at Opis. According to *SIG*³ 312, the decree concerning Samos, the decree was first announced 'in the camp'. See A.B. Bosworth, *Conquest and Empire: the reign of Alexander the Great* (Cambridge 1988) 221-6.

107. As shown by the decree regarding the return of exiles to Tegea (*SIG*³ 306 (Tod 202)) 2ff.: 'the edict shall be inscribed in accordance with the revisions which the city made on the points in the edict which were objected to.'

108. See Diodoros 17.113.3 for embassies disputing the decree with Alexander.

109. Suetonius *Nero* 24; *SIG*³ 814 (*ILS* 8794; E.M. Smallwood, *Documents illustrating the Principates of Gaius, Claudius and Nero* (Cambridge 1967) 64.

4. Unofficial News

Epigraph: W. Shakespeare, *Antony and Cleopatra* II.v.85-8.

1. Theophrastos *Characters* 8.

2. M.I. Finley, *Politics in the Ancient World* (Cambridge 1983) 81; C.G. Starr, *Political Intelligence in Classical Greece* (Leiden 1974), includes in his discussion of less formal intelligence-carrying merchants, travellers and aristocrats. It seems to me that a clearer distinction should be made between the deliberate carrying of news, and its motivations, and travel for other purposes.

3. Xenophon *Hellenika* 3.4.1.

4. Thucydides 1.91. A similar idea about travellers' news is expressed in Aischylos *Agamemnon* 864-7.

5. *IG* ii² 29 (Tod 116). The historical setting is taken to be that of Xenophon *Hellenika* 5.1.25-8, during Antalkidas' campaign in the Hellespont.

6. Aristotle *Athenaion Politeia* 43.6.

7. *IG* ii² 133.

8. Diodoros 16.21.1-4; see A. Gerolymatos, *Espionage and Treason: a study* of the proxenia in political and military intelligence gathering in Classical Greece (Amsterdam 1986) 46-8.

9. Thucydides 3.3.1.

10. F.E. Adcock, *The Greek and Macedonian Art of War* (Berkeley 1957) 40-1, comments on the comparative rarity of surprises in Greek warfare, and attributes this both to poor systems of intelligence-gathering, and fear of taking calculated risks. L.A. Losada, *The Fifth Column in the Peloponnesian War* (Leiden 1972) 114-15, disputes this conclusion, but he is concerned only with the betrayal of cities, which is by his own argument a special case. It is true that Greek systems of scouting were poor, but also that there was, as Adcock notes, little useful tactical information that could be discovered. Spies were often caught (Starr, *Political Intelligence* 10-11), and Herodotos' tale (7.146-8) of the Greek spies who were discovered by Xerxes in 480, given a tour of inspection and returned to Greece, illustrates how little value was placed on their information.

Thucydides' account of Athenian and Spartan manoeuvres in the Aegean in Book 8 reveals the inadequacy of both sides' scouts: most information on the position of the enemy was gained from local inhabitants (8.23, 26, 27, 41); at 8.103 the scouts posted by Thrasylos fail to see the Spartan fleet pass, and at 33 the two fleets anchor for the night on opposite sides of a headland, each unaware of the others' presence. Xenophon *Hipparchikos* 4.7-8 comments on the use of spies in warfare, that *even if* their information is correct, it is still difficult for them to report at the right time (see also *Anabasis* 4.4.15 (scout particularly recommended as an accurate reporter), Thucydides 6.34). When the Spartans did manage to surprise the Athenians in 411, it was the result of an accident (8.42), not of information received. There is much emphasis in ancient authors on the role of the unexpected in warfare, and Adcock suggests that for this reason surprise was seen as 'an enemy rather than a useful friend'.

11. Herodotos 8.75; Xenophon *Hellenika* 4.4.10.

12. Herodotos 8.75, Xenophon *Anabasis* 2.4.15-22; at Hdt. 3.153, the Persian Zopyros mutilates himself in an exceptional bid to make himself credible as a deserter, in order to betray Babylon to Darios.

13. Thucydides 6.64, Plutarch *Nikias* 16.2 (also Diodoros 13.6.2, Polyainos 1.40.5, Frontinus *Strategemata* 3.6.6); other instances of the same ruse: Xenophon *Hellenika* 5.1.25; Plutarch *Alkibiades* 31.2-3.

14. Sestos was recaptured and a cleruchy established in 353 (Diodoros 16.34).

15. Lykourgos *Against Leokrates* 14-15.

16. Plutarch *Nikias* 30.2, also at *Moralia* 509B-C.

17. Thucydides 6.32.3 (news of the launch of the Athenian expedition), 8.1 (news of defeat in Sicily); Demosthenes 4.48-9 (Philip's actions); Lysias 22.14 (news of shipwrecks).

18. Thucydides 6.38.2.

19. Thucydides 2.94, 8.94, Xenophon *Hellenika* 5.1.22.

20. Lysias 22.14.

21. Demosthenes 56.7-8.

22. Aristophanes *Knights* 647-50.

23. Demosthenes 4.48-9.

24. Ibid. 3.5, 4.10-11.

25. Ibid. 4.50.

26. Ibid. 19.288; 4.10.

27. Xenophon *Hellenika* 4.5.6, and in general M.B. Walbank, *Athenian Proxenies of the Fifth Century B.C.* (Toronto 1978) 2-3.

28. Demosthenes 35.6-8, and similarly [Demosthenes] 52.4.

29. Aischines 2.12-16; Demosthenes 19.230.

30. Polyainos 3.13.1.

31. Xenophon *Hellenika* 3.4.1.

32. Ibid. 7.5.10.

33. Thucydides 3.2-3.

34. Ibid. 3.4.4.

35. Gerolymatos, *Espionage and Treason* (above n. 8) 56, comments on this passage that the man would be less trustworthy, being seen as a traitor, but this does not explain why the Mytileneans would have chosen him as ambassador.

36. G. Herman, *Ritualised Friendship and the Greek City* (Cambridge 1987) 139.

37. Gerolymatos, *Espionage and Treason* 4-5.

38. Aischines 2.133-5.

39. Xenophon *Hellenika* 6.1.4. This episode is taken at face value by Mosley, *Envoys and Diplomacy* 5.

40. Xenophon *Hellenika* 6.1.13. Losada, *The Fifth Column* (above n. 10) 82-3, comments similarly on the motives of the *proxenoi* at Mytilene.

41. Demosthenes 14.33, 15.15; below p. 105.

42. Gerolymatos, *Espionage and Treason* 45-6.

43. IG IV i 748. The decree probably dates from 369, when Thebes under Epaminondas attacked, but failed to capture, Epidauros and Troezen.

44. P. McKechnie, *Outsiders in the Greek Cities* (London 1989), 181, 183-5.

45. Demosthenes 35.1-3, 7, 26; C. Mossé, 'The "World of the Emporium" in the private speeches of Demosthenes' in P.D. Garnsey, K. Hopkins and C.R. Whittaker (eds.), *Trade in the Ancient Economy* (London 1983) 53-63.

46. Aristotle *Politics* 951-3; Plato *Laws* 952D-53E.

47. Demosthenes 33.4-5, 37.52-3; also Andokides 1.137.

48. O. Taplin, *The Stagecraft of Aeschylus* (Oxford 1977) 81; J.M. Bremer 'Why messenger-speeches?' in J.M. Bremer, S.L. Radt and C.J. Ruijgh (eds), *Miscellanea Tragica in honorem J.C. Kamerbeek* (Amsterdam 1976) 29-48, 33; W.S. Barrett, Hippolytos (Oxford 1964), on l. 1151 defines the *aggelos* (messenger) as 'a minor character whose sole dramatic function is to report events which have taken place offstage'.

49. The tragic messenger is enough of a convention to be parodied in comedy. In Aristophanes *Birds* 1121-3 a messenger arrives out of breath:

Peisthetairos: But here comes someone running like an Olympic sprinter.

Messenger: *pou pou 'sti, pou pou pou 'sti, pou, pou, pou, 'sti, pou pou Peisetairos estin archôn?* (Where-where is he, where-where-where is he, where-where-where is he, where-where is your leader Peisthetairos?)

See P. Rau, *Paratragodia: Untersuchung einer komischen Form des Aristophanes* (Munich 1967) 164 (on this passage), 162-8 (on parody of messenger scenes in general).

50. Euripides *Phoenissai* 1072-4; *Troades* 235-7.

51. Euripides *Elektra* 765-9; *Herakleidai* 638-40; It is always possible to suspect Euripides of playing with conventions, drawing attention to them in order to ridicule, and certainly the idea that the messenger is someone who has been present, visible or not, in every scene, is being called into question here. Nevertheless such elements can also be included for the sake of realism.

52. In extant Greek tragedy deception scenes occur in *Choephoroi, Elektra* and *Philoktetes*, and also in the lost Kresphontes. U. Parlavantza-Friedrich, *Täuschungsszenen in den Tragödien des Sophokles* (Berlin 1969) 49, divides the scenes into four typical elements, the plan, the execution, the deceit and the discovery.

53. Aischylos *Choephoroi* 560-4; Sophokles *Elektra* 42-6, 668-70.

54. Arrian *Indika* 17.6; *Anabasis* Pref. 2. The idea of the trustworthiness of kings, because they would be more ashamed than other men to lie, became a commonplace in Hellenistic literature, but Arrian's sentence here implies that it was a serious consideration, over and above the fact that Ptolemy was present on Alexander's campaigns.

55. Herodotos 9.16 (Thersander), 2.3 (priestly information), 2.28 (scribe of Saïs). D. Fehling, *Herodotos and his 'Sources': citation, invention, and narrative art* (Leeds 1989) 117, rejects all Herodotos' source citations as invention, even the named Thersander, whom Fehling describes as an authority for a prophetic utterance of a conventional kind. He does not, however, attack the credibility of Herodotos' other named sources, Archias of Pitane (3.55.2) and Tymnes (4.76.6), directly, admitting that there is nothing inherently unbelievable about them.

56. Thucydides 1.21; A.W. Gomme, *A Historical Commentary on Thucydides* i (Oxford 1945) 141.

57. This was suggested to me by Simon Hornblower.

58. Herodotos 8.23 (see below p. 89); Xenophon *Hellenika* 7.5.10.

59. P.A. Brunt, review of P.D. Garnsey, *Social Status and Legal Privilege in the Roman Empire*, *JRS* 62 (1972) 169; Theognis 383-92, 177-8, 267-70; Old Oligarch 1.5: 'Among the people there is the greatest ignorance, disorder and vice; for poverty rather leads them to base deeds'; Thucydides 3.45; Antiphon *Tetralogies* 2.9.

60. Euripides *Andromeda* 768-76, fr. 362. 14-15. Wealth is more important: *Phoenissai* 422, fr. 95, fr. 362. Nobility of the soul: *Helen* 728-33, fr. 232, fr. 336, fr. 495. 41-4.

61. Euripides *Elektra* 36-8, 253, 367-72, 403ff.

62. Aristophanes *Wealth* 88-90, 386-9, 489-97.

63. *Wealth* 527-34, 557-61.

64. In Aristophanes' *Wasps* 1121-69 the old-fashioned Athenian poverty of the jurors is contrasted with the Eastern-style luxury of Bdelykleon and his friends; Xenophon praises the Spartan adoption of poverty (*Lakedaimonion Politeia* 7.2-6, 14.2-4) and contrasts the luxury of the Persians unfavourably with the hardiness of the Spartans (*Hellenika* 3.4.19, 4.1.30). This last is an idea which has its roots in Herodotos (9.82).

65. Plato *Republic* 422A, 590B.

66. Demosthenes 57.35, 46; 'poor but honest' appears in Demosthenes 21.95 (a slightly problematic case because Straton had been deprived of citizen rights, so the jury had reasonable grounds to suspect that he was indeed dishonest, irrespective of wealth or poverty).

67. The attitude of the jury on this point is discussed by S.C. Todd, 'Lady Chatterly's Lover and the Attic Orators', *JHS* 110 (1990) 146-73, a reply to M.M. Markle, 'Jury pay and assembly pay at Athens', in P.A. Cartledge and F.D. Harvey (eds), *Crux: Essays presented to G.E.M. de Ste. Croix* (London 1985) 265-97. Orators certainly indulge in the incitement of prejudice against the rich (Demosthenes 21.159, Lysias 19.10, 21.16-17; Lykourgos *Against Leokrates* 140). However, Todd does not quite do justice to the implications of attitudes towards poor litigants in the speeches. He sees hostility only towards the banausic, not the poor peasant, but this disregards the extent to which wealth was a moral issue. Defendants apologise for their poverty because of the message it carries about their character, and a jury will not sympathise with an impoverished farmer any more than a poor shopkeeper. Aristophanes, it is true, suggests in the *Wasps* (230-47, 291-315) that a poor litigant might appeal to a jury for sympathy, but the speeches tend to indicate the opposite – poverty was a condition to be excused or explained, not brought forward as a plea.

68. R.J. Bonner and G. Smith, *The Administration of Justice from Homer to Aristotle* (Chicago 1938); R. Volkmann, *Die Rhetorik der Greichen und Romer* (Hildesheim 1963) 187.

69. Demosthenes 57.35, 46.

70. This topic aroused discussion at the time, and was a commonplace in forensic speeches, orators arguing both for and against the effectiveness of such measures. There is doubt as to how often torture was in fact used – we possess no record of any case in which evidence given under torture actually came before the court. See Bonner and Smith *Administration of Justice* ii 126-30, and P. Du Bois, *Torture and Truth* (London 1991) 63-8.

71. Antiphon 6.25: 'it is possible to compel free men with oaths and pledges, which are the most serious and most respected methods for the free, and it is possible to use other methods of compulsion on slaves, by means of which, even if they will die as a result of their confession, nevertheless they can be compelled to tell the truth.'

72. On the place of *timê* (honour) in the Roman judicial system, P.D. Garnsey, *Social Status and Legal Privilege in the Roman Empire* (Oxford 1970).

73. Herodotos 8.136.1.

74. Herodotos 8.23. Starr, *Political Intelligence* 16, implicitly distinguishes between the treatment of upper-and lower-class prisoners.

75. Xenophon *Hellenika* 6.5.25.

76. Herodotos 8.94.3.

77. Thucydides 1.91.2: 'he bade them ... send whichever of their citizens were worthy, and would give reliable reports, to see for themselves.' The same thinking may underlie the Spartan institution of the *agathoergoi* (Herodotos 1.67), whereby the five oldest men leaving the cavalry each year became state agents for a year. Membership of the cavalry implies wealth, and Lichas, at 1.67, was certainly on a fact-finding mission.

78. Xenophon *Hellenika* 6.2.31: 'for he had not heard at first-hand what had happened to Mnasippos, and he suspected that the report might be intended to deceive. Accordingly he was on his guard.' Powell, 'Mendacity and Sparta's use of the visual' 179, sets this in the context of Spartan deceitfulness.

79. Homer *Iliad* 13.99-101, 24.312, 392-5, *Odyssey* especially 3.92-6 and 4.322-6, 8.459, 10.179-83, 14.341-3. See G. Nenci, 'Il motivo dell' autopsia nella storiografica greca', *Studi Classici e Orientali* 3 (1953) 14-16.

80. Herodotos 2.29: 'As far as the city of Elephantine my account is firsthand; beyond here, my report is hearsay', 7.152, 2.123. He emphasises that his information is second-hand at 1.201, 4.16, 23. For a discussion of Herodotos' use of autopsy and hearsay, F. Hartog, *The Mirror of Herodotos* (Berkeley 1988) 261-9.

81. Cf. Thucydides 1.22.2.

82. Polybios 12.27a; see E. Hussey, 'The beginning of epistemology', in S. Everson, *Epistemology* (Cambridge 1990) 11-38, 34-5, and Plato *Theaitêtos* 201B-C.

83. Euripides *Medea* 653-4 (Aischylos *Choephoroi* 852 has the same kind of observation); Aischylos *Persai* 266, *Supplices* 684; Euripides *Troades* 481; also Sophokles *Oedipus Tyrannos* 6; Euripides *Herakleidai* 390-1, *Iphigeneia in Tauris* 901.

84. Euripides *Helen* 117-18 (compare the language of Homeric passages at n. 79 above).

85. Xenophon *Hellenika* 4.3.1-2.

86. Thucydides 1.91; Herodotos 8.23.

87. Thucydides 6.45.1.

88. Theophrastos *Characters* 8.2.

89. Plutarch *Pelopidas* 14.2 (a spy disguised as a merchant); Thucydides 3.3.5: 'A man went from Mytilene to Athens, crossing over to Euboia and going on foot to Geraistos, where he found a merchant-ship on the point of setting sail; he made a quick crossing, and on the third day reached Mytilene, where he told them of the Athenian attack.'

90. Sophokles *Philoktetes* 551-2.

91. Sophokles *Trachiniai* 187-90.

92. Diodoros 15.74.1.

93. Starr, *Political Intelligence* 15.

94. Herodotos 8.110.3.

95. Plutarch *Moralia* 178B, Diodoros 16.24, Cicero *Ad Att.* 1.16.12; Demosthenes 19.259-71, 18.295.

96. Demosthenes 20.59-60.

97. Herodotos 9.45.3; Demosthenes 20.60; see Gerolymatos, *Espionage and Treason* 42-3.

98. Thucydides 3.29.1-2.

99. Ibid. 6.41.

100. Ibid. 6.45.

101. Plutarch *Solon* 9.

102. Polyainos 3.9.20; Aineias Tacticus *Poliorketika* 9.1-2. Compare the Athenian response in marching in force to the Piraeus when they thought it was under threat, Thucydides 2.94, 8.94, Xenophon *Hellenika* 5.1.22.

103. *Hellenika Oxyrhynchia* 18; Xenophon *Hellenika* 3.5.4 places the appeal after the invasion, which seems less likely, but one could still see a temporising measure allowing time to muster an army.

104. Demosthenes 3.5.

105. Thucydides 6.65.1: 'The Syracusan generals, since they were encouraged by other events, and had intended even without this to prepare an attack on Katana, trusted the man in a most thoughtless way (*pollô(i) aperiskeptoteron*).'

106. Thucydides 3.3.1.

107. Ibid. 8.1.1.

108. Xenophon *Hellenika* 5.2.12, 20.

109. Demosthenes 3.4-5.

110. M.I. Finley, *Democracy Ancient and Modern* (London 1985) 157-9.

111. Plutarch *Nikias* 30.2.

112. Herodotos 5.87.2, also Plutarch *Moralia* 241B, Sophokles *Antigone* 238-40.

113. Finley, *Politics in the Ancient World* (above n. 2) 80.

114. Demosthenes 2.17.

5. The Assembly

Epigraph: J. Boswell, *Life of Johnson*, ed. G. Birkbeck Hill, rev. L.F. Powell (Oxford 1934-50), iii.293.

1. M.H. Hansen, *The Athenian Assembly in the Age of Demosthenes* (Oxford 1987) 123; C.G. Starr, *Political Intelligence in Classical Greece* (1974) 29-38.
2. Aristotle *Athenaion Politeia* 43.4-6. Deme assemblies concerned solely internal matters, and a narrow range of topics: finance, religion and honours; see R.G. Osborne, *Demos: the discovery of Classical Attika* (Cambridge 1985) 79-80.
3. Demosthenes 19.154 and Aischines 2.61 refer to the regular assemblies being used up; M.H. Hansen, 'How often did the Ecclesia meet?', in *The Athenian Ecclesia* (Copenhagen 1983) 35-72 concludes that only four assemblies could be held in each prytany, whether summoned by regular procedure or called at short notice *(ekklêsia sungklêtos)*. This was true only for the later fourth century; in the fifth and early fourth century there was no such limitation (Thucydides 2.22.1 and J. Christensen and M.H. Hansen, 'What is *syllogos* at Thukydides 2.22.1?' CM 34 (1982) (= Hansen, *The Athenian Ecclesia II* (Copenhagen 1989) 195-211).
4. P.J. Rhodes, *The Athenian Boule* (Oxford 1972) 54.
5. Xenophon *Hellenika* 6.4.19-20. This episode is discussed further in ch. 3 pp. 66-7.
6. Thucydides 6.40.2: 'And if there is no truth in these rumours, as I believe, the city is not going to be thrown into panic by your reports and willingly hand itself over into slavery by choosing you as its rulers.' For the Mysteries case see below p. 119.
7. Hartley, *Understanding News* 77-9; the formulation of newsworthiness follows that of J. Galtung and M. Ruge, 'Structuring and selecting news', in S. Cohen and J. Young (eds), *The Manufacture of News: social problems, deviance and the mass media* (London 1973) 62-72.
8. Aischines 2.169.
9. Plato *Charmides* 153B-C.
10. Demosthenes 18.169-170.
11. Aristotle *Athenaion Politeia* 43.4.
12. Hansen, *The Athenian Assembly* 27.
13. Demosthenes 18.120 comments on the reasons for the proclamation of crowns in the theatre: the proclamation is to the benefit of those granting the crown, as those who hear it are encouraged to benefit the state themselves. The conferring of civic honours was intended to encourage political initiative; the same phenomenon is found with the publication of honorary decrees on stone (Demosthenes 20.5). This idea is explored in more detail below pp. 133-4.
14. Aristotle *Athenaion Politeia* 44.2; Hansen *The Athenian Assembly* 145 nn. 159-61.
15. Thucydides 3.36.5.
16. Aristophanes *Ekklesiazusai* 394-5, *Acharnians* 37-9.
17. Demosthenes 18.169-70; Thucydides 6.8.3-4; 3.36.4-6; Xenophon *Hellenika* 2.2.4.
18. Plutarch *Nikias* 12.1; *Alkibiades* 17.3.
19. G. Herman, *Ritualised Friendship and the Greek City* (Cambridge 1987) 130-42, discusses the use made by states of the personal contacts of *xenia* in official communications. Not until the fourth century does the suggestion of

segregating foreign ambassadors from the citizens appear (Aineias Tacticus *Poliorketika* 10.11).

20. For example, Demosthenes 1.6, 3.4, 7.37, 10.10, 23.104.

21. Aristotle *Athenaion Politeia* 43.3, 6.

22. Aristotle *Rhetorika* 1359b19-23. G.A. Kennedy, *Aristotle on Rhetoric: a theory of civic discourse* (Oxford 1991) 53 n. 87, suggests that both accounts may be derived from a lost handbook of politics.

23. *Rhetorika* 1359b24-7, Xenophon *Memorabilia* 3.6.5-6.

24. Xenophon *Memorabilia* 3.6.12.

25. Aristophanes *Wasps* 655-64.

26. Xenophon *Memorabilia* 3.5.2; see Starr, *Political Intelligence* 41.

27. Demosthenes 4.16-22 sets out plans for two Athenian forces to oppose Philip, one of fifty ships and one of ten. The expense of the larger force of fifty ships is not discussed at all, while detail of the manning of both forces is vague: 'of whatever age you think fit ... serving for as long as you think right.'

28. A. Powell, 'Mendacity and Sparta's use of the visual' in A. Powell (ed.), *Classical Sparta: techniques behind her success* (London 1989) 173-92, 183. Plutarch *Lykourgos* 20.9 (and *Apophthegmata Lakonika* 215D, 218A), records the answers of various Spartan kings to the question 'How many Spartiates are there?', answers notable for their evasiveness.

29. Demosthenes 11.12; also 1.22, 2.17, 19, 8.14, 10.8, 11.8-10.

30. Demosthenes 1.22-3.

31. Plato *Protagoras* 319B-323A comments on the Athenian use of experts to provide advice in the assembly on technical matters, but allowing anyone to advise on political matters. See R.K. Sinclair, *Democracy and Participation in Athens* (Cambridge 1988) 216.

32. Demosthenes 2.17.

33. Thucydides 6.32.3; Aischines 3.82; cf. Demosthenes 7.37.

34. Aristotle *Rhetorika* 1359b37-1360a5.

35. Unease about Thebes: Demosthenes 14.33; about the Rhodians: Demosthenes 15.15.

36. Aischines 2.141, also 106.

37. Aischines 3.160.

38. Demosthenes 23.104: 'I will remind you of a past event with which you are all familiar.'

39. Aischines 3.82; answered by Demosthenes 18.27; Aischines 3.77.

40. Letters from Chares: Aischines 2.90; from Proxenos: 2.134; from Timotheos and Iphikrates: Demosthenes 23.151.

41. See above ch. 4, section 2.i.

42. W.E. Thompson, 'Athenian leadership: expertise or charisma?', in G.S. Shrimpton and D.J. McCargar (eds), *Classical Contributions: studies in honour of M.F. McGregor* (New York 1981) 153-9.

43. Thucydides 1.138.3 (on Themistokles) 2.65, 59 (Perikles); Demosthenes 18.246.

44. Starr, *Political Intelligence* 37: 'Rather, it was men like Themistocles, Pericles, Demosthenes, the elders who had sat in the Council, and more generally across Greece the aristocrats who held in their minds the information which made the intelligence useful.'

45. The opposite view is expressed by, for example, A.H.M. Jones, *Athenian Democracy* (Oxford 1957) 132-3.

46. Particularly G.L. Cawkwell, *Philip of Macedon* (London 1978) 79-82, 87-8, 126-31.

47. Demosthenes 18.71.

48. Plutarch *Phokion* 15.

49. Demosthenes 18.295.

50. Polybios 18.14

51. M.I. Finley, *Politics in the Ancient World* (Cambridge 1983), 80.

52. Demosthenes 1.23.

53. [Demosthenes] 50.4-6.

54. Thucydides 6.33-41.

55. Demosthenes 18.17.

56. Ibid. 225-6.

57. Ibid. 150.

58. Ibid. 249; also Demosthenes 47.44: 'and I ask whichever of you served on the Boule in the archonship of Agathokles to tell it to those sitting next to you'; 40.11 – 'as indeed most of you know, for the matter was much talked of '; 18.249; Aischines 2.44, 3.166.

59. R. Thomas, *Oral Tradition and Written Record in Classical Athens* (Cambridge 1989) 62.

60. Herodotos presents variant accounts without discriminating at 3.86, 5.44-5, 6.137 and 7.152, stating that the decision between versions is left to the reader. D. Lateiner, *The Historical Methods of Herodotus* (London 1989) 80-4, discusses Herodotos' use of variant accounts, and concludes that among Herodotos' concerns the desire not to exclude sources was stronger than the wish to produce an authoritative history.

61. S.C. Todd, 'The purpose of evidence in Athenian courts', in P.A. Cartledge, P.C. Millett and S.C. Todd (eds) *NOMOS: essays in Athenian law, politics and society* (Cambridge 1990) 19-40, 23. Occasionally special procedures could be used with the object of establishing the truth, for example *IG* i³ 102 (M-L 85) ll. 38-47, on the enquiry into Phrynichos' assassins, but this was rare.

62. One of the most striking examples is Andokides' account of the Pentekontaitia, 3.3-9; see Thomas, *Oral Tradition* 118-23.

63. G.E.R. Lloyd, *Magic, Reason and Experience* (Cambridge 1979) 85 and n.137; G.A. Kennedy, *The Art of Persuasion in Greece* (Princeton 1963) 51-2 says that this belief led to the development of the principle that everyone, no matter how bad their case, has a right to present it.

64. Aristotle *Rhetorika* 1375a27-9: 'for it is clear that, if the written law is unfavourable to the case, one must appeal to general law and what is reasonable, as being more just.'

65. Todd, 'The purpose of evidence ...' (above n. 61) 32.

66. *Rhetorika ad Alexandrum* 1431b7ff. This states that it is necessary first to present the evidence of witnesses and confessions, 'and to confirm by means of maxims and general considerations, if the evidence is convincing', but if it is not convincing, arguments from probability, signs and so on should be used.

67. Above n. 23.

68. This is not to say that the testing of theories is never to be found; in Hippokrates *On Joints* 47 the writer recounts an experiment that failed and states the value of this: 'I have recorded this deliberately; for these things are still useful for instruction, which have been tried and found unsuccessful, and show why they failed.' On the whole, however, such an attitude is rare, and few medical writers were confident enough of their position to present opportunities for criticism to their rivals.

69. R.G.A. Buxton, *Persuasion in Greek Tragedy* (Cambridge 1982) 5.

70. Buxton, *Persuasion in Greek Tragedy* 21; Hippokrates *On Joints* 70.

71. Demosthenes 18.226, 276; 19.217.

72. Ibid. 9.2.

73. Ibid. 18.225-6: '... he has selected from a mass of old dates and decrees ones which no one knew of before, and which no one expected to be mentioned today, in order to misrepresent them, and he has altered dates and assigned false motives to past actions so he will appear to have a case'; also 211-12, 282.

74. Demosthenes 3.21-2, 4.38, 51, 6.3, 9.2-5.

75. Thucydides 7.8.2, and also 4.27.3, where Kleon suggests that the messengers from Pylos may not be reporting accurately; Demosthenes 9.4, 3.3, 21.

76. Thucydides 3.3.1.

77. Demosthenes 10.1.

78. Thucydides 2.65.10-11. The Mytilene Debate is a difficult passage to use as evidence, because the speeches were written by Thucydides to make his point, even if they do reflect essentially what the speakers said and how they said it on the occasion. On the other hand, the speeches do represent a valid criticism of the assembly, albeit from a man with oligarchical sympathies. The speeches are also very self-referential, and C.W. MacLeod, 'Reason and Necessity: Thucydides iii 9-14, 37-48' (*JHS* 98 (1978) 64-78 (= *Collected Essays* (Oxford 1983) 88-102) suggests that Thucydides is attempting to illustrate the impossibility of rational debate. But even so, some points about truth and rhetoric can still be drawn from the passage.

79. Thucydides 3.38.4; 3.42.2-4.

80. Demosthenes 23.97; also 18.282, 19.70, Dinarchos 1.47.

81. Thucydides 3.42.4: 'the city would be most likely to succeed if citizens of the kind I have mentioned were unskilled in oratory; for it would far less often be persuaded into making mistakes.'

82. Ibid. 6.24.1-2; Xenophon *Hellenika* 1.7.35.

83. Thucydides 8.1.

84. This view of the assembly also appears in Aristophanes, notably in the *Knights* – Demos is easily led by his slaves and relies on them to make decisions. The fantasy of the plot ends with the rejuvenation of Demos and the return of his ability to make decisions for himself, effectively a return to the 'good old days'.

85. Demosthenes 18.142; also 20.3.

86. Sinclair, *Democracy and Participation* (n. 25) 204-5 makes the point that oratorical sources may be suspect here, because a speaker had to condemn his rivals while upholding the democratic system.

87. Thucydides 2.65.8; Demosthenes 3.21-22.

88. As in the Mytilene debate, and also the debate at Syracuse (6.32-41).

89. Xenophon *Hellenika* 1.7.29; see G.A. Kennedy, 'Focusing of arguments in Greek deliberative oratory', *TAPA* 90 (1959) 131-8, on the modes of argument in the fifth and fourth centuries: he argues that the emphasis on expediency was a particularly fifth-century development, and was less used in the fourth, popular sentiment being unwilling to accept arguments from self-interest only.

90. *Hellenika Oxyrhynchia* 6.1-3.

91. Diodoros 11.42; Demosthenes 2.6. G.E.M. de Ste. Croix, 'The alleged secret pact between Athens and Philip II concerning Amphipolis and Pydna', *CQ* 13 (1963) 110-19, 115 n.1 collects the instances of secret meetings of the Boule.

92. Aischines 3.125: 'when this fellow was not able to cause the downfall of the city openly, he went into the council-chamber, cleared it of non-members, and brought from there a draft proposal for the assembly.'

93. Andokides 2.19.

94. Ibid. 21: 'I would give a great sum of money if I could safely tell you the benefits which I have communicated in secret to the Boule, so that you could know them now in advance.'

95. Andokides 1.12.

96. Rhodes, *The Athenian Boule* 40.

97. Diodoros 11.42.1.

98. Demosthenes 4.18; Aischines 3.103.

99. Demosthenes 25.23; bystanders: 8.4, 19.17.

100. Aristophanes *Ekklesiazusai* ll.441-4; Lysias 31.31.

101. Xenophon *Hellenika* 2.2.3: 'The *Paralos* arrived in Athens by night with news of the disaster, and as one person told the news to the next, the cry of lamentation ran from the Piraeus, along the Long Walls, to the city.'

102. Aristophanes *Acharnians* 37-40, 56-60; *IG* i³ 78 (M-L 73), ll.46-61.

103. Aischines 3.125; see Rhodes, *The Athenian Boule* 56.

104. Aristophanes *Knights* 647-50.

105. Thucydides 8.66: 'thinking that the conspiracy was much greater than it actually was, people were overcome by their fears, and were unable to find out the truth ....'

106. Xenophon *Hellenika* 6.4.19-20.

107. Aristotle *Athenaion Politeia* 42 for registration; Demosthenes 9.3 for the exclusion of slaves and metics; Hansen, *The Athenian Assembly* 139 n. 51 on ephebic training and participation in the assembly.

108. Hansen, *The Athenian Assembly* 16ff.

109. Andokides 1.11.

110. Ibid. 27.

111. Aristotle *Athenaion Politeia* 43.4; [Demosthenes] 50.6.

112. Lysias 22.14.

113. Aristotle *Athenaion Politeia* 41.3; by the time of *Ekklesiazusai* (393/2) it had reached the rate of three obols. Its effect on participation is discussed by S. Todd, '*Lady Chatterley's Lover* and the Attic orators: the social composition of the Athenian jury', *JHS* 110 (1990) 146-73, 170-3.

114. Attacks on poverty: Demosthenes 18.256-67, 19.237; cf. 22.30.

115. Xenophon *Hellenika* 3.3.8.

116. Aristotle *Politics* 1272a10-12, 1273a9-13; see A. Andrewes, 'The government of classical Sparta', in *Ancient Society and Institutions: studies presented to V. Ehrenberg* (Oxford 1967) 1-20, and D.H. Kelly, 'Policy-making in the Spartan assembly', *Antichthon* 15 (1981) 47-61.

117. See Andrewes, 'The government of classical Sparta', 8-13.

118. Thucydides 1.87.1-3.

119. Plutarch *Agis* 9-11; Plutarch says that Lysander 'discussed the ideas with the citizens' (9).

120. On the Macedonian assembly, R.M. Errington, 'The nature of the Macedonian state under the monarchy', *Chiron* 8 (1978) 77-133; E.M. Anson, 'Macedonia's alleged constitutionalism', *CJ* 80 (1985) 303-16; N.G.L. Hammond, *The Macedonian State: the origins, institutions and history* (Oxford 1989) 58-65.

121. E.g. *IG* 1³ 89, Tod *GHI* 111 (although there is no standard practice); Aischines 2.22-35, 38-9, 108-20.

122. Diodoros 16.3.1, 17.2, Justin 11.1.8.

123. See E.N. Borza, *In the Shadow of Olympus: the emergence of Macedon* (Princeton 1990) 232-6. I follow the arguments of Errington and Anson (above n. 120) here.

124. Arrian *Anabasis* 3.26.2-4. The resentment of the army at Parmenio's death is made clear by Diodoros 17.80.4 and Quintus Curtius Rufus 10.1.6, but this resentment was not expressed in an assembly until later on.

125. Arrian *Anabasis* 5.28.4; 7.8.

6. News and Writing

Epigraph: J. Boswell, *Life of Johnson* ed. G. Birkbeck Hill, rev. L.F. Powell (Oxford 1934-50) ii. 170.

1. W.V. Harris, *Ancient Literacy* (Cambridge, Mass. 1989); R. Thomas, *Literacy and Orality in Ancient Greece* (Cambridge 1992); M. Beard (ed.), *Literacy in the Roman World* (Ann Arbor, MI 1991) (a collection of essays in response to Harris).

2. T.A. Boring, *Literacy in Ancient Sparta* (Leiden 1979), 97; see also F.D. Harvey, 'Literacy in the Athenian democracy', *REG* 79 (1966) 585-635, P.A. Cartledge, 'Literacy in the Spartan oligarchy', *JHS* 98 (1978) 25-37, Ø. Andersen, 'Mündlichkeit und Schriftlichkeit im frühen Griechentum', *Antike und Abendland* 33 (1987) 29-44.

3. Harris, *Ancient Literacy* 114-15; Thomas, *Literacy and Orality* 11.

4. R. Thomas, *Oral Tradition and Written Record in Classical Athens* (1988) 38-40; Demosthenes 45.44; Harris 71-2.

5. Thomas, *Literacy and Orality* 88.

6. Ibid. 82-4. Demosthenes 46.11 attributes reasons to depositions made on different materials: 'for those who are giving evidence in response to a challenge, coming forward of their own accord, it is appropriate to write their testimony on wax tablets, so that if anything needs to be added or erased, it can easily be done.'

7. Aristotle *Athenaion Politeia* 42.1; Isokrates 15.237; Plutarch *Nikias* 14.5 (a dubious story, but interesting in that it emphasises that records were normally kept outside the city); D. Whitehead, *The Ideology of the Athenian Metic* (Cambridge 1977). On the *lexiarchikon grammateion*, R. Osborne, *Demos: the discovery of classical Attika* (Cambridge 1985) 72-3; D. Whitehead, The *Demes of Attica* (Princeton 1986) 17-23.

8. Demosthenes 57.20-9, 37-43, 46-7, Demosthenes 39.4-5; also Lysias 23.5-7.

9. Plato *Laws* 785A-B.

10. J.H. Kroll, 'An archive of the Athenian cavalry', *Hesperia* 46 (1977) 83-140, Thomas, *Oral Tradition* 82-3.

11. Xenophon *Memorabilia* 3.5.2-5; Starr, *Political Intelligence in Classical Greece* (1974) 41 and nn. 3-5.

12. Sparta: Xenophon *Hellenika* 6.5.28, 3.3.5; Athens: Thucydides 2.13.2-5, *IG* 1³ 52 (M-L 58), Aristophanes *Wasps* 656-64.

13. Private inscriptions on stone (funerary monuments, dedications, horoi) are of a slightly different order, and are less directly concerned with news.

14. Riepl, *Das Nachrichtenwesen des Altertums*, is mainly interested in the mechanisms of news transmission, but the only written method he considers for the Greek period is the letter.

15. For states which did restrict the use of writing, see below section 3.

16. Most, but not all honorary decrees were published at state expense (see below p. 134). Troops to Melos: *IG* i³ 60.

17. M.H. Hansen, 'How many Athenians attended the *Ecclesia?*', *GRBS* 17 (1976) 115-34 (= *The Athenian Ecclesia* (Copenhagen 1983) 1-20) 130-3.

18. J. Pouilloux, *Récherches sur l'histoire et les cultes de Thasos* i (Paris 1954) 37, no. 7.

19. Theophrastos *Characters* 4 (Agroikos); Aristophanes Lysistrata 518-20; see also *Ekklesiazusai* 243-4.

20. *IG* ii² 1184. This and the decrees that follow are collected in C. Schwenk, *Athens in the Age of Alexander* (Chicago 1985); this decree, 26 ll.18-21.

21. Schwenk 43 (*REG* 91 (1978)) ll. 43ff.

22. *IG* ii² 1198 (Schwenk 66); also H. Engelmann and R. Merkelbach (eds), *Die Inschriften von Erythrai und Klazomenai* i (Bonn 1972) no. 21, an honorary decree from Erythrai from 330, expressing the same idea.

23. Placing of deme decrees: deme agora, *IG* ii² 1174, 1176, 1180, 1188; theatre, *IG* ii² 1197, 1198 (above), 1202; temples, *IG* ii² 1177, 1182, 1184, 1186, 1187, 1199, 1203, 1206, 1214; wherever best, *IG* ii² 1193 l.30. Of the decrees placed in temples, 1186, 1187, 1203 and 1214 are honorific, including both Athenian and foreign honorands (1186). Decrees of Athenian tribes were usually placed in the temple of their respective hero, on or near the Akropolis. See R.G. Osborne, 'The *Demos* and its divisions in classical Athens', in O. Murray and S.R.F. Price (eds), *The Greek City from Homer to Alexander* (Oxford 1990) 265-93.

24. Andokides 1.84; also Demosthenes 24.18, the requirement for new laws to be posted in front of the statue of the Eponymous Heroes; see Thomas, *Oral Tradition* 60-1 (and n. 151).

25. M. Gagarin, *Early Greek Law* (Berkeley 1986) 133.

26. [Demosthenes] 59.76. This was a religious decree, set up in a sanctuary which was opened only once a year, 'so that the majority should not know the content of the decree'.

27. M. Detienne, 'L'espace de la publicité: ses operateurs intellectuels dans la cité' in Detienne (ed.), *Les savoirs de l'écriture en Grèce ancienne* (Paris 1988) 29-81.

28. See B.D. Meritt and J.S. Traill, *The Athenian Agora* vol. xv, *Inscriptions: the Athenian Councillors* (Princeton 1974); G.V. Lalonde (ed.), *The Athenian Agora* vol. xix, *Inscriptions: horoi, poletai records, leases of public lands* (Princeton 1991).

29. *SEG* 33 (1983) 682 (I. Délos 15); *SEG* 12 87.

30. *SEG* 12 87, ll. 16-20.

31. *Hesperia* 43 (1974) 157-88.

32. *IG* ii² 125 (Tod, *GHI* 154).

33. '... they are to inscribe the [decree on a stele of st]one and set it up on the Akrop[olis and in the Agora] and in the harbour.' The reconstruction of the provision for publication is uncertain; the noun *stêlêi* is singular, which led Kirchner to see one stele and two whitened boards, on the analogy of *IG* xii (8) 262, but others (including Tod) reconstruct a provision for three stelai.

34. Plutarch *Moralia* 292B.

35. There was no sense in which the documents in the Metröon were more authoritative than those inscribed on stelai; see Thomas, *Oral Tradition* 45-8.

36. *IG* i³ 110 (M-L 90).

37. Meiggs and Lewis, *GHI* p. 277.

38. *IG* i³ 101 (M-L 89); the erasure is in l.7. Photo in *BSA* (1951) 200-9.

39. A.S. Henry, *Honours and Privileges in Athenian Decrees* (Hildesheim 1983) 262-3.

40. *IG* ii² 1275, Schwenk 77.

41. O. Kern, *Inschriften von Magnesia am Maeander* (Berlin 1900) 32. A Magnesian copy of an Epirote decree. Establishment at shrines ll. 33-9.

42. M.I. Finley, *Studies in Land and Credit in Ancient Athens* (New Brunswick 1952); Thomas, *Oral Tradition* 53-5: 'Often the destruction of the document signifies the end of the transaction it recorded, the end of the honour or agreement. This is sometimes connected with the extremely close identification of the written document and the transaction it records, of which it is in a sense a memorial.'

43. Diodoros 13.69.2.

44. *IG* ii² 6 (Tod 98), *IG* ii² 9.

45. Plutarch *Perikles* 30.1-2.

46. *IG* ii² 1 (Tod 97).

47. E.g. *IG* ii² 360 (Schwenk 68); *IG* ii² 366 (Schwenk 80).

48. Henry, *Honours and Privileges* 228ff.

49. Aischines 3.43.

50. Demosthenes 18.169.

51. Aristophanes *Peace* 1179-82; *Acharnians* 1073-9.

52. Thomas, *Oral Tradition* 60-83.

53. Isokrates *Panegyrikos* 120; Andokides 3.12. The consultation of stelai at Athens is not well documented.

54. Thomas, *Oral Tradition* 66.

55. Lysias 13.70-2, cf. M-L 85; Aristotle *Rhetorika* 1400a32-6. As noted above, the destruction of decrees under the Thirty, and subsequent reinscriptions, created a period of considerable epigraphic confusion.

56. This was the length of time stated in the decree formula: see *IG* ii² 4(1) Appendix p. 39 sv. *anagraphein*. *IG* i³ 85, a decree of unknown content, provides that a stele be set up *hôs tachista* (as soon as possible).

57. Demosthenes 24.17-24.

58. The record of the confiscated property of the Hermokopidai and profaners of the Mysteries in 415 was inscribed on a stele and set up in the Eleusinion at Athens (*IG* i³ 421, 426; M-L 79). Although the inscription was of a religious nature, it was nevertheless designed for public attention and for the disgrace of those involved.

59. [Demosthenes] 58.16, 47.22. The story of Plutarch, that the Megarian Decree was inscribed on a *pinakion*, should be treated with caution.

60. A. Burford, *The Greek Temple Builders at Epidauros* (Liverpool 1969) 11.

61. Suggested by Burford, *The Greek Temple Builders* 11.

62. *IG* ii² 125 (Tod *GHI* 154).

63. See D.M. Lewis, 'Democratic institutions and their diffusion', *Proceedings of the Eighth International Conference on Greek and Latin Epigraphy* (Athens 1984) 55-61.

64. This is the conclusion reached by Cartledge, 'Literacy in the Spartan oligarchy' (above n. 2). Boring, *Literacy in Ancient Sparta* 7, says: 'a more likely explanation [for the small number of public inscriptions] can be seen in the traditional secrecy and virtual isolation of the Spartans after the mid-sixth century.'

65. S. Dow, 'Corinthiaca', *HSCP* 53 (1942) 89-119, claims that 'for a tyrant to put up decrees invites unwelcome publicity or defacement, but demos likes to read what demos has done' (119); herms: [Plato] Hipparchos 228B-229D; *IG* i² 837 is an example from Koropi. Harris draws attention both to the propaganda purpose, and to a general interest in the written word among tyrants, instancing 'the alleged Pisistratan redaction of Homer and the large libraries ascribed to Pisistratus and to Polycrates of Samos' (53 and note); on Hipparchos' aims see B.M. Lavelle, 'Hipparchos' Herms', *Echos du Monde Classique* 29 (n.s. 4) (1985) 411-20.

66. Thucydides 4.80.

67. Lewis, 'Democratic institutions and their diffusion', n. 63; Thomas, *Orality and Literacy* 131-2.

68. For rulers and letters see below pp. 146-8.

69. The fifth-century inscriptions are collected in Boring's Appendix (A Select Catalogue of Inscriptions), 89-90; the others are to be found in *IG* v 1. A new fragment of the war contribution list is announced by A.P. Matthaiou and Y.A. Pikoulas, '*Edon tois Lakedaimoniois potton polemon. Neo thrausma tes IG* V¹ 1', *Horos* 6 (1988) 117, and '*Edon tois Lakedaimoniois potton polemon*', *Horos* 7 (1989) 77-124.

70. Thucydides 5.18.10.

71. *IG* v 1 1564.

72. Plutarch *Lysander* 30.3.

73. Sosibios: Jacoby *FGH* 4 85.

74. Plutarch *Lykourgos* 27.2. The exemption for women extended either to priestesses who died in office, or more probably to women dying in childbirth.

75. Xenophon *Lak. Pol.* 8.1-4, *Agesilaos* 6.4.

76. *IG* xii (2) 1 (Tod *GHI* 112) ll.1-4.

77. *Hesperia* 43 (1974) 157-188, ll. 55-6.

78. Thessaly: *IG* ii² 116 (Tod *GHI* 147); Ioulis: *IG* ii² 111 (Tod *GHI* 142) l.31ff.; Demosthenes 16.27; Thomas, *Oral Tradition* 52.

79. D.M. Lewis, 'The Athenian rationes centesimarum', in M.I. Finley (ed.), *Problèmes de la terre en Grèce ancienne* (Paris 1973) 187-212, 193.

80. Thucydides 5.18.10; 5.47.

81. O. Longo, 'Techniche della comunicazione e ideologie sociali', *QUCC* 27 (1978) 63-92, 72.

82. V. Martin, *La Vie internationale dans la Grèce des cités* (Paris 1940) 404: 'The sites chosen demonstrate that the aim was to make the agreements undertaken known beyond the immediately interested states, in order to inform panhellenic opinion .... This opinion, it was thought, once informed of the terms agreed by the Greek states, would be in a position to respond if a violation of those terms became known.'

83. Thucydides 1.71.5-6; also 1.36: 'and to the man who thinks what we have said would be advantageous, but is still afraid of being persuaded to break the treaty ....'

84. Thucydides 3.8.

85. Aristotle *Politics* 1338a15-19. The other use of writing for communication, implied by Aristotle, is of course the book. I have not included books in this chapter, since they can by their nature be concerned only with information, not news. The use of books to disseminate technical knowledge for certain trades is interesting in view of the proliferation of technical treatises in the fourth century, but many of these manuals are as concerned with theory as practice, and as such reflect the preoccupations of a small class of intellectuals. Technical information, so far as can be judged, continued to be taught orally throughout the period; books were never the concern of more than a small minority. See in general A. Burford, *Craftsmen in Greek and Roman Society* (London 1972) 82-8,

P. McKechnie, *Outsiders in the Greek Cities* (1989) 148-9, 157-8, Harris, *Ancient Literacy* (above n. 1) 82, 84-5.

86. Letters among the wealthy: Lysias 20.27, Demosthenes 27.14, 47, 50.62, Isokrates 17.52; less wealthy: letters on ostraka, Herris, *Ancient Literacy* 89 and n. 116. Pausanias 4.22-47 has a story of letters being used anachronistically early, while Plutarch includes anecdotes of Spartan women writing letters to their sons (*Moralia* 241A, D-E), but this probably results from a later perspective. Graffiti: Tod *GHI* 7; letters in trade: J. Chadwick, 'The Berezan lead letter', *PCPS* 19 (1973) 35-7, 'The Pech-Maho lead', *ZPE* 82 (1990) 161-6.

87. Euripides *Iphigeneia in Tauris* 760-5; Plutarch *Dion* 26.7.

88. F. Hartog, *The Mirror of Herodotos* (Berkeley 1988), 278; O. Longo, 'Scrivere in Tucidide: comunicazione e ideologia' in E. Livrea and G.A. Privitera (eds), *Studi in onore di A. Ardizzoni* (Rome 1978) 517-54.

89. Antiphon 5.53-4.

90. Aineias Tacticus *Poliorketika* 31; One could also add Aischines 2.124-8, Demosthenes 19.36 (the midnight letter), and Plato 314C (a letter to Dionysios II containing the instruction to burn the letter after reading). A striking parallel, suggested to me by Tom Harrison, appears in T.E. Lawrence, *The Seven Pillars of Wisdom* (Harmondsworth 1935, repr. 1977) 51: 'Feisal's correspondence with his father was an adventure in itself. They communicated by means of old retainers of the family, men above suspicion, who went up and down the Hejaz Railway, carrying letters in sword-hilts, in cakes, sewn between the soles of sandals, or in invisible writings on the wrappers of harmless packages.'

91. I follow the argument of S. West, 'Archilochus' Message-stick', *CQ* (1988) 42-8, which seems far more satisfactory in its interpretation of the *skytale* as a method of authenticating a message, rather than an encoding device.

92. Thucydides 1.132.

93. Aineias Tacticus *Poliorketika* 31.9; also Xenophon *Anabasis* 1.6.3; *Poliorketika* 31.33-4, Plutarch *Moralia* 596E-F; Arrian *Anabasis* 2.4.9-10.

94. Aischines 3.164, 225, Demosthenes 19.279, 25.50; 42.14, 56.8, Lykourgos fr. C10.

95. Longo, 'Scrivere in Tucidide' (above n. 88).

96. Thucydides 7.10-15; 1.128-134; 137-8 (Pausanias and Themistokles intriguing with Xerxes).

97. Longo, 'Scrivere in Tucidide' 528.

98. P.E. Easterling, 'Anachronism in Greek tragedy', *JHS* 105 (1985) 1-10.

99. Homer *Iliad* 6.168-177; also Thucydides 1.132, Plutarch *Lysander* 20.1-4.

100. Aischylos *Supplices* 446-8.

101. Euripides *Hippolytos* 1296-1312.

102. Euripides *Iphigeneia in Tauris* 760-5

103. Euripides *Iphigeneia in Aulis* 98-105 (true letter); 303-26 (false letter).

104. Herodotos 1.123-4, 5.35, 7.239.

105. Hartog, *Mirror of Herodotos* (above n. 88) 278-9.

106. Herodotos 1.125, 3.128, 3.40-2.

107. Thucydides 1.137, 1.128-32, 8.45, 50-1; also 4.50.

108. Xenophon *Hellenika* 1.7.4, Polyainos 4.2.8 (cf. Frontinus *Stratagems* 1.4.13), 4.11.2. Harris, *Ancient Literacy* 128 and n. 60, comments that the same attitude to letters is detectable in Polybios, with letters either forgeries or plots: 5.43.5-6, 50.11-12, 57.5, 61.3.

109. Letters from Philip: (direct) [Demosthenes] 12, 18.39, 77-8, 157, 166, 167, 19.38, 40, 51, 161, 187; (references) Demosthenes 2.7, 4.37, 7.1, 33, 8 (written in reply to a letter), 11 (in reply), 12.22, 18.221; Aischines 2.45, 50, 128; Plutarch *Moralia* 233E = 235A-B = 513A; 218E-F. Persian kings: examples from Thucydides and Herodotos at nn. 104-7 above; Aischines 3.238, Xenophon *Agesilaos* 8.3 (= Plutarch *Agesilaos* 33), Plutarch *Moralia* 213D-E, 225C-D. Thracian kings: Demosthenes 23.115, 174, 178.

110. Chios: *SIG*³ 283 (Tod 192); Eresos: *IG* xii 2.526 (Tod 191); Skepsis: *OGIS* 5; Teos: *SIG*³ 344.

111. Aischines 2.45, 129, Demosthenes 18.38.

112. Diodoros 13.58, 76, Xenophon *Hellenika* 7.1.36.

113. Herodotos 8.136.

114. Alexander: Diodoros 17.117.3, Curtius 10.54, Justin 12.15.12; Augustus: Dio 53.30.2.

115. Xenophon *Hellenika* 5.1.30, Thucydides 1.129; see also *Hellenika* 7.1.39.

116. Thucydides 4.20, [Demosthenes] 12.2, Xenophon *Hellenika* 1.1.23. F.E. Adcock and D.J. Mosley, *Diplomacy in Ancient Greece* (London 1975) 176, comment that the Greeks' ability to intercept envoys from other states may have had as much to do with the predictability of diplomatic moves, as with the receipt of successful intelligence.

117. Plutarch *Moralia* 799E.

118. Thucydides 2.67, also mentioned at Herodotos 7.137.

119. P. Ducrey, *Le Traitement des prisonniers de guerre dans la Grèce antique* (Paris 1968) ch. 4A. The Ten Thousand in Asia questioned their prisoners (Xenophon *Anabasis* 3.5.14-17, 4.1.22, 4.4.16-18), but mainly for geographical information, which they also discovered from native guides (for example 4.1.21).

120. Aischines 3.249-50.

121. Demosthenes 18.225-6, 19.39-40.

122. Ibid. 23.115, 151, 153, 159-63, 175-8, 183.

123. Aischines 2.134-5.

124. S. Hornblower, *Thucydides* (London 1987) 39-40; for the opposite view, Harris, *Ancient Literacy* 78. W.K. Pritchett, *The Greek State at War* ii (Berkeley 1974) 47, comments on the titles '*epistoleus*' and '*epistoliaphoros*', given to the vice-admiral in a Spartan command, for the importance of dispatch-writing. At Sparta writing, even at an official level, was still more concerned with secret information – compare the letters of Pedaritos and Astyochos (Thucydides 8.33,38, 50-1), and the list of those to be arrested by Kinadon (Xenophon *Hellenika* 3.3.8).

125. Demosthenes 23.153.

126. *IG* ii² 553; see also 387 and 213; Pritchett, *The Greek State at War* ii 45-7 has a list of such inscriptions.

127. *IG* ii² 213 ll. 6-9.

128. Demosthenes 23.168.

129. Eupolis fr. 308, Lucian *Pro Lapsu* 3, Schol. Ar. *Plut.* 322.

130. Aischines 2.90.

131. Thucydides 7.8-10.

132. Demosthenes 19.174

133. Xenophon *Hellenika* 1.7.1-7, 17.

134. A. Andrewes, 'The Arginusai trial', *Phoenix* 28 (1974) 112-22; Diodoros 13.100-3.

135. Demosthenes 23.156-8.

136. Ibid. 159-61.

137. Demosthenes 19.36, Aischines 2.124-5, Lykourgos fr. 105, Demosthenes 25.50.

138. See Herodotos 8.98; Marco Polo book 2 ch. 26 (= Marco Polo, *The Travels*, trans. R.E. Latham (Harmondsworth 1958) 150-5); Riepl *Das Nachrichtenwesen des Altertums* section 4.1.

Conclusion

1. For example, M. MacLuhan, *The Gutenberg Galaxy: the making of typographic man* (London 1962), esp. 58-61, G. Achard, *La Communication à Rome* (Paris 1991).

Bibliography

Achard, G., *La Communication à Rome* (Paris 1991).

Adcock, F.E., *The Greek and Macedonian Art of War* (Berkeley/Los Angeles 1957).

Adcock, F.E. and Mosley, D.J., *Diplomacy in Ancient Greece* (London 1975).

Aleshire, S.B., *The Athenian Asklepieion: the people, their dedications, and the inventories* (Amsterdam 1989).

Andersen, Ø., 'Mündlichkeit und Schriftlichkeit im frühen Griechentum', *Antike und Abendland* 33 (1987) 29-44.

Andrewes, A., 'The government of classical Sparta', in *Ancient Society and Institutions: Studies presented to V. Ehrenberg* (Oxford 1967).

——'The Theramenes Papyrus', *ZPE* 6 (1970) 35-8.

—— 'The Arginusai trial', *Phoenix* 28 (1974) 112-22.

Anson, E.M., 'Macedonia's alleged constitutionalism', *CJ* 80 (1985) 303-16.

Austen, J., *Emma*, ed. James Kinsley, (Oxford 1990).

Aymard, A., 'Philippe de Macédoine ôtage à Thèbes' *REA* 56 (1954), 15-36.

Barrett, W.S., *Hippolytos* (Oxford 1964).

Baslez, M-F., *L'Étranger dans la Grèce antique* (Paris 1984).

Beard, M. (ed.), *Literacy in the Roman World* (Ann Arbor, MI 1991).

Bonner, R.J. and Smith, G., *The Administration of Justice from Homer to Aristotle* (Chicago 1930-8) (2 vols).

Boring, T.A., *Literacy in Ancient Sparta* (Leiden 1979).

Borza, E.N., *In the Shadow of Olympus: the emergence of Macedon* (Princeton 1990).

Boswell, J., *Life of Johnson*, ed. G. Birkbeck Hill, rev. L.F. Powell (Oxford 1934-50).

Bosworth, A.B., *Conquest and Empire: the reign of Alexander the Great* (Cambridge 1988).

Bradford, A.S., 'The duplicitous Spartan', in A. Powell and S. Hodkinson (eds), *The Shadow of Sparta* (London 1994) 59-85.

Brandes, S., *Kinship, Migration and Community* (New York 1975).

Bremer, J.M., 'Why messenger-speeches?', in J.M. Bremer, S.L. Radt and C.J. Ruijgh (eds), *Miscellanea Tragica in honorem J.C. Kamerbeek* (Amsterdam 1976) 29-48.

Bremmer, J., 'Adolescents, *symposion*, and pederasty', in O. Murray (ed.), *Sympotica: a symposium on the symposion* (Oxford 1990) 135-48.

Brunt, P.A., review of Garnsey, P.D., *Social Status and Legal Privilege in the Roman Empire*, *JRS* 62 (1972) 169.

Burford, A., *The Greek Temple Builders at Epidauros* (Liverpool 1969)

—— *Craftsmen in Greek and Roman Society* (London 1972).

Buxton, R.G.A., *Persuasion in Greek Tragedy* (Cambridge 1982).

Camp, J.M., *The Athenian Agora* (London 1986).

Carey, C. and Reid, R.A., *Demosthenes: selected private speeches* (Cambridge 1985).

Cartledge, P.A., *Sparta and Laconia* (Cambridge 1977).

—— 'Literacy in the Spartan oligarchy', *JHS* 98 (1978) 25-37.

—— 'The Greek religious festivals', in P.E. Easterling and J.V. Muir (eds), *Greek Religion and Society* (Cambridge 1985), 98-127.

—— *Agesilaos and the Crisis of Sparta* (London 1987) 414-17.

Casson, L., *Ships and Seamanship in the Ancient World* (Princeton 1971).

—— *Travel in the Ancient World* (Oxford 1977).

—— 'Mediterranean communications', in *Cambridge Ancient History* vi, ed² (Cambridge 1994) 512-26.

Cawkwell, G.L., *Philip of Macedon* (London 1978).

Chadwick, J., 'The Berezan Lead Letter', *PCPS* 19 (1973) 35-7.

—— 'The Pech-Maho lead', *ZPE* 82 (1990) 161-6.

Christensen, J. and Hansen,M.H., 'What is *syllogos* at Thukydides 2.22.1?', *CM* 34 (1982) (= Hansen, *The Athenian Ecclesia II* (Copenhagen 1989) 195-211).

Cohen, D., 'Seclusion, separation and the status of women in Classical Athens', *G&R* 36 (1989) 3-15.

—— *Law, Sexuality and Society: the enforcement of morals in classical Athens* (Cambridge 1991).

Collard, C., *Euripides Supplices* ii (Groningen 1975).

Connor, W.R., *The New Politicians of Fifth-Century Athens* (Princeton 1975).

Daremberg, C. and Saglio, E., *Dictionnaire des antiquités grecques et romaines* (Paris 1877-1919).

David, E., 'Laughter in Spartan society', in A. Powell (ed.), *Classical Sparta: techniques behind her success* (London 1989) 1-25.

Delebecque, E., *Euripide et la guerre du Peloponnèse* (Paris 1951).

Detienne, M., 'L'espace de la publicité: ses operateurs intellectuels dans la cité' in Detienne, M. (ed.), *Les Savoirs de l'écriture en Grèce ancienne* (Paris 1988) 29-81.

Dover, K.J., *Greek Popular Morality in the time of Plato and Aristotle* (Oxford 1974).

—— Aristophanes: *Frogs* (Oxford 1993).

Dow, S., 'Corinthiaca', *HSCP* 53 (1942) 89-119.

du Bois, P., *Torture and Truth* (London 1991).

Ducrey, P., *Le Traitement des prisonniers de guerre dans la Grèce antique* (Paris 1968).

Duncan-Jones, R., *Structure and Scale in the Roman Economy* (1990).

Easterling, P.E., 'Anachronism in Greek tragedy', *JHS* 105 (1985) 1-10.

Eco, U., *The Open Work*, trans A. Cancogni (London 1989).

Edelstein, E.J. and Edelstein, L., *Asclepius* (Baltimore 1945).

Edmunds, L., *Chance and Intelligence in Thucydides* (Cambridge, Mass. 1975).

Engelmann, H. and Merkelbach, R. (eds), *Die Inschriften von Erythrai und Klazomenai* i (Bonn 1972).

Errington, R.M., 'The nature of the Macedonian state under the monarchy', *Chiron* 8 (1978) 77-133.

Fehling, D., *Herodotus and his 'Sources': citation, invention and narrative art*, trans. J.G. Howie (Leeds 1989).

Finley, M.I., *Studies in Land and Credit in Ancient Athens* (New Brunswick 1952)

—— *Democracy Ancient and Modern* (Cambridge 1973, ed² 1985).

—— *Politics in the Ancient World* (Cambridge 1983).

Finley, M.I. and Pleket, H.W., *The Olympic Games* (London 1976).

Fontenrose, J., *The Delphic Oracle* (Berkeley 1978).

Forbes, R., *Studies in Ancient Technology* ii (Leiden 1955).

Fornara, C.W., *The Nature of History in Ancient Greece and Rome* (Berkeley 1983).

Frost, F.J., 'The dubious origins of the "Marathon" ', *AJAH* 4 (1979) 159-63.

Gagarin, M., *Early Greek Law* (Berkeley 1986).

Galtung, J. and Ruge, M., 'Structuring and selecting news', in S. Cohen and J. Young (eds), *The Manufacture of News: social problems, deviance and the mass media* (London 1973).

Garnsey, P.D., *Social Status and Legal Privilege in the Roman Empire* (Oxford 1970).

Gerolymatos, A., *Espionage and Treason: a study of the proxenia in political and military intelligence gathering in Classical Greece* (Amsterdam 1986).

Goldhill, S., 'The Great Dionysia and civic ideology', in J.J Winkler and F.I. Zeitlin (eds), *Nothing to Do with Dionysos?* (Princeton 1990) 97-129.

Gomme, A.W., Andrewes, A. and Dover, K.J., *A Historical Commentary on Thucydides* (Oxford 1945-81).

Halliwell, S., 'Comic satire and freedom of speech in classical Athens', *JHS* 111 (1991) 48-70.

Hammond, N.G.L., *The Macedonian State: the origins, institutions and history* (Oxford 1989).

Hansen, M.H., 'How many Athenians attended the *Ecclesia*?', *GRBS* 17 (1976) 115-34 (= *The Athenian Ecclesia* (Copenhagen 1983) 1-20) 130-3.

—— 'How often did the Ecclesia meet?', in *The Athenian Ecclesia* (Copenhagen 1983) 35-72.

—— *The Athenian Assembly in the Age of Demosthenes* (Oxford 1987).

Harding, P., 'All pigs are animals, but are all animals pigs?', *AHB* 5 (1991) 145-9.

Harris, W.V., *Ancient Literacy* (Cambridge, Mass. 1989).

Hartley, J., *Understanding News* (London 1982).

Hartog, F., *The Mirror of Herodotos* trans. J. Lloyd (Berkeley 1988).

Harvey, F.D., 'Literacy in the Athenian democracy', *REG* 79 (1966) 585-635.

Havelock, C.M., 'Art as communication in ancient Greece', in E.A. Havelock and J.P. Hershbell (eds), *Communication Arts in the Ancient World* (New York 1988) 95-118.

Havelock, E.A. and Hershbell, J.P. (eds), *Communication Arts in the Ancient World* (New York 1988).

Henry, A.S., *Honours and Privileges in Athenian Decrees* (Hildesheim 1983).

Herman, G., *Ritualised Friendship and the Greek City* (Cambridge 1987).

Hershbell, J.P., 'The ancient telegraph: war and literacy', in E.A. Havelock and J.P. Hershbell (eds), *Communication Arts in the Ancient World* (New York 1988) 81-92.

Hirsch, S.W., *The Friendship of the Barbarians: Xenophon and the Persian Empire* (Hanover and London 1985).

Hodot, R., 'Le vice, c'est les autres', in Lonis, R. (ed.), *L'Etranger dans le monde grec* ii (Nancy 1992).

Holladay, A.J. and Goodman, M.D., 'Religious scruples in antiquity' *CQ* 36 (1986) 151-71.

Hornblower, S., *The Greek World 479-323 BC* (London 1985).

—— *Thucydides* (London 1987).

How, W.W. and Wells, J., *A Commentary on Herodotus* (Oxford 1912).

Humphreys, S.C., *The Family, Women and Death: comparative studies* (London 1983).

Hunter, V.J., 'Gossip and the politics of reputation in Classical Athens', *Phoenix* 44 (1990) 299-325.

—— *Policing Athens: social control in the Attic lawsuits 420-320 BC* (Princeton 1994).

Hussey, E., 'The beginning of epistemology', in S. Everson, *Epistemology* (Cambridge 1990) 11-38.

Jameson, M., 'Private space and the Greek city', in O. Murray and S.R.F. Price (eds), *The Greek City from Homer to Alexander* (Oxford 1990) 171-95.

Jones, A.H.M., *Athenian Democracy* (Oxford 1957).

Kase, E.W., Szemler, G.J. and Wilkie, N.C. (eds), *The Great Isthmus Corridor Route: explorations of the Phokis-Doris expedition* i (Iowa 1991).

Kelly, D.H., 'Policy-making in the Spartan assembly', *Antichthon* 15 (1981) 47-61.

Kennedy, G.A., 'Focusing of arguments in Greek deliberative oratory', *TAPA* 90 (1959) 131-8.

—— *The Art of Persuasion in Greece* (Princeton 1963).

—— *Aristotle on Rhetoric: a theory of civic discourse* (Oxford 1991).

Kern, O., *Inschriften von Magnesia am Maeander* (Berlin 1900).

Keuls, E.C., *The Reign of the Phallus: sexual politics in ancient Athens* (New York 1985).

Kroll, J.H., 'An archive of the Athenian cavalry', *Hesperia* 46 (1977) 83-140.

Lalonde, G.V., Langdon, M.K. and Walbank, M.B., *The Athenian Agora* vol. xix, *Inscriptions: horoi, poletai records, leases of public lands* (Princeton 1991).

Lateiner, D., 'Heralds and corpses in Thucydides', *Classical World* 71 (1977) 97-106.

—— *The Historical Methods of Herodotus* (London 1989).

Lavelle, B.M., 'Hipparchos' herms', *Echos du Monde Classique* 29 (n.s. 4) (1985) 411-20.

Lawrence, T.E., *The Seven Pillars of Wisdom* (Harmondsworth 1935, repr. 1977).

Lewis, D.M., 'The Athenian rationes centesimarum', in Finley, M.I. (ed.), *Problèmes de la terre en Grèce ancienne* (Paris 1973) 187-212.

—— 'Democratic institutions and their diffusion', *Proceedings of the Eighth International Conference on Greek and Latin Epigraphy* (Athens 1984) 55-61.

Lloyd, G.E.R., *Magic, Reason and Experience* (Cambridge 1979).

Longo, O., 'Scrivere in Tucidide: comunicazione e ideologia' in E. Livrea and G.A. Privitera (eds), *Studi in onore di A. Ardizzoni* (Rome 1978) 517-54.

—— 'Techniche della comunicazione e ideologie sociali', *QUCC* 27 (1978) 63-92.

Losada, L.A., *The Fifth Column in the Peloponnesian War*, Mnemosyne Supplement 21 (Leiden 1972).

MacDonald, B.R., 'The import of Attic pottery to Corinth', *JHS* 102 (1982) 113-23.

McKechnie, P., *Outsiders in the Greek Cities in the Fourth Century B.C.* (London 1989).

MacLeod, C.W., 'Reason and Necessity: Thucydides iii 9-14, 37-48', *JHS* 98 (1978), 64-78 (= C.W. MacLeod *Collected Essays* (Oxford 1983) 88-102).

MacLuhan, M., *The Gutenberg Galaxy: the making of typographic man* (London 1962).

—— *Understanding Media* (London 1964).

Marco Polo, *The Travels*, trans. R.E. Latham (Harmondsworth 1958).

Markle, M.M., 'Jury pay and assembly pay at Athens', in P.A. Cartledge and F.D. Harvey (eds), *Crux: essays presented to G.E.M. de Ste. Croix* (London 1985) 265-97.

Martin, V., *La Vie internationale dans la Grèce des cités* (Paris 1940).

Matthaiou, A.P., and Pikoulas, Y.A., '*Edon tois Lakedaimoniois potton polemon. IG V¹ 1*', *Horos* 6 (1988) 117.

—— '*Edon tois Lakedaimoniois potton polemon*', *Horos* 7 (1989) 77-124.

Meiggs, R., *The Athenian Empire* (Oxford 1972).

Meiggs, R. and Lewis, D.M., *A Selection of Greek Historical Inscriptions: to the end of the fifth century BC* (Oxford 1969) (ed² 1988).

Merrit, B.D. and Traill, J.S., *The Athenian Agora* vol. xv, *Inscriptions: the Athenian councillors* (Princeton 1974).

Morrison, J.S. and Williams, R.T., *Greek Oared Ships* (Cambridge 1976).

Mosley, D.J., 'Spartan kings and proxeny', *Athenaeum* 49 (1971) 433-5.

—— *Envoys and Diplomacy in Ancient Greece*, Historia Supplement 22 (Wiesbaden 1973).

Mossé, C., 'The "World of the Emporium" in the private speeches of Demosthenes' in P. Garnsey, K. Hopkins and C.R. Whittaker (eds), *Trade in the Ancient Economy* (London 1983) 53-63.

Murray, O., *Early Greece* (London 1980).

—— 'The affair of the Mysteries: democracy and the drinking group', in Murray (ed.), *Sympotica: a symposium on the* symposion (Oxford 1990) 149-61.

Murray, O. and Price, S.R.F., (eds), *The Greek City from Homer to Alexander* (Oxford 1990).

Mylonas, G.E., *Eleusis and the Eleusinian Mysteries* (Princeton 1961).

Nenci, G., 'Il motivo dell' autopsia nella storiografica greca', *Studi Classici e Orientali* 3 (1953) 14-46.

Nilsson, M.P., *Greek Popular Religion* (New York 1940).

Ober, J., *Mass and Élite in Democratic Athens: rhetoric, ideology and the power of the people* (Princeton 1989).

Ollier, F., *Le Mirage spartiate: étude sur l'idéalisation de Sparte dans l'antiquité grec* (Paris 1943).

Osborne, R.G., *Demos: the discovery of classical Attika* (Cambridge 1985).

—— 'The *Demos* and its divisions in classical Athens', in O. Murray and S.R.F. Price (eds), *The Greek City from Homer to Alexander* (Oxford 1990) 265-93.

Parke, H.W., *The Oracles of Zeus* (Oxford 1967).

Parker, R.C.T., 'Greek states and Greek oracles', in P.A. Cartledge and F.D. Harvey (eds), *Crux: essays in Greek history presented to G.E.M. de Ste. Croix* (London 1985) 298-326.

Parlavantza-Friedrich, U., *Täuschungsszenen in den Tragödien des Sophokles* (Berlin 1969).

Pelling, C.B.R., 'Thucydides' Archidamus and Herodotus' Artabanus', in *Georgica: Greek studies in honour of G.L. Cawkwell*, BICS Supplement 58, (London 1991) 120-42.

Pouilloux, J., *Récherches sur l'histoire et les cultes de Thasos* i (Paris 1954).

—— *Choix d'inscriptions grecs* (Paris 1960).

Powell, A., 'Mendacity and Sparta's use of the visual', in A. Powell (ed.), *Classical Sparta: techniques behind her success* (London 1989) 173-92.

Price, S.R.F., 'Delphi and divination', in P.E. Easterling and J.V. Muir (eds), *Greek Religion and Society* (Cambridge 1985) 128-54.

Pritchett, W.K., *The Greek State at War* ii (Berkeley 1974).

—— *Studies in Ancient Greek Topography* iii (Berkeley 1980).
—— *The Greek State at War* iv (Berkeley 1985).
Purcell, N., 'Mobility and the *polis*' in O. Murray and S.R.F. Price (eds), *The Greek City from Homer to Alexander* (Oxford 1990) 29-58.
Rau, P., *Paratragodia: Untersuchung einer komischen Form des Aristophanes* (Munich 1967).
Rawson, E., *The Spartan Tradition in European Thought* (Oxford 1969).
Reed, C.M., *Maritime Traders in the Greek World of the Classical and Archaic Periods* (Oxford D.Phil thesis 1981).
Rhodes, P.J., *The Athenian Boule* (Oxford 1972).
Riepl, W., *Das Nachrichtenwesen des Altertums (mit besondere Rücksicht auf die Römer)* (Leipzig 1913).
Romilly, J. de, 'Guerre et paix entre cités' in J-P. Vernant (ed.), *Problèmes de la guerre en Grèce ancienne* (Paris 1968) 207-20.
Ste. Croix, G.E.M. de, 'The alleged secret pact between Athens and Philip II concerning Amphipolis and Pydna', *CQ* 13 (1963) 110-19.
Schwenk, C., *Athens in the Age of Alexander* (Chicago 1985).
Seabrook, J., *The Unprivileged* (1967).
Sherwin-White, S.M., *Ancient Cos*, Hypomnemata Supplement 51 (Göttingen 1978).
Sinclair, R.K., *Democracy and Participation in Athens* (Cambridge 1988).
Smallwood, E.M., *Documents Illustrating the Principates of Gaius, Claudius and Nero* (Cambridge 1967).
Snodgrass, A., 'Interaction by design: the Greek city-state', in C. Renfrew and J.F. Cherry (eds), *Peer Polity Interaction and Socio-political Change* (Cambridge 1986) 47-58.
Sommerstein, A.H., 'The Decree of Syrakosios', *CQ* 36 (1986) 101-8.
Stephens, M., *A History of News from the Drum to the Satellite* (New York 1988).
Starr, C.G., *Political Intelligence in Classical Greece*, Mnemosyne Supplement 31 (Leiden 1974).
Taplin, O., *The Stagecraft of Aeschylus* (Oxford 1977).
Thomas, R., *Oral Tradition and Written Record in Classical Athens* (Cambridge 1988).
—— *Literacy and Orality in Ancient Greece* (Cambridge 1992).
Thompson, W.E., 'Athenian Leadership: expertise or charisma?', in G.S. Shrimpton and D.J. McCargar (eds), *Classical Contributions: Studies in Honour of M.F. McGregor* (New York 1981) 153-9.
Tigerstedt, E.N., *The Legend of Sparta in Classical Antiquity* i (Stockholm 1965).
Todd, S.C., '*Lady Chatterley's Lover* and the Attic orators', *JHS* 110 (1990) 146-73.
—— 'The purpose of evidence in Athenian courts', in P.A. Cartledge, P.C. Millett and S.C. Todd (eds), *NOMOS: essays in Athenian law, politics and society* (Cambridge 1990) 19-40.
Trollope, A., *Framley Parsonage* (Oxford 1980).
Vidal-Naquet, P., 'Slavery and the rule of women in tradition, myth and utopia', in R.L. Gordon (ed.), *Myth, Religion and Society: structuralist essays* (Cambridge 1981) 187-200 (= 'Esclavage et gynécocratie dans la tradition, le mythe et l'utopie', in C. Nicolet (ed.), *Recherches sur les structures sociales dans l'antiquité classique* (Paris 1970) 63-80).
Volkmann, R., *Die Rhetorik der Greichen und Römer* (Hildesheim 1963).

Walbank, M.B., *Athenian Proxenies of the Fifth Century B.C.* (Toronto 1978).

Wankel, H., *Demosthenes: Rede Für Ktesiphon Über den Kranz* i (Heidelberg 1976).

Wéry, L.M., 'Le meutre des hérauts de Darius en 491 et l'inviolabilité du héraut', *AC* 35 (1966) 468-86.

West, S., 'Archilochus' message-stick', *CQ* (1988) 42-8.

Whitehead, D., *The Ideology of the Athenian Metic* (Cambridge 1977).

—— *The Demes of Attica* (Princeton 1986).

Winkler, J.J. and Zeitlin, F.I. (eds), *Nothing to do with Dionysos?: Athenian drama in its social context* (Princeton 1990).

Woodman, A.J., *Rhetoric in Classical Historiography: four studies* (London 1988).

Yavetz, Z., *Plebs and Princeps* (Oxford 1969).

Zanker, P., *The Power of Images in the Age of Augustus* (Michigan 1988).

Zuntz, G., 'Contemporary politics in Euripides', *Opuscula Selecta* (Manchester 1972) 54-61.

Index